Annual Editions: Comparative Politics, 33/e

Edited by Caroline Westerhof

http://create.mheducation.com

ISBN-10: 1259350649   ISBN-13: 9781259350641

Contents

Preface

In publishing ANNUAL EDITIONS we recognize the enormous role played by the magazines, newspapers, and journals of the public press in providing current, first-rate educational information in a broad spectrum of interest areas. Many of these articles are appropriate for students, researchers, and professionals seeking accurate, current material to help bridge the gap between principles and theories and the real world. These articles, however, become more useful for study when those of lasting value are carefully collected, organized, indexed, and reproduced in a low-cost format, which provides easy and permanent access when the material is needed. That is the role played by ANNUAL EDITIONS.

Comparative politics focuses on the empirical and experiential studies of political behaviors, institutions, actors, legitimate and illegitimate regulations and rules to facilitate explanations, predictions, projections, and theory-building. This book sets as its task the presentation of information based on systematic study of such behaviors, institutions, and rules.

The volume is organized to emphasize political behaviors, institutions, actors, and rules from a comparative perspective. Current comparative political texts make similar arguments regarding the need for such a focus. This is a comparative study, which may or may not be specifically regional or country specific.

Annual Editions: Comparative Politics, 33/e develops, where possible, comparative relationships about how people and governments behave and interact politically. Such is determined by rules, institutions, and actors that are in place across a range of countries and political systems, at the time of "putting this edition to bed." Systematic generalizations that address the questions of why, what, and how regarding political behaviors and institutions apply across countries and political systems. We do not dispute that country-relevant information contextualizes behavior and interactions. Rather, we consider it necessary to clarify the generalizations that provide baseline knowledge regarding why, what, and how of political behaviors and institutions. With this baseline in place, particularities that are observed become even more interesting or unusual and are more easily understood.

We address the relevant political questions of why, what, and how regarding political behaviors, actors, and within institutions. Students are introduced to debates, questions, and circumstances that create the issues involved within the diversity of the global arena; such data is drawn from the news, public press, current governmental readings, and referred journals across different nation-states. We recognize that in this period of history, world actors are continuously changing and the morals and morale of society are in turbulence in many parts of the world. Many of the writings are from third-party actors, not primary observers.

We take into context at this time the tragedies, dilemmas, tortuous behavior, and fierce battles taking place in areas that are "undeclared war territories." In the midst of these global agonies, including the infectious Ebola crisis, in which thousands have already died, the 69th General Assembly of the United Nations met at the UN headquarters in New York City. The delegates and representatives from over 100 countries laid out the plans for the 70th General Assembly meeting in 2015.

Each of the readings has Learning Outcomes, Critical Thinking questions, and Internet References to help facilitate the student's learning and understanding of the topics. This academic structure ensures that students explore how the discipline and issues connect with other nation–states and are involved in the practicum of world politics, whether in individual countries, in multinational relationships, or within world organizations.

We become aware of the ever-changing footsteps, military and civilian, involved in globalization, including governmental and outside influents. There are the political changes going on in the Arab states, in the Middle East, in Burma, the instability of other nation–states, and the economic and political crises.

Such data underscores the crucial importance of knowledge regarding foreign governments and societies. In the global society and within the world economic issues, poor or weak governments, institutions, and changing actors have direct consequences on our lives.

Comparative politics is a dynamic subfield in political science. It reveals how other academic and social disciplines study and interact with governments and politics, recognizing the significance of the comparative political science approach, and the examining and understanding of diversity in culture and behavior. We approach democratic theory, its ramifications and varied interpretations, emphasizing the nature of comparative politics. It is a theoretically driven enterprise, with its requisite debates, tests, and counterarguments raised and evaluated over time.

The reality of discussions on democratic theory highlights the relevance of citizen participation and addresses why and how citizen participation is organized and in what forms. The emphasis is on the particularities of interest groups and political parties, advocacy groups, and pressure politics as outlets of political behavior that, if repressed or ignored, may lead people to find "less democratic ways" to participate.

The political discipline of the social sciences must consider the actors and the institutions of government in addressing questions regarding the roles they play in the political process, how they affect political behaviors, and, perhaps most importantly, how their successes or failures are evaluated.

The executive, in the study of comparative politics, plays the leadership role of accountability and responsiveness to the public. How that role is handled in both democratic and autocratic systems of government determines the nation–states' responses to world issues.

Accountability in the nation's legislature may increase citizen participation if it is within a democratic system. It can be implemented as the mouthpiece of the autocratic leader. Given the importance of representation aspect, some nation–states may seek to improve participation of minorities, including issues of gender, and to understand how electoral systems may hinder or improve that representation.

The unelected bureaucrats and members of the government include the judiciary, military, civil servants, and others who are involved in policymaking. Is there resentment against unelected officials, even in democratic governments? In fact, it was recently noted that many, at times, find the political activism of the U.S. Supreme Court discussions to be distasteful and believe that such judicial policy making should be left to the elected political actors and evaluated over time.

How do institutional changes occur: by election, by military coups, and by other means? We also know that elections may mean a one-party candidate. Institutional actions and political behaviors are reciprocal.

Many challenges and increasing problems are bombarding the politics and political trends and decision making within globalization. We are living in a wave of challenges from downsizing public funds, reducing the size of the U.S. military, sending U.S. troops to Liberia in the midst of the Ebola crisis, and Iraq asking the United States for ground troops.

The transitions in the Middle East certainly reveal that our thinking about how transitions occur needs to be revisited. Domestic demand and new pressures are essential for initiating institutional changes; however, it is not culture but, rather, tolerance and equality that fuel the strengthening of democracy. Equally important are ways

that authoritarian governments circumvent this push for democratic accountability and responsiveness. Autocratic leaders, sooner or later, recognize that the world scene views accountability, responsiveness, representation, and civic participation as crucial, even under a dictatorial regime.

What do we need to know in order to project how the political arenas on the global scene will develop? It is important to understand foreign political institutions and policy processes. Whether we look at Asia and the eastern part of the world or Europe, the Middle East, or the Americas, can we uncover what regions will embrace the transition to democracy and what regions will be controlled by authoritarianism, a reminder of how important it is to understand foreign political institutions, sensitive to cultural differences, understand the policy processes— what is reality; what is political bubble; what are legitimate threats?

There are several individuals to thank for this current volume. Thanks go to the editorial staff at McGraw-Hill, particularly Mary Foust, Product Developer, for clear and insightful advice, support, and gentle reminders of deadlines. Also, thanks to the many colleagues at the Australian National University and the University of Kansas, whose support, advice, and critiques are gratefully recognized. The responses of the advisory board members in critiquing and suggesting selections in this edition are instrumental; we are indebted to their painstaking efforts and commitment to see an improved, accessible, and academically rigorous edition. Finally, thanks to the readers, whose comments helped with the selection of readings. We hope that you will continue to help improve future editions by keeping us informed of your reactions and suggestions for change.

Caroline Westerhof
Editor

Editor

Caroline Shaffer Westerhof is an online adjunct professor for several universities across the United States. Her students participate from all parts of the world, including Afghanistan, Iraq, Qatar, Ghana, Germany, Japan, Puerto Rico, and other areas. She was a tenured full professor within The City University of New York; she is an international management organization analyst and mediator; among the publications she has authored is "The Executive Connection . . ." the first management study on press secretaries to elected mayors, and she has researched press secretaries to presidents of the United States from the time of Roger Tubby to the week before James Brady and President Reagan were shot. She is also the author of *The Petology Series: Letters to Charlye,* has had poetry published in several collections, as well as articles in professional journals and newspapers. Dr. Westerhof was a special negotiator to the U.S. Presidential Commission on Regulatory Affairs; the first female visiting professor at the U.S. Air War College; and in cooperation with the U.S. State Department set up public and business management programs in Ghana. She has spoken on U.S. presidential elections on BBC, London, was a political analyst for ABC News, and lectured at the CIA. Westerhof is a member of the Academy of International Business, has been CEO of a transportation-related corporation, as well as director of regulatory affairs for a multinational business, and has worked actively with Underwriter's Laboratory in both the United States and Canada. She is also a member of the American Society of Public Administration, the MidSouth Sociological Association, as well as other professional groups. She has recently spoken at the Academy of International Business on China and Vietnam—The China Sea Conundrum: Where is the United Nations muscle?

Academic Advisory Board

Members of the Academic Advisory Board are instrumental in the final selection of articles for the *Annual Editions* series. Their review of the articles for content, level, and appropriateness provides critical direction to the editor(s) and staff. We think that you will find their careful consideration reflected in this book.

Unit 1

UNIT

Prepared by: Caroline Shaffer Westerhof,
California National University for Advanced Studies

Why Comparative Politics?

Why do we study foreign government institutions or the policies they make? Clearly, part of the answer is "interest" and to create understanding and develop awareness. That is, we study foreign government institutions, their policymaking processes, and the resultant policies. We need to comprehend what is similar or different from us, encapsulating our interests in foreign governments, institutions, and the policies that follow from such governments and institutions. It is important that we understand what happens in other countries, the ways they are different, and what motivates their changes.

It is imperative that we recognize issues, similarities, and dissimilarities in understanding comparative politics. Studying comparative politics helps us to become aware so that we may make projections regarding what will happen next to some of our closest allies or affect our largest trading partners. There is the strong humanitarian consideration: Before we are able to help, we need to gain knowledge and insights into foreign government institutions, their policymaking processes, and actual policies.

The security, political, and economic considerations capture the other parts of globalization: Globalization, which has brought with it many advantages from economic, social, and cultural exchange, has also left us more exposed to the frailties of foreign governments and policy failures. Whereas geography may previously pose a viable line of defense against weak or erratic governments, the increasing interconnectedness of countries through trade, migration, and the Internet—a process termed *globalization*—has rendered physical boundaries almost meaningless. As a result, we are no longer insulated from the ramifications of recalcitrant governments or citizens in foreign countries. Instead, issues ranging from the political unrest in the Middle East, civil war in Africa, and the economic crises across Europe are directly affecting our lives and livelihoods. These reverberations stress that we need to be cognitive to the activities, citizens, and actors in other countries.

The need to understand institutions and policy processes is all the more relevant given that we do not have successful regional or international institutions for mediating conflicts or addressing the humanitarian, welfare, or social problems that arise. History reminds us that many such regional or international agencies are far from functional. Further, with information disseminated at lightning speed, we are prone to inaccurate interpretations and incorrect conclusions without a basic political and social knowledge of any country. Even though we are witness to a country ravaged by civil strife, we must also be attentive to the fact that our offers of aid are often delivered with simplistic and unrealistic expectations. Such expectations may do more damage in the long run, particularly to political socioeconomic relations within and between countries.

Thus, consider, for instance, that the long history of aid extension to Africa has brought few successes, in part because the aid was fueled by the clamor to "do something." And, the poor success has spurred an "anti-aid" position that almost seems ideological. What does this tell us? More so than before, there is a need to for us to be equipped to participate as a global citizen: to gain knowledge and understanding of political institutions, processes, and systems in order to contribute meaningfully and empathetically. Also, the porous financial and geographical borders of globalization mean that we come face to face with the fallout of political and social instability more often and sooner than previous eras. And, these occur across industrialized democracies such as Norway and Britain, as well as less-industrialized countries of India, Afghanistan, and in the African continent. If we think we are insulated from the problems of failed political institutions and corruption, take a look at the reports of the felony and criminal charges that the United States Securities and Exchange Commission has filed, and think again. Should we consider—in light of the economic doldrums in the United States—that the experience in Britain may be more relevant to us than we would like to admit?

Clearly, there are humanitarian, economic, and social imperatives to learning about foreign government institutions and policy processes. This is relevant, not only from the perspective of an aid-giver; it is also important given that the porous borders of globalization may lead us to face the same political, social, or economic circumstances.

Now comes the challenge: How do we learn about foreign governments and policies? What do we need to take away from that learning? This is no small task: The UN recognizes 192 countries; this number does not include several that are not UN members.[1] The United States government recognizes 195 autonomous countries in the world.[2] The list easily expands beyond 250 if we include nations that are self-governing as well as those that are not. A nation is defined as "a group of people whose members share a common identity on the basis of distinguishing characteristics and claim to a territorial homeland."[3] Each of these nations or countries has long histories that may bear on the government's behaviors or the responses of their people and also influence what institutions and rules are considered and adopted. Clearly, learning about the particularities, of even one country, requires considerable time and effort, let alone the more than 100 formally recognized ones.

How do we accomplish this? From the political science perspective, it means we start with some fundamentals, such as:

What is comparative politics? What do we compare? How do we compare? Why do we compare? Who are the actors? How do we define the culture or multicultural aspects of the environment and its particular boundaries?

What is comparative politics? *Comparative Politics* refers to the study of governments and the potential of inter-relationships. That seems clear. Yet, popular dictionaries such as the Merriam-Webster's and Oxford Dictionary contain no less than five and as many as ten different ways of conceiving the word "government." They include[4]:

1. The exercise of authority over a state, district, or territory.
2. A system of ruling, controlling, or administering.
3. The executive branch of a government.
4. All the people and institutions that exercise control over the affairs of a nation or state.
5. The study of such systems, people, and institutions.

These definitions emphasize several concepts integral to comparative politics: authority, system, people and institutions, and state, district, or territory. In the broadest sense, comparative politics involves the systematic comparison of authority, systems, people, and institutions across states, districts, or other territories. Its focus is both formal and informal. Comparative politics focuses on the patterns of politics within a domestic territory, where political parties, interest groups, civil servants, the public, and the press interact under specified laws to influence who gets what, when, how, and why.

Comparative politics emphasizes careful empirical study as the way to gain knowledge about how people and governments behave and interact politically, given rules and institutions that are in place. It is important to note that other disciplines also study how people and governments behave; however, their goals or ends for such study are different.

We compare nation-states for several reasons: First, it provides a way to systematically consider how people and institutions across different countries, districts, or systems balance the competing goals of stability, change, security, freedom, growth, accountability, and responsiveness. Thus, for the political practitioner, analyst, or scholar, comparative politics is applied to describe, clarify, and, subsequently, understand change or stability. Second, we compare in order to enhance theory-building. Theory building is predicated on examination and evaluation, testing and retesting, in order to achieve, if possible, generalization and projections for the future, either negative or positive, or both. The comparative method in political science is one of the means toward this end of theory building.

Thus, comparative politics provides systematic generalizations regarding political behaviors, processes, and institutions to promote learning with greater efficiency. This understanding of why we compare in political science is important because it distinguishes political science from other disciplines. For example, the history discipline may also study governments; however, the focus of such study is directed at fact-finding and gathering to enhance interpretation and accuracy. Importantly, then, knowing a lot about a country or an area does not make one a comparative political scholar. It is the interrelationships that matter, and the baseline knowledge that is derived from particularities of observation, description, explanation, and through projection, possibly anticipated.

Our awareness of possible generalizations may be drawn regarding which countries democratize, how countries democratize, and why they democratize. At the most fundamental, what the people want from their governments in terms of accountability and representation is key. Thus, international political actors—including foreign governments and institutions such as the UN—will do well by paying attention to the domestic political conditions that contextualize how solutions are formulated and implemented. This is an ongoing process—no matter how far along a country appears in the political development spectrum (consider India)—the context of what people want drives their support of the government and the institutions. And, notwithstanding different countries and systems, there are fundamental behaviors, processes, and institutions needed to achieve the balance among the factors of stability, change, security, freedom, growth, accountability, and responsiveness. We seek the tasks of the identification of those behaviors, processes, and institutions in order to map out what is needed for the balance, and when possible, a global peace.

Note

1. The United Nations. un.org/News/Press/docs//2007/org1479.doc.htm

2. United States Department of State. www.state.gov/s/inr/rls/4250.htm

3. Michael Sodaro. 2007. *Comparative Politics: A Global Introduction,* 3rd edition. New York: McGraw Hill.

4. *Oxford Dictionary.* oxforddictionaries.com/definition/government?region 5 us; *Merriam-Webster's Online Dictionary.* www.merriam-webster.com/dictionary/government

Article

Prepared by: Caroline Shaffer Westerhof,
California National University for Advanced Studies

David Cameron's Dangerous Game

The Folly of Flirting with an EU Exit

MATTHIAS MATTHIJS

Learning Outcomes

After reading this article, you will be able to:

- Explain the economic argument of why the United Kingdom should leave the EU.

- Explain the politics and policies of why many members of the Conservative Party in the United Kingdom have turned against Europe.

- Distinguish the politics of Franklin Roosevelt and Charles deGaulle relative to Prime Minister Winston Churchill's statement that if he had to pick between the two, he would always choose the leader of the United States.

Despite his innate caution and usually sound political instincts, British Prime Minister David Cameron is gambling with his country's future. In January, in a long-anticipated speech, he called for a wide-ranging renegotiation of the terms of the United Kingdom's membership in the European Union and promised to put the result up for a straight in-or-out popular referendum by the end of 2017 (assuming his party wins the next election, due in 2015). A British exit from the EU is now more likely than ever—and it would be disastrous not only for the United Kingdom but also for the rest of Europe and the United States.

If London does ultimately cut the rope, it will not be the result of rational political or economic calculations. British Euroskepticism boils down to a visceral dislike of Brussels—the host of a number of European institutions and the EU's de facto capital—on the part of an ill-informed conservative minority that clings to an antiquated notion of national sovereignty. These sentiments are on display every day in the right-wing tabloids, which play on voters' fears with vitriolic commentary and sensationalistic headlines, such as "Eu Wants to Merge UK With France" and "EU Will Grab Britain's Gas," both of which recently appeared in the *Daily Express*.

By caving in to the demands of the right wing of his party, Cameron appears to be falling into the same trap that his predecessors fell into. Both Margaret Thatcher and John Major, the previous two Conservative prime ministers, were eventually thrown out of office as their party tore itself apart over the issue of European integration during the late 1980s and mid-1990s. In 1995, these divisions among the Conservatives led a young Labour opposition leader named Tony Blair to ridicule Major on the floor of the House of Commons, scoffing, "I lead my party; he follows his." Even Cameron himself, back in 2006, less than a year after he took over the Conservative Party, wisely counseled his colleagues to "stop banging on about Europe" if they ever wanted to win elections again.

And yet, seven years later, Cameron faces a simmering rebellion on an issue that most Britons still do not care much about but that has once again turned toxic in his party. In a 2012 survey of the British electorate, only six percent of respondents described Europe as the most salient issue facing the country, compared with 67 percent who prioritized the economy, 35 percent who worried most about unemployment, and just over 20 percent whose main concerns were immigration and race relations.

With his January speech, Cameron had hoped to achieve four short-term objectives. First, he wanted to stop the growing threat on his party's right flank from the anti-EU and anti-immigration UK Independence Party, whose populist leader, Nigel Farage, positions himself as a champion of British common sense and defender of British sovereignty against Brussels' encroachment. Second, Cameron aimed to neutralize his own party's increasingly restless Euroskeptic backbenchers, many of whom also advocate a British exit from the EU. Third, he hoped to put the losing political issue of Europe to rest until the next parliament. Fourth, he tried to portray the country's economic woes as a result of the eurozone crisis rather than of his own government's biting austerity measures.

On all four fronts, however, it appears that Cameron miscalculated. The UK Independence Party wildly outperformed expectations in the local elections in May, earning close to a quarter of the overall vote. The Euroskeptics in the Conservative Party are still insisting on a referendum during the current parliament, underscoring once again that they cannot be appeased on the European question and do not trust the prime minister to deliver on it. Cameron's leadership is more tenuous than ever, especially after he pushed through a contentious bill in support of gay marriage, a stance that many party activists find hard to swallow. (The fact that one of Cameron's close advisers referred to these activists as "mad, swivel-eyed loons" has not helped.) And finally, a slew of recent scholarly studies, including one published by the International Monetary Fund, have blown a giant hole in the intellectual case for austerity, undercutting the government's economic strategy. But far more is at stake than one prime minister's political career. If the United Kingdom ends up abandoning Europe, it will feel the negative economic and political effects for decades to come.

A Marriage of Convenience

The United Kingdom's relationship with Europe has never been warm, much less passionate; it is more like a loveless arranged marriage. Based on cost-benefit analysis rather than lofty rhetoric about a common European destiny, the country's European affair has been fraught with abysmal timing and shattered hopes. When the country first knocked on Brussels' door in the 1960s, it found its applications unceremoniously rejected by France's Charles de Gaulle. In 1973, when Edward Heath, a Conservative prime minister, successfully steered the United Kingdom toward membership in the European Economic Community, the Western world was about to slip into its first deep postwar recession. The subsequent Labour government, facing opposition to European integration from its left-wing backbenchers, felt the need to put Heath's decision to a national referendum, which eventually passed in 1975 by a two-to-one margin.

During the 1980s, Thatcher told her European partners that the United Kingdom wanted "a very large amount of [its] own money back" and warned them that she had not successfully rolled back the frontiers of government at home only to see them reintroduced through the backdoor by Brussels. At the beginning of the next decade, against her better judgment, she let her country join Europe's Exchange Rate Mechanism, a precursor to the monetary union. Major, then chancellor of the exchequer, had convinced her that this was the best way to tame inflation, which had been creeping up again at the end of the 1980s. But joining the ERM meant dancing to the tune of Germany's monetary policy, and soaring German interest rates to fight inflation and finance German reunification meant that the Bank of England had to follow the Bundesbank's lead in hiking up interest rates. Doing so at the onset of another domestic recession meant political suicide, however, and the United Kingdom was forced to leave the ERM only a few years after it joined.

After succeeding Thatcher as prime minister, Major negotiated various areas in which the United Kingdom could opt out of the Maastricht Treaty, which created the EU, most notably keeping the United Kingdom out of the common currency while allowing it to retain full EU membership. Blair, who as prime minister passionately told the French National Assembly in a 1998 speech that be shared the European ideal, at one point sought to bring his country onto the euro, but he was blocked by his powerful chancellor of the exchequer, Gordon Brown.

In some ways, the United Kingdom's quandary today looks like it did 40 years ago, when the country first joined the European Economic Community. Then, as now, the British were in deep, mostly self-inflicted economic trouble. In the 1970s, however, the politics of the issue were flipped: the Conservatives saw integration with Europe as a liberalizing move, and the Heath government believed it was the only way to reverse the country's relative economic decline. Thatcher, for her part, campaigned strongly in favor of staying in the European Economic Community during the referendum of 1975, arguing that access to the large and growing continental market would fuel British growth. At the same time, a majority of Labour Party members, although not the leadership, resolutely opposed membership on the grounds that Brussels was too market-friendly.

Today, the British economy is again struggling to emerge from a slump, but this time, Europe is seen as the source of the malaise, not its cure. In an attempt to play down the negative effects of their austerity policies, both Cameron and his chancellor of the exchequer, George Osborne, have been blaming the European sovereign debt crisis for the British economy's lack of growth. They usually justify their draconian spending cuts by pointing to Greece's fiscal tragedy. And whereas Labour is now moderately in favor of staying in the EU, seeing the union as the guarantor of certain social rights in the United Kingdom, the majority of Conservatives have turned against Europe and want to see the repatriation of key powers back to the national government. According to the most recent opinion polls, more Britons are in favor of leaving the EU than are in favor of staying in it.

Cameron's stance on Europe constitutes a break with Conservative tradition. Although Thatcher was never enamored with Brussels, she was a driving force behind the effort to establish a European common market in the 1980s, which culminated in the signing of the Single European Act in 1986. She was always careful to nurture relationships with like-minded leaders on the continent and keen to avoid British isolation. Major had a tougher time navigating the European question, but in the end, he signed the Maastricht Treaty, albeit while opting out of the euro. But when Cameron decided in December 2011, during the height of the euro crisis, to completely stay out of a new fiscal pact, forcing the EU to move forward with an intergovernmental agreement without the United Kingdom, he radically changed that Conservative tradition. His demand for a renegotiation of his country's EU membership terms went one step further, and it has infuriated many European leaders, who fear it will reignite old debates that were settled through compromise a long time ago.

Better Together

The economic argument for why the United Kingdom should leave the EU goes something like this: The continent is preoccupied with fighting a full-fledged sovereign debt crisis, one that has fundamentally changed the dynamics of European integration. The crisis has made integration a much more inward-looking project, requiring all kinds of new regulations in the financial sector aimed at completing the monetary union with common banking supervision, joint deposit insurance, and closer fiscal cooperation. These new regulations will allegedly hurt the City of London (the United Kingdom's financial hub) and therefore the entire British economy. And since fixing the euro once and for all can be achieved only by granting more powers to European institutions, the role of the British parliament and government as the legitimate representatives of the country's citizens will be threatened. This would further widen the democratic deficit within the EU, a particularly sensitive issue for the United Kingdom.

But on close inspection, none of these concerns holds up. The idea that the United Kingdom would be better off outside the EU is misguided, since it is based on a finance-centric view of the British economy. This view holds that the United Kingdom's comparative advantage is in financial services, a sector that needs to be protected at all costs from burdensome regulations. According to this school of thought, Thatcher's liberalization and deregulation of the economy in the 1980s and Blair's consolidation of finance as the core sector of the British economy in the late 1990s were unmitigated successes.

Proponents of this view suffer from collective amnesia about what has happened to the British economy over the past five years. Although finance lifted many boats during good times (some much more than others), when the sector crashed in 2008, it led to a collapse in government revenue, as close to one-quarter of all the Treasury's income came from finance. Even as the government's coffers were emptying, London had to dole out large bailouts to the very banks that had caused the crisis. The Cameron government then chose to respond with big expenditure cuts, and the pain seems set to continue for at least another five years. And that is the optimistic scenario.

Surely, the Cameron government's alternative to the EU banking regulations designed to thwart future crashes is not to get rid of financial rules altogether. For better or worse, this is now a post–Lehman Brothers era, and some amount of regulation is politically inevitable. What is more, London would certainly not be able to maintain its status as the leading financial center in Europe if the British left the Common Market, since doing so would make capital flows from the continent to the United Kingdom more regulated and thus more restricted than they are now.

The moment the United Kingdom leaves the EU is also the moment it loses all influence on European economic policymaking. And London would still have to accept most of Brussels' regulations and standards if it wanted free access to a market of over 400 million well-off European consumers, who currently buy more than 50 percent of all British exports. By leaving, the United Kingdom would also miss out on the free movement of labor, forfeiting the ability to attract many of Europe's best brains and the ability to take advantage of an influx of low-wage workers from central Europe.

The fact that the United Kingdom today remains in the EU but out of the eurozone means that it can have its cake and eat it, too. An independent monetary policy has allowed the country to keep down the value of the pound, boosting British exports to Europe and the rest of the world. And thanks to its membership in the Common Market, the United Kingdom remains influential in setting its rules. It is difficult to imagine a better position.

A British exit from the EU would be equally disastrous for the United Kingdom's standing in the world. Speaking at West Point in 1962, former U.S. Secretary of State Dean Acheson observed that the United Kingdom had lost an empire and had yet to find a role. By the 1970s, that role had started to take shape: the British would help shepherd European integration and maintain a "special relationship" with the United States. The alliance between the United Kingdom and the United States saw its heyday during the 2003 invasion of Iraq, when U.S. Defense Secretary Donald Rumsfeld spoke of Europe as divided into an antagonistic "old Europe"—led by the United Kingdom's traditional rivals, France and Germany—and a more supportive "new Europe."

But at that time, Washington still feared a common European defense policy, seeing a unified continent as a potential competitor. A decade later, the Americans no longer hold that view. Because of Germany's renewed economic strength and quasi-hegemonic status within the eurozone, Washington now sees Berlin, not London, as its preferred partner in Europe. The interests of the United States and Europe are more closely aligned than they used to be, as both try to cope with an economic slump, rising powers, and common security threats. Although the Obama administration has made clear that it sees Asia as the strategic battleground of the future, it is also encouraging European countries to cooperate more closely on defense so that they can help the United States bear the burden of global security. It would be a strategic mistake for London to leave the EU just as Washington is starting to warm to it.

As austerity takes its toll on the British armed forces, the only way for the United Kingdom to play any role in global security is if it pools its resources with the rest of Europe. In a sign of things to come, Europe's two nuclear powers, the United Kingdom and France, have agreed to share their aircraft carriers. A truly common European defense policy, however, has remained elusive. As a French diplomat recently told me, "You cannot do anything without Britain, but you also cannot do anything with Britain."

Still, as the wars in Iraq and Libya demonstrated, EU membership has not stopped the United Kingdom from acting in its own interests. Those campaigns have shown that the EU member states less inclined to intervene militarily, such as Germany, will not prevent others from resorting to force. NATO countries have adopted the flexible strategy of acting in "coalitions of the willing"; there's no reason why a formal EU defense alliance could not do the same thing. And now is the right time for such a move, since London's strategic interests have never been more closely aligned with those of the rest of Europe.

The End of the Affair

On the eve of the Allied troops' landing in Normandy in June 1944, British Prime Minister Winston Churchill warned de Gaulle that "every time we have to decide between Europe and the open sea, it is always the open sea that we shall choose." Elaborating on his point, Churchill explained that if he ever had to make a choice between de Gaulle and Franklin Roosevelt, between Europe and the United States, he would always pick the latter.

Ironically, Churchill was one of the first European leaders to call for a "United States of Europe," not long after World War II. De Gaulle, however, would never forget Churchill's wartime rebuke, and it certainly was on his mind both times he vetoed the United Kingdom's application to join the European Economic Community. Today, almost 70 years after Churchill's comment, U.S. President Barack Obama is sending the opposite message to his British counterpart, in equally firm terms: if the United Kingdom wants to retain any influence on the open sea, it must choose Europe.

But Cameron might well have already set his country inexorably on the road to isolation and irrelevance. Even if some European leaders would be willing to make substantive concessions to the United Kingdom to help keep it in the club, they are unlikely to ever go far enough for Cameron to appease the Euroskeptics in his party, much less to convince those British voters who favor withdrawing from the EU. There is a real danger, then, that the United Kingdom will end its relationship with Europe—making the tragic mistake of trading genuine power for the mirage of national sovereignty.

Critical Thinking

1. Why are London's strategic interests more closely aligned with the rest of Europe than they have ever been?

2. What are the reasons that the British electorate is not too concerned with the EU at the present time?

3. Did Charles deGaulle's decision to twice veto the United Kingdom's application to join the European Economic Community after World War II affect the future of Great Britain?

Create Central

www.mhhe.com/createcentral

Internet References

Foreign Affairs
www.ForeignAffairs.com

Nigel Nelson on David Cameron
www.mirror.co.uk/news/uk-news/nigel-nelson-david-cameron-win-2149434

BBC News—UK and the EU: Better Off Out or In?
www.bbc.co.uk/news/uk-politics-20448450

U.K. Lawmakers Debate Leaving the European Union
www.washingtonpost.com/blogs/worldviews/wp/2013/05/13/u-k-lawmakers-debate-leaving-the-european-union/

UK Economy Grows Again
www.express.co.uk/news/uk/417369/UK-economy-grows-again-as-economist-says-a-real-tailwind-now-behind-the-recovery

Matthias Matthijs is Assistant Professor of International Political Economy at Johns Hopkins University's School of Advanced International Studies.

Matthijs, Matthias. From *Foreign Affairs*, September/October 2013, pp. 10–16. Copyright © 2013 by Council on Foreign Relations, Inc. Reprinted by permission of Foreign Affairs. www.ForeignAffairs.com

Prepared by: Caroline Shaffer Westerhof,
California National University for Advanced Studies

Article

Ukraine Declares One-Week Cease-Fire in Fight with Pro-Russia Rebels

West Hopes to Pressure Putin, but Kremlin Reacts Coolly and Pro-Russia Rebels Demand Kiev First Withdraw Its Troops.

LUKAS I. ALPERT AND WILLIAM MAUDLIN

Learning Outcomes

After reading this article, you will be able to:

- Understand why Ukraine has been teetering between violence and peace and that a temporary ceasefire is not holding.
- Explain the geopolitical crisis affecting Crimea with Ukraine's failure to turn around Crimea's political fortunes.
- Explain the political and economic dynamics of U.S. political leaders threatening Russia with economic sanctions.

Ukraine's new president declared a one-week cease-fire Friday in the fight to put down a pro-Russia rebellion, starting a process the West hopes will pressure Moscow to rein in separatists it has been accused of supplying with weaponry.

The Kremlin responded coolly, however, calling the cease-fire an ultimatum rather than an invitation to talk. "The plan is missing the key element—a proposal to start negotiations," it said in a statement.

In the U.S., officials added several Ukrainian separatist figures and leaders in Crimea, which Russia annexed in March, to its sanctions list. A senior U.S. official said Russia would face economic "scalpel sanctions" from the U.S. and the European Union if it continues to destabilize Ukraine.

President Barack Obama on Friday spoke separately with German Chancellor Angela Merkel and French President François Hollande to discuss the crisis in Ukraine, and the leaders agreed that Russia must take significant steps to ease tensions or face new costs, according to a White House statement.

Ukraine's President Petro Poroshenko announced the cease-fire on a visit to Sviatohirsk, a town in the Donetsk region near the separatist stronghold of Slovyansk, the Interior Ministry in Kiev said.

He has portrayed the unilateral cease-fire as a first step in a peace plan that aims to end the two month-old uprising. It calls for the insurgents to lay down their weapons and offers an amnesty to those not guilty of grave crimes. Ultimately, the government would move to a more decentralized system, granting more autonomy to the regions.

Diplomats in the West say they now intend to step up pressure on Russian President Vladimir Putin to stop the separatists from fighting and secure the border or face more sanctions.

However, a separatist leader in Luhansk, the other border regions largely under rebel control, said his men wouldn't lay down their arms unless government troops withdrew completely from the region.

The senior U.S. official said the U.S. is reviewing Ukraini[an] assertions that Russia had sent another 10 tanks to rebels acro[ss] the border, but was able to confirm Friday only that they h[ad] left a deployment site in southwest Russia a day earlier.

Ukraine and Western leaders have accused Russia of allo[w]ing arms and fighters to cross into Ukraine, which Moscow h[as] denied. The Obama administration said a week ago it had c[on]firmed separatists had acquired some tanks and rocket launc[h]ers from Russia.

The senior U.S. official said Friday that the material be[ing] provided consists of equipment widely used in Ukraine, but [...]

Russia, enabling separatists to claim that they had captured it n the battlefield in Ukraine.

Ukraine's Interior Ministry said the cease-fire would last ntil June 27—the same day Mr. Poroshenko is scheduled to ign an agreement cementing stronger trade and political ties ith the EU. It added that the military will respond if attacked, nd those rebels who don't lay down their arms by June 27 will be destroyed."

The move comes as Ukrainian forces made a last-ditch effort o regain control of the border with Russia, long stretches of hich had fallen into rebel hands. Mr. Poroshenko had said that ould be a condition for a halt in the fighting.

Earlier in the day, Ukraine's defense minister and the peaker of parliament both claimed that government forces had egained control of several border posts abandoned two weeks go to the separatists. But the national defense council later cknowledged much of the border in the Luhansk region was ill unsecured. A rebel leader also said the border remained in eparatist hands.

The Kremlin acknowledged it had moved troops back to s side of the border, weeks after Mr. Putin had ordered sol-iers in the region back to their bases. But Mr. Putin's spokes-an, Dmitry Peskov, told Russian news agencies the country asn't massing soldiers again, but had shifted some troops to rengthen border security.

Pointing to the Russian troop movements, White House pokesman Josh Earnest said the Obama administration "will not accept any use of Russian military forces under any pretext in eastern Ukraine."

Mr. Earnest also faulted comments by Russian Foreign Minister Sergei Lavrov this past week that equated Ukrainian demands for the departure of militants with ethnic cleansing. "We see these statements for what they are—an attempt to cre-ate pretext for further illegal Russian intervention in Ukraine," he said.

A rebel convoy with tanks, armored vehicles and trucks driv-ng Friday toward Donetsk in east Ukraine. Associated Press.

Fighting has raged in recent days even as Ukraine and Russia epped up diplomatic contacts.

Late Thursday, Messrs. Putin and Poroshenko spoke by hone to discuss the Ukrainian leader's peace plan, the Kremlin aid. Mr. Putin said he was hopeful that it could be implemented nd that the demands of people living in the predominantly ussian-speaking regions should be taken into account. He also peated that Kiev needed to cease its military operation imme-ately, the statement said.

The Kremlin said Mr. Putin met afterward with members of ussia's security council to discuss the situation.

Ukraine's newly appointed Foreign Minister Pavlo Klimkin so spoke by phone for the first time since taking the job with

his Russian counterpart to discuss the peace plan, Ukraine's foreign ministry said.

The Kremlin also said Mr. Putin was expected to speak by phone with Mr. Obama, Ms. Merkel, and Mr. Hollande in the coming days. The Russian president is scheduled to travel to Vienna on Tuesday for meetings with Austria's president and the head of the Organization for Security and Cooperation in Europe.

The U.S. move to freeze assets and restrict travel for the sep-aratist leaders is the latest step in a sanctions program that has targeted high-ranking Kremlin officials, leaders of the break-away Crimea region and several Russian business leaders and firms tied to the Russian state.

Beyond that, the U.S. and its allies have said Russia would face more serious sanctions—aimed at significant sectors of Russian industry, for example—if Moscow doesn't move to promote stability in Ukraine.

Russian Prime Minister Dmitry Medvedev said Friday that Russia would contest American sanctions before the World Trade Organization.

Heavy fighting was reported Friday near two border cross-ings and in the towns of Krasny Partisan and Krasny Liman in the Donetsk region. Rebel leaders told Russian news agencies that government planes had dropped bombs near the regional capital of Luhansk, which had triggered air raid sirens in the city.

The defense ministry also reported that rebel fighters had attacked a tank repair depot in Artemivsk in the early-morning hours, firing rocket-propelled grenades at the gate, but the gov-ernment forces had managed to repel the assault.

The Kremlin said Ukrainian shelling near the border Friday had struck a post on the Russian side, seriously wounding a customs officer. Russia's foreign ministry said it was issuing a formal protest and the Kremlin demanded an explanation or apology.

While the U.S. could ratchet up sanctions against Russia at any point, the European Union will have to wait until a meet-ing of EU leaders in Brussels on June 26 and 27. At that point, European officials say, the leaders could add to its existing list of dozens of individuals and two Crimea-based companies sub-ject to an EU-wide visa ban and asset freeze.

Critical Thinking

1. What prompted the newly elected Ukrainian president to believe he could pressure Moscow to reign in separatists?
2. Does the threatening of economic sanctions against Russia affect Russian business leaders and corporations?
3. Can you ever foresee a state of peace between Ukraine and Russia?

Internet References

Pro-Russian separatists agree to honour Ukraine ceasefire
www.theguardian.com/world/2014/jun/23/ukraine-separatists-ceasefire-luhansk-donetsk

Ukraine cease-fire falters as rebels down copter
www.dispatch.com/content/stories/national_world/2014/06/24/0624-Cease-Fire-in-Ukraine-Falters-as-Rebels-Down-Copter.html

Ukraine Rebels Agree to Temporary Ceasefire Separatist Leader
www.youtube.com/watch?v=JdGOk2UVxX4

Why Ukraine's free trade agreement with EU puts all eyes Moscow
www.cityam.com/1403867987/ukraine-signs-historic-free-trade-pa eu-all-eyes-moscow

---

LUKAS I. ALPERT is a reporter for *The Wall Street Journal* and Do Jones Newswires in Moscow, where he covers foreign investme **WILLIAM MAUDLIN** is a reporter for *The Wall Street Journal*.

Article

Prepared by: Caroline Shaffer Westerhof,
California National University for Advanced Studies

Leaders Sound Alarm in General Assembly Debate on Unprecedented Mix of Challenges in Middle East, Taking "Terror to a New Era and a New Level"

UNITED NATIONS DEPARTMENT OF PUBLIC INFORMATION

Learning Outcomes

After reading this article, you will be able to:

Understand why the diverse group of Heads of State at the United Nations General Assembly meetings has sounded the alarm about the unprecedented combination of challenges facing the troubled Middle East as terror is being taken "to a new era and a new level."

Understand why the President of Namibia pointed to numerous crises confronting the international community, including several African countries facing an outbreak of Ebola, the 200 girls abducted in Nigeria, and Gaza having received "indiscriminate" bombardment . . . and that terrorist groups were disrupting peace and stability in different parts of the world.

Understand why the enduring values and principles of the United Nations Charter do not always guide the international community, as demonstrated by the theme of the sixty-ninth session of the United Nations General Assembly, "Delivering on and Implementing a Transformative Post-2015 Development Agenda."

A geographically and sociopolitically diverse group of Heads of State sounded the alarm today about the unprecedented combination of challenges facing the troubled Middle East that was taking "terror to a new era and a new level," as the General Assembly continued its high-level debate.

The President of Iraq said the "ISIS" attacks on innocent civilians had established a "State" based on hatred. The terrorist group, with its huge financial and military assets, had committed crimes against humanity, inflicted suffering on the Iraqi people and was attracting militants and extremists from around the world, including the United States and Europe, he said.

A "terrorist onslaught" in Lebanon, said the country's Council of Ministers President, was causing loss of military and civilian lives and considerable material damage. The terrorists also obstructed the indirect negotiations conducted by his Government to calm the turbulent region. The international mobilization against terrorist activities, however, reflected a global awareness of the urgent need to extinguish the "blazing flames" in the Middle East.

Events unfolding in Syria and Iraq, he continued, also had caused unprecedented waves of displaced persons, and destabilized n   s, divided societies and destroyed human and material re   ces. The Syrian war had driven 1.5 million displaced perso   to Lebanon, which was equivalent to one third of its total p   lation. That unbearable burden could not be borne by any o   untry, he said.

In that vein, th   esident of the State of Palestine, Mahmoud Abbas, noted   t following the last war on Gaza—the third in five years—   t half a million people had been displaced. The number   lestroyed homes, schools, hospitals, public buildings, mos   factories and even cemeteries was incalculable and repres   d a series of war crimes. The idea that it was possible to re   to past patterns, which repeatedly failed, was naive, and in   ase, wrong.

Also examining the e   crippling the Middle East was Malaysia's Prime Minister,   said his Government had convened an international cont   e of scholars of Islamic law, where it had been agreed tha   State to be called "Islamic," it must deliver economic, p   and social justice, and it must advance the six objectiv   Islamic law, namely, the right to life, religion, family, p   ty, dignity, and intellect. "ISIL," he said, had violated eve   gle one of those. It was therefore neither Islamic, nor a St

The Prime Minister of Luxemb   choed that point, saying that ISIL tarnished Islam and se   only to spread its terror to destabilize Syria, Iraq, and bey   He reiterated support for measures aimed at cutting off fina   preventing radicalization and stemming the flow of foreign   hters, and he urged the world community to tackle the root causes of the grave crisis in Iraq.

The world was witnessing a "globalization of hatred," proclaimed Malta's Prime Minister. He urged a resumption of meaningful negotiations in the Middle East, as "too many innocent civilians have died; too many children have been buried," and he called on the Security Council to act urgently and decisively to end the bloodshed in Syria. Closer to home, he stressed more attention was needed to the plight of illegal immigrants in the Mediterranean. Both Malta and Italy were doing their utmost to save lives, he said, but the States receiving waves of migrants could not stand up to the challenge alone.

Adding to the day's multifaceted debate was a Member of the Presidency of Bosnia and Herzegovina, who, noting the many events dedicated to the anniversary of the Sarajevo assassination, said Bosnians asked themselves whether they had learned the lessons from the past. Regrettably, he said, given the local wars fought on all sides of the world today, it seemed the international community had not learned those lessons, but rather had repeated old mistakes and made new ones.

Serbia's President was one of several speakers referring to the benefits of European Union integration, noting that pursuit of membership was his country's top foreign policy priority.

The Prime Minister of Georgia also discussed efforts to esta lish European political, economic, social and legislative nor and standards, as part of an integration strategy.

Also speaking in the debate were Heads of State and G ernment of Namibia, Guyana, Cyprus, Lithuania, Côte d'Ivoi Slovenia, Guinea, El Salvador, Congo, Samoa, Pakistan, Som lia, Haiti, Federated States of Micronesia, Dominica, the form Yugoslav Republic of Macedonia, Comoros, Marshall Islan Kiribati, Nepal, Belgium, and Trinidad and Tobago.

Speaking at the ministerial level were representatives Azerbaijan, Kazakhstan, Uzbekistan, Sudan, Guatemala, a Zambia.

Speaking in exercise of the right of reply were represen tives of India, Armenia, and Azerbaijan. . . .

Academic Editor Note

Excerpts of statements from various country representatives cluded the following, which, in part, hinge on the theme of 69th session, "Delivering on and Implementing a Transform tive Post-2015 Development Agenda."

- Negotiations within the United Nations Framework Convention on Climate Change (UNFCCC) seek the ultimate aim of reaching a coordinated global agreement i 2015.
- Voicing concern about the "political instability" and arme conflict in South Sudan, Mali, and the Central African Republic.
- Condemning the "barbaric and grotesque" killings of jour nalists, humanitarian aid workers and other hostages, and the loss of lives of civilians by the murderous extremists.
- Calling the Ebola epidemic a global problem that require an immediate response of a scale far beyond what was currently being done.
- Witnessing the emergence of ISIL particularly in Libya, Lebanon, Syria, and Iraq, should not leave delegates indifferent or passive.
- Peaceful and sustainable coexistence between countries a societies requires collective efforts, determination and national commitment.
- The international community must maintain undivided security and exert all its efforts to stop ISIS and Al-Qai and restore peace and security in the Middle East.
- Priorities of developing nations should be paid particular attention, and intergovernmental negotiations on the post-2015 development agenda must be inclusive and balanced.
- Noted that the world was in turbulence with humankind facing numerous tensions and conflicts, terrorism, old

and new epidemics, persisting disparities and climate change.

Climate change is a major threat to the planet.

ISIS is a real danger, and that group's attacks on innocent civilians had taken terror to a new era and level, establishing a state based on hatred.

The United Nations is at the heart of multilateralism.

Extreme weather was disrupting world economies particularly in developing countries.

Peace must be based on right and justice, while respecting the sovereignty of nations, upholding their security and safeguarding the fundamental rights of individuals and groups.

Spectre of the deadly Ebola disease and the scourge of HIV/AIDS and noncommunicable diseases had significant potential impacts and threatened the gains made so far by small island developing States.

Rule of law is impossible without respect for human rights.

Young people are victims of the violations in international order made by past and present generations.

Human activities were responsible for the accelerated degradation of the global environment in the pursuit of short-term economic gains, without regard to the health of oceans and the environment.

International peace and security cannot be achieved amid the continuing arms race.

No country should act unilaterally and each must adjust to a "new and multipolar world order.

The nature of global security had changed dramatically, with non-State actors, religious fundamentalists and rebellious criminal gangs terrorizing the world and threatening the safety of peaceful people.

Some States are supporting terrorists and have become hubs and shelters for growing violence.

Existing opportunities in the fight against climate change.

The illegal exploitation and illicit trade of flora and fauna represented another threat to the biodiversity and environment.

Right of Reply

Speaking in exercise of the right of reply, the representative of India responded to "unwarranted references" made by Pakistan's Prime Minister in his speech, stressing that Jammu and Kashmir had peacefully chosen their future. He rejected in their entirety the comments made.

The representative of Armenia, also speaking in exercise of the right of reply, said Azerbaijan's statement relied on falsified information. They repeated the same lies yearly, so he wondered if the leadership now believed what they were saying. He provided several examples that he said refuted what Azerbaijan

claimed and called on Azerbaijan to engage constructively on the basis of principles of sovereignty, territorial integrity, non-use of force or the threat of force.

The representative of Azerbaijan took the floor in exercise of the right of reply, pointing to a "moral and legal irresponsibility" on the part of Armenia. Four United Nations resolutions were the most authoritative rulings on the situation, all demanding the withdrawal of Armenia's occupying forces. No withdrawal was happening. A state of aggression continued because of the ongoing occupation. The representative had referred to self-determination, but the Armenian ethnic minority did not fit into any of the three categories recognized as being entitled to self-determination.

The representative of Armenia took to the floor for a second time, stressing that the people of Nagorno-Karabakh had been clear about their wishes and that any aggression against them would be considered as such. Armenians might not have been the majority population in Azerbaijan, but they were the majority population in Nagorno-Karabakh. He described Armenia's efforts to integrate Azeri refugees and stressed that no Azeri had any historical, legal, or moral right to tell Nagorno-Karabakh how to live or how independent they should be.

The representative of Azerbaijan also took to the floor for a second time, saying the claim of Nagorno-Karabakh's independence was "an outright lie." Armenia had been responsible for the creation of a "subordinate, puppet regime" and had given vital political, military and economic means to the separatist regime. She added that the ethnic make-up of the region was due to ethnic cleansing and stated that Armenia's Head of State took pride in his involvement in atrocities.

Academic Editor Note

Many delegates voiced concerns that were similar to each other. Delegates and the general public seek to recognize the authority of the United Nations. However, the realities of power, greed, and geopolitics always seem to interfere with individual and collective stumbling blocks. As the 2014 United Nations General Assembly completes its meetings, and sets the agenda for the General Assembly meeting of 2015, we trust that the maturing of nation-states and their leaders will achieve values that can give sustenance to a more peaceful world.

Critical Thinking

1. In relation to these crises and the world tragedies, do you believe that UN Secretary-General Ban Ki-moon can lead in establishing world peace in the next decade?
2. Understand why many global world leaders suspect that the disruption of peace and stability in different parts of the world will always be a part of globalization.

3. Given the local wars fought on all sides of the world today, is the international community of today in dire need of learning the lessons of previous wars of the 20th century and is continuing to repeat old mistakes and make new ones? Is it not the member states' responsibility to improve security in the world in the interest of development and progress?

Internet References

EU Statement—United Nations General Assembly: Organizational modalities for September 2015 Summit
www.eu-un.europa.eu/articles/en/article_15375_en.htm

General Debate General Assembly of the United Nations
www.un.org/en/ga

Global Ebola Response
www.un.org/ebolaresponse/resources.shtml

UN General Assembly Beyond 2015
www.beyond2015.org/un-general-assembly

UN General Assembly—Meeting Summaries—United Nations
www.un.org/en/ga/meetings/summaries.shtml

Prepared by: Caroline Shaffer Westerhof,
California National University for Advanced Studies

Article

A Korea Whole and Free

Why Unifying the Peninsula Won't Be So Bad after All

SUE MI TERRY

Learning Outcomes

After reading this article, you will be able to:

Explain why some scholars and practitioners believe a merger of North and South Korea would not spell disaster.

Explain China's concern if such a merger ever did happen.

Discuss the financial and industrial geopolitical consequences of reunification.

When Kim Il Sung, North Korea's founding ruler, died in 1994, many outside observers predicted that his state would die with him. That never happened, of course, and his son Kim Jong Il managed to keep the regime alive until his own death, in 2011. When his son Kim Jong Un took the reins that year, numerous Korea watchers again predicted a collapse. Once again, they were proved wrong. Despite its extreme poverty, North Korea is still very much alive and a major threat to its southern neighbor.

But cracks are appearing. Last December, Kim Jong Un took the unprecedented step of publicly executing his uncle Jang Song Thaek, the second most powerful official in the regime. Although Jang's removal may help strengthen Kim's rule in the short run, it could have the opposite effect in the long run, convincing North Korean elites that the 31-year-old heir to the throne is too hotheaded to be trusted. The regime's patrons in China, meanwhile, were undoubtedly unsettled by the execution of Jang, who was Pyongyang's chief envoy to Beijing and a proponent of Chinese-style reforms.

But Beijing is unlikely to start putting more pressure on Pyongyang, at least not anytime soon. China's leaders may not like the current regime, but they like the alternative far less. North Korea's collapse would likely flood China with refugees and precipitate a military intervention that would bring South Korean and U.S. forces to China's border. So Beijing sees supporting Kim as its least bad option.

Seoul, for its part, has also traditionally avoided doing anything to destabilize Pyongyang, and for similar reasons. For South Korea's leaders, living with the North's occasional pinprick attacks and the ever-present threat of another war is preferable to bearing the crippling social and financial burdens that would accompany reunification.

Contrary to popular belief, a merger of North Korea and South Korea would not spell disaster.

Even the United States and Japan, which have much less to fear from North Korea's demise, have quietly decided to live with the regime. Both the Clinton and the George W. Bush administrations struck generous aid deals with Pyongyang in exchange for limits on its nuclear program. Japan agreed to spend $1 billion as part of one of those deals, the 1994 Agreed Framework, to finance two light-water nuclear reactors in the North (a project that was formally suspended in 2002), and Tokyo has contributed generous amounts of food aid. Policymakers in Washington and Tokyo know that they have little leverage to bring down the North Korean regime. But they also fear the regional chaos that regime change would bring.

Such concerns are legitimate, and all outside parties need to take them into account when planning for the regime's inevitable demise. Even under the best of circumstances, the reunification of North and South Korea will prove more expensive and challenging than that of East and West Germany, given how far apart the two Koreas are in terms of their economies, education levels, and ideologies.

But it is a mistake to conclude that reunification should therefore be avoided. Contrary to popular belief, a merger would not spell disaster for South Korea, nor would it pose an unacceptable risk for the United States, China, and Japan.

Rather, it would produce massive economic and social benefits for the peninsula and the region. There can be only one happy ending to the long-running saga of the North: the emergence of a single, democratic Korea. Outsiders should do all they can to promote and plan for this outcome.

The Good, the Bad, and the Ugly

Reunification is likely to come about in one of three basic ways. The scenario South Koreans hope for most is a soft landing, in which Pyongyang adopts the Chinese economic model, eschews militarism, and undertakes a gradual rapprochement with Seoul. The second scenario is far less attractive: North Korea, staggering under the weight of economic and social forces, implodes and gets absorbed by South Korea. The third scenario is even worse: the peninsula could be reunified through military conflict, in which, following a major attack from the North, South Korean and U.S. forces finally destroy the regime. Of these three outcomes, a soft landing is the least likely, given how little interest Kim has shown in reform. The third scenario is also improbable; for all his pugnacity, Kim is no more suicidal than his father or his grandfather was. That leaves the second scenario, a hard landing, as the most plausible. So that's what policymakers should plan for.

The collapse of Kim's regime would pose many immediate problems, the most pressing of which, from the standpoint of the United States, being how to secure North Korea's nuclear weapons. U.S. and South Korean forces would have to maintain the command structure of North Korea's army in order to prevent factional fighting and attacks by die-hard elements. They would also need to provide security, food, and basic public services, such as water, electricity, and telecommunications, in order to avert a humanitarian crisis that would send the long-suffering North Korean population flooding across the borders into China and South Korea and across the sea to Japan.

These are major challenges, but with enough planning, South Korea—backed by the United States, the UN, and other international actors—could deal with them. In fact, South Korea's Ministry of Unification, in cooperation with U.S. defense officials, has spent decades preparing to do just that. In the event of the North Korean regime's collapse, South Korea's large, well-equipped, and highly trained military should be able to rapidly assume control of North Korea and provide basic services until a civilian government takes over. The task would prove all the easier if South Korea could involve China in the planning process. So far Beijing has refused to publicly entertain the possibility that the Kim regime may not last forever. But even without Chinese participation, South Korea and its partners should be able to handle the fallout of collapse.

The real fear of South Koreans, however, is not that Seoul won't be able to deal with the immediate effects of an implosion; it is that the financial price would ruin them. Reun[ing] Korea would likely cost more than reunifying Germa[ny] did: the Halle Institute for Economic Research has estimat[ed] Germany's bill at $1.9 trillion over 20 years. According [to] South Korea's finance ministry, reunification would consu[me] seven percent of South Korea's current GDP—a share equal [to] $80 billion—every year for a minimum of 10 years. An ad[vi]sory body appointed by South Korean President Lee Myun[g]-bak in 2011 put the price tag of reunification even higher, [at] over $2 trillion. Whatever the final figure, there is little do[ubt] that the endeavor will prove expensive and that the difficulti[es] will be exacerbated by the social challenges of integrating [an] isolated, impoverished, and brainwashed population.

Regional powers, notably South Korea and the Unit[ed] States, should stop propping up the Kim dynasty.

When Two Become One

Although South Koreans tend to focus on the obvious cos[ts], those costs would be outweighed by the benefits of reunific[a]tion. Most immediate among these would be the disappearan[ce] of Northeast Asia's primary source of instability. Assuming t[hat] the regime's nuclear weapons and ballistic missiles could [be] secured and its army peacefully demobilized, its dissoluti[on] would leave not only Seoul but also Washington and Tok[yo] much more secure. The United States would no longer ha[ve] to worry about North Korea selling nuclear weapons abroad [or] drawing U.S. forces into a second Korean war. Japan would [no] longer have to fear North Korean missile strikes or the abdu[c]tion of more of its citizens. And South Korea could stop w[or]rying about North Korea's artillery pulverizing Seoul, its na[vy] torpedoing South Korean ships, or its commandos targeti[ng] South Korean leaders.

Even China would have reason to rejoice. It could repla[ce] its unrequited transfers of fuel, food, and other goods to Pyo[ng]yang with capital investments that yielded income. And on[ce] it stopped propping up the most despotic regime in the wor[ld,] Beijing would find it far easier to portray itself as a responsi[ble] international stakeholder.

The end of the Kim regime would also have huge huma[ni]tarian benefits, freeing 25 million people from the grip of [the] world's last remaining Stalinist state and integrating them i[nto] a modern democracy. The majority of North Korea's 80,00[0 to] 120,000 state prisoners could leave the government's sla[ve] labor camps, where most have been consigned for politic[al,] rather than criminal, offenses. Average North Koreans co[uld] move from a starvation diet, both literally and intellectually, [to] the plentiful availability of food, information, consumer pr[od]ucts, and all the other benefits of modern capitalism. So[uth] Koreans, an intensely nationalist people, would also fina[lly] get to celebrate the reunification of the Korean family. Ko[re-]

ould once again become a single state, as it was from the
ear 668, when the Silla dynasty unified the three Korean king-
oms, until 1945, when the Soviet Union and the United States
vided it at the 38th parallel.

But the greatest benefits for the South would be economic.
eunification would be far more profitable than is commonly
sumed. For starters, Seoul could sharply reduce its defense
pending, which currently stands at $30 billion a year, or
5 percent of GDP—A figure that excludes the $1 billion it
ves every year to Washington to help cover the costs of the
.S. military's presence on the peninsula. South Korea could
d universal conscription and shrink its 680,000-man mili-
ry to 500,000 personnel or fewer, freeing large numbers of
oung Korean men to enter the work force years earlier than
ey currently do. Also joining them would be the 1.1 million
eople, most of them young, that North Korea now employs in
s military.

The prospect of extra young workers should be especially
ntalizing given the rapid aging of South Korea's population.
hanks to the country's growing wealth, life expectancy in
outh Korea has reached 81 years and continues to improve,
hereas its birthrate, at only 1.2 children per woman, is among
e lowest in the world. As a result, according to projections by
e Organization for Economic Cooperation and Development,
2050, South Korea will have the second-oldest population in
e developed world, with nearly seven people over the age of
5 for every working-age adult. Absent reunification, the num-
er of South Koreans aged 15–64 will start to decline in 2017;
2030, so will the overall population.

In North Korea, by contrast, 91 percent of the population is
rrently younger than 65, and the fertility rate is higher than in
e South, at 2.0 children per women. Following reunification,
orth Korea would add more than 17 million potential workers
ed 15–64 to the nearly 36 million already in the South. South
orea could thereby avoid turning to Southeast Asia or other
gions for low-wage workers, who would be hard to assimilate.
outh Korean firms could even move their factories from China
North Korea, where wages would be even lower initially.

Reunification would yield big gains in the mining sector.
outh Korea's high-tech economy is among the most advanced
the world, but the country possesses virtually no mineral
ealth and must import 97 percent of its energy and mineral
eds. North Korea, by contrast, has vast deposits of coal, ura-
um, magnesite, and rare-earth metals—together valued at
trillion—but it cannot currently access them. With technology
om the South, however, this mother lode could be unlocked at
st, providing a welcome boost to the global economy.

A reunified Korea would also boast a newly expanded
mestic market, experience a spike in tourism revenues—
ce some of the most scenic parts of the peninsula lie in the
orth—and see its sovereign risk rating improve. As the risk

of war finally disappeared, credit would become cheaper and
foreign capital would flow more freely into the country.

Once the landmine-fortified demilitarized zone vanished,
moreover, trade would get easier and cheaper. South Korea
currently functions as an island economy, paying high trans-
portation prices for raw materials. With the border gone, a
long-envisioned gas pipeline from Vladivostok to Seoul could
finally be built, sending badly needed Russian oil and gas south.
Energy costs, which drag down the South Korean economy,
would fall dramatically. Korean companies could also begin
shipping goods to China and Russia over land.

Over time, a reunified Korea, with a hard-working population of 75 million, could emerge as a consumer and industrial powerhouse—the Germany of Asia. As two economies
became one, abundant new investment opportunities would
arise. According to a 2009 report by Goldman Sachs, within
30–40 years, the peninsula, if reunified, could overtake France,
Germany, and even Japan in terms of GDP. South Korea's current trading partners—especially the biggest two, China and
the United States—would benefit immensely from this new-
found source of economic vitality.

Neighborhood Watch

Despite all these benefits, selling Korea's neighbors on the
geopolitical consequences of reunification will be difficult.
Leaders in China fear losing a bulwark against U.S. power, but
Washington could assuage these concerns by privately assuring
Beijing that following reunification, no U.S. troops would be
stationed north of the current demilitarized zone—or on any
part of the peninsula, if that's what it takes to win Chinese support. Nationalist South Koreans might insist on this anyway;
relieved of the threat from the North, they could well demand
that Washington withdraw its forces.

Although such a move might feel jarring in Washington, it
would not be a foreign policy setback. If anything, the departure of U.S. forces would represent a happy culmination of
the long U.S. commitment to the peninsula, which began in
the dark days of the Korean War. The United States could still
hedge against Chinese expansionism from its bases in Japan
and Guam, and it would undoubtedly maintain good relations
with a reunified Korea, just as it does with a reunified Germany.

As for Beijing, its ties with Seoul are already better in some
ways than its vexing relations with Pyongyang—and they
should stay that way after reunification. Historically, Korea was
a tributary state of China, and although that submissive relationship will never be reestablished, China need not fear reunification. The new Korea would become an even better trade
partner, and given its desire to avoid a hostile relationship with
its giant neighbor to the north, it would likely triangulate its
foreign policy between Beijing and Washington.

Japan, for its part, would no doubt look askance at the emergence of a stronger, single Korean state. Nearly 70 years after World War II, the Japanese–South Korean relationship remains fraught thanks to Japan's dark colonial legacy. But the emergence of a democratic, capitalist Korea would not truly threaten the region's other big democracy. In fact, reunification would give Tokyo a golden opportunity to dispel anti-Japanese sentiment among Koreans by donating food and medicine and sending aid workers and medical personnel. Japan already ranks as one of the top foreign aid donors in the world, and it could win considerable goodwill by helping rebuild the North.

Ready for Reunification

Given all these advantages, the international community should promote reunification, not postpone it. There may be little that any outsider can do to make Pyongyang change course. But regional powers, notably South Korea and the United States, should stop propping up the Kim dynasty in return for fleeting assurances of better behavior, as they have in the past; Kim Jong Un is no more likely to keep these promises than his father or his grandfather was.

Nor should the West resist the urge to tighten sanctions or retaliate proportionally in response to North Korea's provocations for fear of destabilizing the country. Even if the North were to implode now, that would be preferable to allowing the state to limp along for decades and waiting for reforms that will never come. South Korea has the most to gain from reunification, so it should confront the prospect with confidence, not trepidation. South Korean President Park Geun-hye caused a stir earlier this year when she called reunification a possible "bonanza," and she gave a major pro-unification speech in Germany (a symbolic choice) at the end of March. Her government should continue with its public relations campaign to get South Koreans educated and excited about the benefits of reunification—a task that is particularly important as the younger generation in South Korea grows increasingly wary of it. And Park should make good on her pledge to stay resolute in the face of the North's threats and provocations, even as she attempts to establish a renewed dialogue with the Kim regime and pursue initiatives such as holding cross-border family reunions. Seoul should not shy away from retaliating—which it has never really done—the next time Pyongyang torpedoes a South Korean vessel or shells a South Korean island for fear that doing so could destabilize or aggravate North Korea. Even China would be well advised to stop pouring resources into Pyongyang, unless a new cadre of reform-minded rulers takes power.

To get China and Japan on board, the United States and South Korea should launch a diplomatic initiative aimed at preparing for the contingency of an unexpected collapse. Washington and Seoul should augment their joint military planning by crafting comprehensive political, diplomatic, economic, and legal strategy for reunification. Both governments should designate diplomatic and political representatives to come up with a civilian counterpart to the joint military plans that would be activated in the event of a conflict with or instability in the North. Both states have much to offer: South Korea's Ministry of Unification and other agencies could contribute years of expertise on precisely this scenario, and the United States could contribute the lessons learned from its experiences, good and bad, with nation building in Germany, Japan, Kosovo, Iraq, and Afghanistan.

Once the United States and South Korea develop a common vision, they should encourage Japan to join the planning. Tokyo has legitimate interests in the future of the peninsula and would benefit from preparations designed to address its concerns, such as the prospect of a massive influx of refugees by sea. Japan's logistical support and economic assistance would prove crucial during reunification.

As a final step in this process, the trilateral dialogue among the United States, South Korea, and Japan should expand to include China and possibly Russia. All these key players should be asked to bear some of the costs of reunification in return for a say in how the new Korea behaves in the region. For example, China and Japan could be asked to contribute to the North's reconstruction—the former could help develop the North by providing discounted electricity and assistance in rebuilding infrastructure, and the latter could provide humanitarian and financial aid, investment, and expertise—in return for a guarantee that Seoul will not keep North Korea's nuclear arsenal. Striking such a deal would solve two big problems: South Korea's fears about the costs of integrating North Korea and the rest of the region's fears about an unleashed Korea as a military and economic competitor.

The Kim regime will probably not come to a neat end; the collapse of a state is always messy, and it will be particularly so for a regime so militarized and desperate. But that reality should not blind outside powers to the many upsides of what will come after, nor should it cause them to put off planning the inevitable. In fact, the best way to cope with future instability in the North and reduce the costs of reunification is for the principal powers to start cooperating now. North Korea has the worst government on the planet. Despite all the challenges a transition will entail, everyone will benefit immeasurably from the rise of a new Korea, whole and free.

Critical Thinking

1. Identify the advantages of triangulation in foreign policy between Washington and Beijing with the potential of a "New Korea."

2. What is the possibility of a Chinese-style North Korea, if Kim Jung-un, or post-Kim Jung-un, decides to reform the country, and the North starts to function as a "normal" nation with an open economy?
3. What would be the position of China and Russia with respect to question 2?

nternet References

ina snubs North Korea with leader's visit to South Korea
www.theguardian.com/world/2014/jul/03/china-snubs-north-korea-with-ders-visit-to-south-korea

Guardian Unlimited Special Report: North and South Korea
www.theguardian.com/world/north-korea

North Korean "Peace Proposal" Rejected by South Korea
www.thediplomat.com/2014/07/north-korean-peace-proposal-rejected-by-south-korea

North Korea says it wants 'to create an atmosphere of reconciliation and unity'
www.cnn.com/2014/01/23/world/asia/north-korea-reconciliation

SUE MI TERRY is a former analyst at the CIA and a Senior Research Scholar at Columbia University's Weatherhead East Asian Institute.

Unit 2

UNIT

Prepared by: Caroline Shaffer Westerhof,
California National University for Advanced Studies

Studying Comparative Politics: Evaluating Theories, Learning from Cases, Generalizing Trends

This section builds upon the discussion of why we compare. In part, it describes how theory-building is achieved, that is, it describes the process of examination and evaluation, testing and retesting, verifying sources, and collecting credible evidence in order to achieve generalizability and predictive strength. Generalizations are essential for providing baseline knowledge from which particularities are observed, described, explained, and anticipated. To concretize what this means, this unit looks into one of the oldest theoretical debates in political science: democratic theory. We track how leading scholars ruminate about democratic theory before looking at how additional studies—on participation, mature democracies, transitioning regimes, and the relationship between capitalism and democracy—build on some of the theoretical foundations laid out.

Here, the tone is set for distinguishing between democracy as studied in political science and conventional usage. Democracy is a term most widely used among politicians; scholars actually "hesitate" to use it "because of the 'ambiguity' of the term." Nevertheless, given its popular use in both democratic and autocratic regimes, it is important to clarify what it is and what it is not. Importantly, democracy, clarified by scholars may be interpreted one way, and practitioners may consider other definitions. As the concept is researched, it is important, at the outset, to clarify its interpretations in terms of concepts, procedures, and principles.

There is a review of the study of democracy noting the process of theory-building. The essential parts of theory-building include of theories derived from systematic scholastic examination and evaluation through evidentiary support. Fifteen interesting conclusions or considerations from twenty-five years of democratic study are reviewed and included.

What is political science research? Such research is situated in the debate in the literature and based on evidentiary evaluation. In this regard Middle East studies demonstrate "how theory meets reality." Progress in Middle East studies notes that we need no longer explain Arab in cultural terms and to recognize that there is a belief within the Arab world to acknowledge the popularity of democracy as a concept. We do recognize the broad conflagration that is tearing apart this part of the world. It continues to be a bloody turmoil that is growing worse, day by day. The president of the United States is being faced with hard questions.

Discussion and argumentation, fact-finding, and evidentiary support are the essential elements to theory-building so that the patterns that are identified withstand scrutiny and evaluation. This is the "theoretically informed" comparative study. Indeed, it is because the theoretical fundamentals are in place that we observe particularities that evolve throughout our rationale of comparative politics. We note the promises and problems of citizen participation and mobilization across transitioning countries and mature democracies. Thus, whether in transitioning regimes or mature democracies, viable outlets for citizen participation are the key to maintaining political stability and enhancing development, although these do not always exist.

If we think that the debate is near exhaustion, consider this additional angle: Does capitalism drive democracy or does democracy lead to economic development? Is this a wrinkle to the theory? Or is it an elaboration of the theory, even as protestors appear to demand an end to capitalism or the existing democratic institutions, they are also encouraging alienated groups to return to the political fold by participating? That participation, in turn, leads to less dramatic or less revolutionary forms of change, such as petitions for policy or economic responses.

Must the United States rethink its strategy as it addresses the challenges of maintaining its primacy as a global power? Yet, as the world is becoming increasingly multi-polar, the world center of gravity has shifted to Asia. Although the United States may want to contain China, China is continuing to make history by developing a new shipping frontier.

Clearly, political scholars as well as practitioners will continue to assess how democratization occurs, what it takes to consolidate democracies, and what processes will enrich emergent and mature democracies. That is, theory building is likely to continue— as it well should—and policymakers will continue to evaluate the empirical applications of the theory. Importantly, the discussion, evaluation, and testing reveal to us the problems of letting our own biases dictate who gets to participate and how or when. In the process, we also learn a fundamental and important lesson about participation: If we provide for citizen participation, the expanded venues provide the release of any bottled up responses that may otherwise find relief through dangerous or extremist appeals. That is a generalization and baseline that will enhance political development in any country and region and may yet be a destructive force.

Article

Prepared by: Caroline Shaffer Westerhof,
California National University for Advanced Studies

German Spy Agency Searches for More Moles after U.S. Breach

BND president orders analysis of agency's communications for irregularities, and foreign minister to meet John Kerry.

PHILIP OLTERMANN

Learning Outcomes

After reading this article, you will be able to:

Discuss the implications and reactions of the German intelligence agency with regard to U.S. spying in Germany.

Discuss why a theory is circulating in Germany labeling the U.S. National Security Agency a "mafia with a legal department," and stating that it does not care for laws or basic rights and has no ethics and no morality.

Germany's intelligence agency has reacted to the continuing row over U.S. spying by commissioning an investigation to unmask further moles in its own ranks. Gerhard Schindler, president of the BND, has told the government that he has ordered an analysis of his agency's communications for irregularities, according to Der Spiegel.

Similar searches had previously concentrated on identifying Russian and Chinese spies, the magazine said.

The discovery in the past fortnight of two suspected U.S. spies on the German government's payroll triggered an official request on Thursday for the CIA's station chief to leave the country.

The move met with cross-party approval in Germany on Friday. The foreign minister, Frank-Walter Steinmeier, described the request, which does not amount to a formal expulsion, as a necessary step in response to the U.S. "breach of trust."

Steinmeier confirmed he would meet the U.S. secretary of state, John Kerry, during the Iranian nuclear talks in Vienna

next week. He said he hoped the meeting would lead to a new start for the United States and Germany's damaged relations: "It would be an illusion to assume that conflicts can be defused and political solutions can be worked out without closely collaborating with the US."

A recent survey by Germany's TNS research institute illustrates what a devastating impact the string of spying allegations over the past year have had on the German public's view of the United States. Of those surveyed, 69% told researchers their trust in the United States had shrunk, while 57% called for more independence from the United States. As many as 40% said they would approve of closer collaboration between Germany and Russia.

It remains unclear whether U.S. intelligence services were pursuing a specific goal in their correspondence with contacts within the German authorities. Originally, there was speculation that U.S. spy agencies may have been trying to obtain information about the government's parliamentary investigation into NSA surveillance in Germany.

Members of the Bundestag's supervisory panel said on Thursday that they believed that motive was unlikely. Out of the cache of 215 confidential documents the BND staffer is alleged to have sold to contacts at the CIA for €25,000 (£20,000), only one is said to concern the activities of the NSA committee.

Clemens Binninger, chair of the supervisory panels, said it was currently "impossible to come up with a conclusive analysis" of the importance and relevance of four folders of leaked documents. But according to Die Welt, some of the leaked documents were part of the communication between the office of the chancellor, Angela Merkel, and that of the president of

BND, while others contained an overview of BND locations around the world—which might hint at a more general spying strategy rather than a targeted operation.

That is the most widely circulated theory in Germany. "The NSA digs and rummages wherever it can," wrote Kai Biermann in an op-ed in Die Zeit [http://www.zeit.de/politik/deutschland/2014-07/nsa-botschaft-resident-ausweisung]. "It is a 'mafia with a legal department' and does not care for laws or basic rights. It has no ethics and no morality and only wants one thing: to know everything."

More details have emerged about the second instance of suspected spying. Germany's counter-espionage service was alerted to a defence ministry employee's contacts with a US agent while he was engaged as a political adviser to the Nato-led Kosovo force in the Balkans.

The defence ministry employee is said to have had regular meetings with the US agent since 2010, but insisted these had been of a private nature. A payment of €2,000 into the suspect's bank account had drawn the attention of counter-espionage investigators, but the suspect claimed the money was merely a loan for a wedding party.

Critical Thinking

1. Is cyber-espionage a normal way of doing business today, whether friend or foe? If undetected?

2. How effective is such cyber-espionage against foreign nations and foreign companies?

3. What is accomplished by hiring "cyber-mercenaries"?

Internet References

CIA Was Involved in U.S. Spying on Germany: Report
www.huffingtonpost.com/2014/07/07/cia-spying-germany_n_55645.html

DOJ brings first-ever cyber-espionage case against China officials
www.foxnews.com/politics/2014/05/19/doj-bringing-cyber-espiona case-against-chinese-officials

Germany to escalate counter-espionage efforts in wake of spying allegations
www.theguardian.com/world/2014/jul/07/germany-counter-espiona escalate-bnd-arrest-maziere-policy

Germany Urges US to Explain Suspected "Double Agent" Case
www.newsmaxworld.com/GlobalTalk/germany-us-espionage/2014/07/id/580983

Iranian Cyber Espionage Plot Targeted US-Israel Relations
http://www.newsmax.com/Newsfront/Iran-Israel-cyber-espionage/20 05/29/id/573939

PHILIP OLTERMANN is the Guardian and Observer's Berlin correspondent and the author of *Keeping up with the Germans: A History Anglo-German Encounters*.

Article

Prepared by: Caroline Shaffer Westerhof,
California National University for Advanced Studies

Q & A: What Is This Iron Dome That Is Protecting Israel from Hamas Rockets?

MICHAELA DODGE

Learning Outcomes

After reading this article, you will be able to:

Understand how this Iron Dome shoots down incoming rockets before they hit the target.

Understand the layered missile defense system that Israel is building.

As Hamas launches rockets from the Gaza Strip into Israel, casualties are kept at a minimum thanks to Israel's superior air defense system. In the current conflict, up to 90 percent of the rockets engaged by the "Iron Dome" are intercepted as they approach high-value Israeli targets. The Rafael-Raytheon air defense system has held a high rate of success since it first intercepted a Gaza rocket in April 2011. What is the Iron Dome and how does it operate? Heritage policy analyst Michaela Dodge answers these questions and more.

What is the Iron Dome?

The Iron Dome is an Israeli air defense and a short-range defense system designed to destroy *enemy rockets, mortars, and artillery shells.*

How does it work?

Each Iron Dome battery is comprised of interceptors (Tamir), radars, and command and control systems. The system shoots down incoming rockets mid-air before they hit the target. The system only intercepts rockets that would hit targets of value population centers, military facilities, etc.). This allows the system to preserve interceptors and save more resources than

if it were shooting down every single rocket. In April 2011, the Israelis found out that they needed to launch an interceptor against only about 20 percent of the rockets launched by Hamas.

How often is it activated?

This depends on the threat level. The Iron Dome is deployed close to population centers. It is mobile so it can be deployed to different parts of the country depending on where the threat is coming from. Once radars get information about incoming rockets, the interceptors are fired in a manner that increases the probability of the intercept.

Since it's a short-range air defense system, what type of capabilities does the IDF have for countering long- and medium-range threats?

Israel is building a layered missile defense system, which means that it is developing a range of systems for different ballistic missile threats. Arrow 3 is designed to intercept short- and medium-range ballistic missiles. David's Sling, currently under development, will be designed to intercept short-range ballistic missiles.

What role did the United States play in developing the system?

The United States is contributing funds toward developing the Iron Dome system. In the fiscal year 2014, the Department of

Defense requested more than $220 million to fund the system. Raytheon, U.S. defense contractor, is under contract for co-producing the system's components and interceptors.

How effective is it? What percentage/number of incoming rockets has it intercepted?

In the current conflict, the Iron Dome has intercepted up to 90 percent of rockets that it engages. Note that it does not engage every single rocket, but only the ones that would actually target valued areas.

What other countries have the Iron Dome technology?

Other countries (for example, Russia, the United States, Japan, South Korea) have air defense systems and while they are conceptually similar, other air defense systems are based on different technologies that the Iron Dome uses. No other country in the world has the Iron Dome system today.

Can you briefly address the criticisms of the system?

Critics have argued that the Iron Dome is too expensive, since limited numbers of interceptors (about $60,000 apiece) are fielded against large numbers of cheaper offensive rockets (about $500 to $1,000 apiece). These critics miss the point. What matters is the value of defended area and what would costs of a successful attack. The damage in blood and treasure caused by a successful attack could be much larger than a cost of an interceptor.

Critics also argue that the system does not work based on a "visual analysis" of rockets' contrails. This argument simply does not stand. Blurry videos from cameras and smartphones are not sufficient to make a judgment whether a threat was destroyed or not. The IDF uses different types of radars to confirm intercepts.

There are other significant benefits that the critics of the system often omit from their analysis. Until the deployment of the Iron Dome system, the Israelis faced a stark choice: They could absorb the attacks or escalate the conflict by conducting retaliatory offensive operations against their enemies. Escalation, for justifiable reasons, is what the Israelis chose to do both

against Hezbollah in 2006 and against Hamas periodically. the extent the Israelis used these retaliatory strikes in attempt to destroy enemy rocket launchers—itself a fundamental defensive purpose—they found the offensive counterstrike themselves to have limited effectiveness and cost effectivene The Iron Dome system provides the Israeli leadership w the political, policy, and military options as well as the spa and the time to make the right decision in order to prevent escalation.

The use of the Iron Dome system permits Israel to draw even clearer distinction between itself and its enemies as which side is the aggressor (not that there should be much dou by anyone making an honest assessment). Nevertheless, the is considerable, albeit intangible, value in depriving an ener of plausible arguments against an effective defensive milita system. For Hamas and Hezbollah to argue against Iron Dom they will have to assert that Israeli use of this defensive syste is an aggressive measure. The argument is implausible.

Critical Thinking

1. Is the Iron Dome system necessary for the survival of Israel?
2. Should cost of the Iron Dome system weigh in the decision t implement its use?
3. How is the success rate of the Iron Dome system determined

Internet References

From Inside the *Iron Dome*
www.theatlantic.com/international/archive/2014/07/from-inside-t iron-dome/374580

Israel's mobile missile defense system: What is the Iron Dome?
www.globalnews.ca/news/1203882/israels-mobile-missile-defen system-what-is-the-iron-dome

No safe haven for those living near Israel's Iron Dome
www.theguardian.com/world/2014/jul/17/no-bomb-shelters-reside israel-iron-dome-missiles

The Economist explains: How Israel's "Iron Dome" works
www.economist.com/blogs/economist-explains/2014/07/econom explains-12

U.S. Senate Doubles Funding for Israel's Iron Dome
http://www.thewire.com/global/2014/07/us-senate-doubles-fundi for-israels-iron-dome/374473

MICHAELA DODGE specializes in missile defense, nuclear weapo modernization, and arms control as policy analyst for defense and s tegic policy in The Heritage Foundation's Allison Center for Fore Policy Studies.

rticle

Prepared by: Caroline Shaffer Westerhof,
California National University for Advanced Studies

n Canada, a Fishing Town Faces Its End

Once-Vibrant Newfoundland Community of Little Bay Islands Plans Vote on Whether to Shut Down and Relocate.

LISTAIR MacDonald

earning Outcomes

ter reading this article, you will be able to:

Explain the economic argument of why a village in the Canadian Newfoundland and Labrador province is looking to "shut down."

Distinguish the politics in shutting down the village of Little Bay Islands as compared to a city within the United States, such as Williams, Arizona, which, although on the brink of financial disaster, survived.

Alma Budgell is the last of 12 children born to a fishing family still living in this picturesque community. Now, she hopes to be among the very last people ever to live here. The village has no retail shop and a school with just two ldren. Founded almost 200 years ago, the town thrived with wfoundland's once mighty fishing industry and declined ng with it. Only some 90 people, most of them older than 60, l live here year-round.

Its tale of a dwindling and aging population is not uncom->n among small towns in the Western world, but residents e have an unusual resettlement option.

Sixty years ago, the province of Newfoundland and Labra-· began offering its shrinking outposts money to close down l move on. After a nearly four-decade lull, the number of nmunities seeking resettlement has been ticking up, as the er sea-faring generation fades and the government has raised value of its offers. The province is reviewing inquiries from communities.

Little Bay Islands is set to decide its future in a vote in the ing.

Ms. Budgell, 58 years old, has lived her entire life here. She said she will vote yes to leaving. "It's like a prison here," she said.

She remembers a community filled with children and a vibrant social life, where "steamers" would bring visitors as well as buyers for the plentiful fish and crabs. Signs of the town's fishing past are everywhere, from the piles of lobster traps to the fishermen's huts that hug the rocky bay. Its decline also is on display, in empty streets and abandoned stores.

Fishing jobs in Newfoundland long have been disappearing. In the late 1980s, the industry employed around 13% of the province's workers, according to the provincial Department of Finance. That tailed off sharply to 3% currently, as fish stocks fell and after the government put a moratorium on cod fishing about 20 years ago. Four years ago, the local fish-processing plant closed, hit by lower government quotas for snow crabs, among other factors, said Pete Eveleigh, who was CEO of the company that operated the facility. The closure led to the loss of about a hundred jobs, including Ms. Budgell's. "That is when the island began to die," she said.

Her husband, Dennis Budgell, has lately been helping to take down the shuttered plant, one of the few job opportunities that came his way in 2013.

"I just can't get work here, and I am not ready for retire-ment," the 61-year-old said. Mr. Budgell is the local councilor who first contacted the government to apply for resettlement.

Hundreds of outposts in Newfoundland and Labrador shut down in the mid-20th century, as the fishing industry underwent structural changes and some residents sought better educational opportunities and a wider range of jobs. About 28,000 people relocated between 1954 and 1975, according to the provincial government. The resettlement program faded as government support did, amid complaints from some of those displaced that they were forced out and as some struggled to find jobs in their new communities. Its mark can still be seen in the deserted villages that dot parts of the coast.

Almost every summer, Ernest Taylor, 70, returns to Grole, the fishing village he says his family was "forced" to leave in 1969. Now, all that is left of the village, on the island's rugged southern coast, are gravestones.

"Rural Newfoundland has been pretty much destroyed," said Mr. Taylor, a retired teacher living in Grand Bank, a nearby town.

Little Bay Islands villagers who don't want to leave say the government wants to shut them down to save money on essential services. A spokesman for the Department of Municipal and Intergovernmental Affairs said that while relocations occur only when they save the province money, the province has been responding to requests for resettlement, rather than initiating moves. Residents who don't want to move are not forced to leave, he said.

The ferry service that connects Little Bay Islands to the mainland, a 30-minute journey, costs 2.9 million Canadian dollars (about US$2.6 million) a year to run, according to the provincial government.

In March, the province increased its resettlement offer by about C$150,000 to a range of C$250,000 and C$270,000 per household.

Perry Locke is one of a handful here who wants to stay. He has a full-time job at the local electric utility, and his child is one of the two at the school. He says C$250,000 would barely cover the cost of a house elsewhere.

Those wishing to stay, like Mr. Locke, argue the village has a future in tourism. They point to newly spruced-up houses where they say some Americans spend the summer. Locals say these part-time residents are against the closure, as it would end

electric utility, sewage and ferry service, but they can't take pa in voting.

The measure needs 90% approval to be adopted. Mo islanders expect it will pass.

According to local lore, the town was founded in 1825 by English settler named Budgell. Dennis Budgell, the town cou cilor who approached the province about resettlement, sa islanders often joke about this.

"Everybody says, it was a Budgell who started this place now it's a Budgell who is going to close it down," he said.

Critical Thinking

1. What has caused the fishing industry in Little Bay Islands to lose its financial battle?
2. Does a dwindling and aging population affect the reality of shutting down Little Bay Islands?
3. How can globalization affect Little Bay Islands?

Internet References

In Canada, a Fishing Town Ponders Its End
www.online.wsj.com/news/articles/SB1000142405270230420220457
2510717736366

Little Bay Islands forced to ask Newfoundland for "resettlemen
www.news.nationalpost.com/2013/02/27/little-bay-islands-as
newfoundland-for-resettlement

Newfoundland town awaits vote on accepting relocation deal
www.globalnews.ca/news/852263/newfoundland-town-awaits-vote-accepting-relocation-deal

ALISTAIR MACDONALD is the Wall Street Journal's senior Canada c respondent, covering politics, business and general news. Before that covered U.K. politics and general news in the Journal's London bure

Article

Prepared by: Caroline Shaffer Westerhof,
California National University for Advanced Studies

Why Middle East Studies Missed the Arab Spring: The Myth of Authoritarian Stability

F. GREGORY GAUSE III

Learning Outcomes

After reading this article, you will be able to:

- Understand why Professor Gause states the United States should not encourage democracy in the Arab world.

- Understand the complexity among all forces and factions in the Middle East.

- Understand what is meant by the "Arab Spring."

The vast majority of academic specialists on the Arab world were as surprised as everyone else by the upheavals that toppled two Arab leaders last winter and that now threaten several others. It was clear that Arab regimes were deeply unpopular and faced serious demographic, economic, and political problems. Yet many academics focused on explaining what they saw as the most interesting and anomalous aspect of Arab politics: the persistence of undemocratic rulers.

Until this year, the Arab world boasted a long list of such leaders. Muammar al-Qaddafi took charge of Libya in 1969; the Assad family has ruled Syria since 1970; Ali Abdullah Saleh became president of North Yemen (later united with South Yemen) in 1978; Hosni Mubarak took charge of Egypt in 1981; and Zine el-Abidine Ben Ali ascended to Tunisia's presidency in 1987. The monarchies enjoyed even longer pedigrees, with the Hashemites running Jordan since its creation in 1920, the al-Saud family ruling a unified Saudi Arabia since 1932, and the Alaouite dynasty in Morocco first coming to power in the seventeenth century.

These regimes survived over a period of decades in which democratic waves rolled through East Asia, eastern Europe, Latin America, and sub-Saharan Africa. Even the Arab countries' neighbors in the Muslim Middle East (Iran and Turkey) experienced enormous political change in that period, with a revolution and three subsequent decades of political struggle in Iran and a quasi-Islamist party building a more open and democratic system in secular Turkey.

For many Middle East specialists, this remarkable record of regime stability in the face of numerous challenges demanded their attention and an explanation. I am one of those specialists. In the pages of *Foreign Affairs* in 2005 ("Can Democracy Stop Terrorism?" September/ October 2005), I argued that the United States should not encourage democracy in the Arab world because Washington's authoritarian Arab allies represented stable bets for the future. On that count, I was spectacularly wrong. I also predicted that democratic Arab governments would prove much less likely to cooperate with U.S. foreign policy goals in the region. This remains an open question. Although most of my colleagues expressed more support for U.S. efforts to encourage Arab political reform, I was hardly alone in my skepticism about the prospect of full-fledged democratic change in the face of these seemingly unshakable authoritarian regimes.

Understanding what we missed and what we overestimated in our explanations of the stability of Arab authoritarianism—and understanding why we did so—is of more than just academic significance. Regional analysts must determine what changed in the forces that underpinned four decades of Arab regime stability and what new elements emerged to spark the current revolts. Doing so will allow U.S. policymakers to approach the Arab revolts more effectively by providing them insight into the factors that will drive postrevolutionary politics in the Arab world.

Arab States and Their Militaries

The first task is to establish what academia knew and did not know. To begin with, it is important to recognize that few, if any, political scientists working on the Middle East explained the peculiar stability of Arab regimes in cultural terms—a sign of progress over the scholarship of earlier eras. The literature on how Arab dictators endured did not include old saws about how Islam is inimical to democracy or how Arab culture remains too patriarchal and traditional to support democratic change. We recognized how popular the concept of democracy was in the Arab world and that when given real electoral choices, Arabs turned out to vote in large numbers. We also understood that Arabs did not passively accept authoritarian rule. From Algeria to Saudi Arabia, Arab autocrats were able to stay in power over the past 40 years only by brutally suppressing popular attempts to unseat them, whether motivated by political repression or food prices. Arab citizens certainly demonstrated the desire and ability to mobilize against their governments. But those governments, before 2011, were extremely successful in co-opting and containing them.

As a result, academics directed their attention toward explaining the mechanisms that Arab states had developed to weather popular dissent. Although different scholars focused on different aspects of this question, from domestic institutions to government strategies, most attributed the stability of Arab dictatorships to two common factors: the military-security complex and state control over the economy. In each of these areas, we in the academic community made assumptions that, as valid as they might have been in the past, turned out to be wrong in 2011.

Most scholars assumed that no daylight existed between the ruling regimes and their military and security services. That assumption was not unreasonable. Many Arab presidents served in uniform before they took office, including Ben Ali and Mubarak. In the wake of the Arab military coups of the 1950s and 1960s, Arab leaders created institutions to exercise political control over their armies and, in some cases, established rival military forces to balance the army's weight. Arab armies helped ruling regimes win their civil wars and put down uprisings. As a result, most Middle East experts came to assume that Arab armies and security services would never break with their rulers.

This assumption obviously proved incorrect. Scholars did not predict or appreciate the variable ways in which Arab armies would react to the massive, peaceful protests this year. This oversight occurred because, as a group, Middle East experts had largely lost interest in studying the role of the military in Arab politics. Although this topic once represented a central feature of U.S. scholarship on the Middle East—when the Arab military coups of the 1950s and 1960s occupied the academics of that era—the remarkable stability of the Arab regimes since then led us to assume that the issue was no longer important. Yet a preliminary review of the unfolding revolts suggests that two factors drive how Arab militaries react to public unrest: the social composition of both the regime and its military and the level of institutionalization and professionalism in the army itself.

The countries in which the military, as an institution, sided with the protesters, Egypt and Tunisia, are two of the most homogeneous societies in the Arab world. Both are overwhelmingly Sunni. (The Coptic Christian minority in Egypt plays an important social role there but has little political clout.) Both the Egyptian and the Tunisian armies are relatively professional, with neither serving as the personal instrument of the ruler. Army leaders in both nations realized that their institutions could play an important role under new regimes and thus were willing to risk ushering out the old guard.

In Arab countries featuring less institutionalized forces, where the security services are led by and serve as the personal instruments of the ruler and his family, those forces have split or dissolved in the face of popular protests. In both Libya and Yemen, units led by the rulers' families have supported the regimes, while other units have defected to the opposition, stayed on the sidelines, or just gone home.

In divided societies, where the regime represents an ethnic, sectarian, or regional minority and has built an officer corps dominated by that overrepresented minority, the armies have thus far backed their regimes. The Sunni-led security forces in Bahrain, a Shiite-majority country, stood their ground against demonstrators to preserve the Sunni monarchy. The Jordanian army remains loyal to the monarchy despite unrest among the country's Palestinian majority. Saudi Arabia's National Guard, heavily recruited from central and western Arabian tribes, is standing by the central Arabian al-Saud dynasty. In each country, the logic is simple: if the regime falls and the majority takes over, the army leadership will likely be replaced as well.

The Syrian army's reaction to the crisis facing the Assad regime will offer an important test of this hypothesis. Members of the Assad family command important army units, and Alawites and members of other minority groups staff a good portion of the officer corps in the Sunni-majority country. If minority solidarity with the regime endures, Assad is likely to retain power. Yet if disaffected officers begin to see the army as an instrument of the Assad family itself, they could bring down the regime. Either way, once the dust settles, Middle East scholars will need to reexamine their assumptions about the relationship between Arab states and their militaries—perhaps the key element in determining regime survival in a crisis.

The Reform Factor

State control over the economy in the Middle East was another pillar of regime stability identified by academics. Scholars posited that Arab states with oil reserves and revenues deployed this wealth to control the economy, building patronage networks, providing social services, and directing the development of dependent private sectors. Through these funds, Arab rulers connected the interests of important constituencies to their survival and placated the rest of their citizens with handouts in times of crisis. Indeed, since the current uprisings began, only Libya among the major oil exporters (Algeria, Iraq, Kuwait, Libya, Qatar, Saudi Arabia, and the United Arab Emirates) has faced a serious challenge. Buoyed by high oil prices, the other oil exporters have been able to head off potential opposition by distributing resources through increased state salaries, higher subsidies for consumer goods, new state jobs, and direct handouts to citizens. Qaddafi's example establishes that oil money must be allocated properly, rather than wasted on pet projects and harebrained schemes, for it to protect a regime. The recent Arab revolts, then, would seem to validate this part of the academic paradigm on regime stability.

Yet this year's revolts have called the economic foundations of the regime stability argument into question when it comes to non-oil-producing states. Although Arab petrostates have relied on their oil revenues to avoid economic reform, changes in the world economy and the liberalizing requirements of foreign aid donors have over the past two decades forced non-oil-producing states to modernize their economies. A number of Arab regimes, including in Egypt, Jordan, Morocco, and Tunisia, have privatized state enterprises, encouraged foreign investment, created incentives to kick-start the private sector, and cut subsidies and state expenditures that previously consumed government budgets. Such Washington consensus-style economic reforms exacerbated inequalities and made life more difficult for the poor, but they also opened up new opportunities for local entrepreneurs and allowed the upper classes to enjoy greater consumer choice through liberalized trade regimes. Some Middle East specialists thought that economic liberalization could establish new bases of support for Arab authoritarians and encourage the economic growth necessary to grapple with the challenges of growing populations (as economic reforms in Turkey have led to greater support for the ruling Justice and Development Party there). Meanwhile, Western governments pushed the idea that economic reform represented a step toward political reform.

But these economic reforms backfired on those governments that embraced them most fully: Cairo and Tunis. Although both Egypt and Tunisia had achieved decent economic growth rates and received praise from the International Monetary Fund as recently as 2010, politically driven privatizations did not enhance the stability of their regimes. Instead, they created a new class of superwealthy entrepreneurs, including members of the presidents' families in both countries, which became the targets of popular ire. And the academics' assumption that these beneficiaries of economic reform would support the authoritarian regimes proved chimerical. The state-bred tycoons either fled or were unable to stop events and landed in postrevolutionary prison. The upper-middle class did not demonstrate in favor of Ben Ali or Mubarak. In fact, some members became revolutionary leaders themselves.

It is supremely ironic that the face of the Egyptian revolt was Wael Ghonim, the Egyptian Google executive. He is exactly the kind of person who was poised to succeed in the Egypt of Mubarak—bilingual, educated at the American University of Cairo, and at home in the global business world. Yet he risked his future and life to organize the "We are all Khaled Said" Facebook page, in memory of a man beaten to death by Egyptian police, which helped mobilize Egyptians against the regime. For him and many others in similar economic circumstances, political freedom outweighed monetary opportunity.

Seeing what happened in Cairo and Tunis, other Arab leaders rushed to placate their citizens by raising state salaries, canceling planned subsidy cuts, and increasing the number of state jobs. In Saudi Arabia, for example, in February and March, King Abdullah announced new spending plans of more than $100 billion. The Saudis have the oil money to fulfill such pledges. In non-oil-producing states, such as Jordan, which halted its march down the road of economic reform once the trouble began, governments may not have the money to maintain the old social contract, whereby the state provided basic

economic security in exchange for loyalty. Newly liberated Egypt and Tunisia are also confronting their inherited economic woes. Empowered electorates will demand a redistribution of wealth that the governments do not have and a renegotiation of the old social contract that the governments cannot fund.

Many Middle East scholars recognized that the neoliberal economic programs were causing political problems for Arab governments, but few foresaw their regime-shaking consequences. Academics overestimated both the ameliorating effect of the economic growth introduced by the reforms and the political clout of those who were benefiting from such policies. As a result, they underestimated the popular revulsion to the corruption and crony privatization that accompanied the reforms.

Oil wealth remains a fairly reliable tool for ensuring regime stability, at least when oil prices are high. Yet focused on how Arab regimes achieved stability through oil riches, Middle East scholars missed the destabilizing effects of poorly implemented liberal economic policies in the Arab world.

A New Kind of Pan-Arabism

Another factor missed by Middle East specialists had less to do with state policies and institutions than with cross-border Arab identity. It is not a coincidence that major political upheavals arose across the Arab world simultaneously. Arab activists and intellectuals carefully followed the protests of Iran's 2009 Green Movement, but no Arabs took to the streets in emulation of their Iranian neighbors. Yet in 2011, a month after a fruit vendor in Tunisia set himself on fire, the Arab world was engulfed in revolts. If any doubts remain that Arabs retain a sense of common political identity despite living in 20 different states, the events of this year should put them to rest.

Such strong pan-Arab sentiments should not have surprised the academic community. Much of the work on Arab politics in previous generations had focused on Arab nationalism and pan-Arabism, the ability of Arab leaders to mobilize political support across state borders based on the idea that all Arabs share a common political identity and fate. Yet many of us assumed that the cross-border appeal of Arab identity had waned in recent years, especially following the Arab defeat in the 1967 war with Israel. Egypt and Jordan had signed treaties with Israel, and the Palestinians and Syria had engaged in direct negotiations with Israel, breaking a cardinal taboo of pan-Arabism. U.S.-led wars against Iraq in 1990-91 and beginning in 2003 excited opposition in the Arab world but did not destabilize the governments that cooperated with the U.S. military plans—a sign of waning pan-Arabism as much as government immunity to popular sentiment. It seemed that Arab states had become strong enough (with some exceptions, such as Lebanon and post-Saddam Hussein Iraq) to fend off ideological pressures from across their borders. Most Middle East scholars believed that pan-Arabism had gone dormant.

They thus missed the communal wave of 2011. Although the events of this year demonstrate the continued importance of Arab identity, pan-Arabism has taken a very different form than it did a half century ago under the leadership of Egyptian

President Gamal Abdel Nasser. Then, Nasser, a charismatic leader with a powerful government, promoted popular ideas and drove events in other countries, using the new technology of his day, the transistor radio, to call on Arabs to oppose their own governments and follow him. Now, the very leaderless quality of the popular mobilizations in Egypt and Tunisia seems to have made them sources of inspiration across the Arab world.

In recent decades, Arab leaders, most notably Saddam during the Gulf War, have attempted to embrace Nasser's mantle and spark popular Arab movements. Even the Iranian leader Ayatollah Ruhollah Khomeini-a Persian, not an Arab-appealed to Islam to mobilize Arabs behind his banner. All these attempts failed. When the people of Tunisia and then Egypt overthrew their corrupt dictators, however, other Arabs found they could identify with them. The fact that these revolts succeeded gave hope (in some cases, such as in Bahrain, false hope) to other Arabs that they could do the same. The common enemy of the 2011 Arab revolts is not colonialism, U.S. power, or Israel, but Arabs' own rulers.

Academics will need to assess the restored importance of Arab identity to understand the future of Middle East politics. Unlike its predecessor, the new pan-Arabism does not appear to challenge the regional map. Arabs are not demonstrating to dissolve their states into one Arab entity; their agendas are almost exclusively domestic. But the Arab revolts have shown that what happens in one Arab state can affect others in unanticipated and powerful ways. As a result, scholars and policymakers can no longer approach countries on a case-by-case basis. The United States will have a hard time supporting democracy in one Arab country, such as Egypt, while standing by as other allies, such as Bahrain, crush peaceful democratic protests.

In addition, the new pan–Arabism will eventually bring the issue of Arab–Israeli peace back to the fore. Although none of the 2011 Arab revolts occurred in the name of the Palestinians, democratic Arab regimes will have to reflect popular opinion on Israel, which remains extremely low. Arab public opinion on the United States is influenced by Arabs' views on the Israeli-Palestinian conflict as much as by U.S. actions in other Arab countries. As a result, the United States will need to reactivate Israeli-Palestinian peace talks to anticipate the demands of Arab publics across the Middle East.

Back to the Drawing Board

Academic specialists on Arab politics, such as myself, have quite a bit of rethinking to do. That is both intellectually exciting and frightening. Explaining the stability of Arab authoritarians was an important analytic task, but it led some of us to underestimate the forces for change that were bubbling below, and at times above, the surface of Arab politics. It is impossible for social scientists to make precise predictions about the Arab world, and this should not be a goal. But academics must reexamine their assumptions on a number of issues, including the military's role in Arab politics, the effects of economic change on political stability, and the salience of a cross-border Arab identity, to get a sense of how Arab politics will now unfold.

As paradigms fall and theories are shredded by events on the ground, it is useful to recall that the Arab revolts resulted not from policy decisions taken in Washington or any other foreign capital but from indigenous economic, political, and social factors whose dynamics were extremely hard to forecast. In the wake of such unexpected upheavals, both academics and policymakers should approach the Arab world with humility about their ability to shape its future. That is best left to Arabs themselves.

Critical Thinking

1. Can democracy stop terrorism? Explain.
2. Does the Arab world of today represent stability or instability for the future? Explain.
3. Can it be explained why the young bloggers were the first who demonstrated against Hosni Mubarak? Explain.

Create Central

www.mhhe.com/createcentral

Internet References

Remember Cairo? Brookings Institution
www.journalofdemocracy.org/sites/default/files/Editors-Intro=21-1.pdf

Authoritarianism
pomeps.org/2012/09/authoritarianism

WPR Article Middle East: Authoritarian Democracy and Democratic Authoritarianism
www.worldpoliticsreview.com/articles/3835/middle-east-authoritarian-democracy-and-democratic-authoritarianism

F. Gregory Gause III is a leading Saudi Arabian expert, and Professor of Political Science, University of Vermont.

From *Foreign Affairs*, vol. 90, issue 4. July/August 2011, pp. 81–90. Copyright © 2011 by Council on Foreign Relations, Inc. Reprinted by permission of Foreign Affairs. www.ForeignAffairs.com

Article

Prepared by: Caroline Shaffer Westerhof,
California National University for Advanced Studies

Few Good Choices for the U.S. in Mideast

GERALD F. SEIB

Learning Outcomes

After reading this article, you will be able to:

- Understand the complexity of Sunnis facing off against Shiites.

- Understand why many secularists are filled with bigotry against Islamists, regardless of which part of the world they call home.

- Understand the political instability and tensions that plague the Middle East, the Arabian peninsula, and North Africa.

The Middle East has a tendency to eat up American presidencies, and suddenly that is a real danger facing President Barack Obama.

The region is much closer to a broad conflagration than most Americans realize, with Sunnis now facing off against Shiites, and secularists against Islamists across a wide swath of lands. The dream of fostering a new wave of democratic, multiethnic governments—embraced by two successive American administrations—may be withering before our eyes.

As a result, Mr. Obama is coming face-to-face with two hard questions: Does the U.S., with a shrunken checkbook and a weary military, have the power to steer events? And does the U.S., tired after a decade of war in Iraq and happy to be growing less dependent on Middle East oil, even care enough to try?

The problems start with the bloody turmoil in the streets of Egypt, the cornerstone of American influence in the region for 35 years. There, a new military strongman seems more intent on crushing the Muslim Brotherhood than heeding American counsel to find a way to include the Islamists in a new government.

Meantime, Syria has become a proxy war for the entire region, pitting Shiites against Sunnis and drawing in combatants from all over. The nasty Alawite/Shiite axis of Syrian President Bashar al-Assad, Iran and Hezbollah has fought back to even with Sunni opposition forces, armed by Persian Gulf states and, soon, the U.S.

This now is essentially a sectarian war, and it's starting to spread next door to Lebanon. Sunnis there resent the fact that Hezbollah's Shiite fighters have been using Lebanon as a springboard to enter the fight on behalf of Mr. Assad. Car bombs and street fights between Sunni and Shiite groups are popping up; Lebanon is in danger of sliding back into its familiar rut of sectarian war.

Iraq now also seems infected. While most Americans have largely checked out of Iraqi news, a new wave of Sunni-Shiite violence is building. On Monday alone, 18 bombs exploded, killing at least 58 people. Whatever stability a decade of American military presence left behind seems newly imperiled.

Nearby, Jordan is becoming home to a giant, destabilizing refugee population of Syrians fleeing the fighting in their homeland. An estimated 650,000 refugees have entered Jordan; one refugee camp now is Jordan's fourth-largest city. It is an economic and demographic crisis of the first order for Jordan's king, one of America's most reasonable and reliable allies.

Oh, and Libya, home to a vast stockpile of weapons that seem to be finding their way around the region, is drifting into lawlessness; a thousand inmates were sprung in a giant jail break over the weekend.

In the middle of all this sits Israel. It now is surrounded by trouble and the march of Islamist forces in every direction—in Egypt to the west, Jordan to the east, Syria to the northeast and Lebanon to the north. It's no wonder that Israel agreed, after extensive prodding from Secretary of State John Kerry, to open new peace talks with the Palestinians in Washington this week. Amid this mess, it needs to buy a little stability on the home front if it can.

The impulse is to think the U.S. should do something—anything—to contain the risks.

But what? The U.S. once had great leverage over the Egyptian government because it provided the biggest chunk of aid. No longer. Saudi Arabia now writes much bigger checks, and it is urging the military leader there, Gen. Abdel Fattah Al Sisi, to hang tough against the Muslim Brotherhood. Each of the rival sides in Cairo's streets seems to think Washington is supporting the other, limiting American influence with both.

The U.S. military once might have waded into the mess in Syria, but the president is wary and the Pentagon tends to view engagement in Syria right now as a losing proposition. More broadly, the notion that Mr. Obama's relative popularity in, and overtures of friendship toward, the Islamic world could temper behaviors has faded in a period when hard power is what seems to matter.

The counter temptation is for the U.S. to simply step away, tending to the economy at home and pivoting toward Asia abroad. The problem is that history teaches that the Middle East doesn't like being ignored. Through soaring energy prices, or the scourge of terrorism, or some other calamity, it has a habit of insinuating itself onto the American agenda.

That leaves the U.S. the unsatisfying option of working with allies on a series of half-steps to move the region back from the brink so transformation can start anew: With the Saudis to convince Gen. Sisi in Egypt to contain his security forces; with the Europeans to help Jordan to contain the refugee crisis; with Arab allies to exert enough pressure to expel Syrian President Assad before Syria fractures permanently.

Not a satisfying list, but perhaps the only one available.

Critical Thinking

1. Can the Middle East ever achieve stability?
2. Is such tension in the Middle East generated by deep-seated hatred, or is it a manifestation of bigotry in the 21st century?
3. Is such tension and bombings a result of power politics, regardless of the actors?

Create Central

www.mhhe.com/createcentral

Internet References

In Mideast, Obama Finds He Has Limited Leverage—WSJ.com
http://online.wsj.com/article/SB100014241278873241700045786358100
11536562.html

Islam: Sunnis and Shiites—About.com Middle East Issues
http://middleeast.about.com/od/religionsectarianism/a/me070907
sunnis.htm

The Shia/Sunni Conflict in the Middle East Wars—Syria into Focus
http://worldpoliticsuncovered.wordpress.com/2013/09/28/the-shiasunni-conflict-in-the-middle-east-wars-syria-into-focus/

Video—Fueled by Anger, Iraqi Sunnis Make Push for Power
http://live.wsj.com/video/fueled-by-anger-iraqi-sunnis-make-push-for-power/9266CF4D-8744-4342-A4CE-0D96ACCFEBBB.
html#!9266CF4D-8744-4342-A4CE-0D96ACCFEBBB

The Solution to America's Collapsing Confidence—WSJ.com
http://online.wsj.com/article/SB100014241278873239938045786137825
47946130.html

GERALD SEIB is assistant managing editor, executive Washington editor of *The Wall Street Journal,* and a writer for WSJ. He is also a regulator commentator on Washington news for Fox Business.

Article

Prepared by: Caroline Shaffer Westerhof,
California National University for Advanced Studies

Making Modernity Work: The Reconciliation of Capitalism and Democracy

GIDEON ROSE

Learning Outcomes

After reading this article, you will be able to:

- Examine the concept, as some write, "We are living… through an ideological crisis."

- Understand why the author maintains that we are not living in "ideological upheaval but stability."

- Examine the theory that there are just as many examples of "democracies failing as there are of capitalism failing…"

We are living, so we are told, through an ideological crisis. The United States is trapped in political deadlock and dysfunction, Europe is broke and breaking, authoritarian China is on the rise. Protesters take to the streets across the advanced industrial democracies; the high and mighty meet in Davos to search for "new models" as sober commentators ponder who and what will shape the future.

In historical perspective, however, the true narrative of the era is actually the reverse-not ideological upheaval but stability. Today's troubles are real enough, but they relate more to policies than to principles. The major battles about how to structure modern politics and economics were fought in the first half of the last century, and they ended with the emergence of the most successful system the world has ever seen.

Nine decades ago, the political scientist Harold Laski noted that with "the mass of men" having come to political power, the challenge of modern democratic government was providing enough "solid benefit" to ordinary citizens "to make its preservation a matter of urgency to themselves." A generation and a half later, with the creation of the postwar order of mutually supporting liberal democracies with mixed economies, that challenge was being met, and as a result, more people in more places have lived longer, richer, freer lives than ever before. In ideological terms, at least, all the rest is commentary.

The Birth of the Modern

In the premodern era, political, economic, and social life was governed by a dense web of interlocking relationships inherited from the past and sanctified by religion. Limited personal freedom and material benefits existed alongside a mostly unquestioned social solidarity. Traditional local orders began to erode with the rise of capitalism in the eighteenth and nineteenth centuries, as the increasing prevalence and dominance of market relationships broke down existing hierarchies. The shift produced economic and social dynamism, an increase in material benefits and personal freedoms, and a decrease in communal feeling. As this process continued, the first modern political ideology, classical liberalism, emerged to celebrate and justify it.

Liberalism stressed the importance of the rule of law, limited government, and free commercial transactions. It highlighted the manifold rewards of moving to a world dominated by markets rather than traditional communities, a shift the economic historian Karl Polanyi would call "the great transformation." But along with the gains came losses as well—of a sense of place, of social and psychological stability, of traditional bulwarks against life's vicissitudes.

Left to itself, capitalism produced longterm aggregate benefits along with great volatility and inequality. This combination resulted in what Polanyi called a "double movement," a progressive expansion of both market society and reactions against it. By the late nineteenth and early twentieth centuries, therefore, liberalism was being challenged by reactionary nationalism and cosmopolitan socialism, with both the right and the left promising, in their own ways, relief from the turmoil and angst of modern life.

The catastrophic destruction of the Great War and the economic nightmare of the Great Depression brought the contradictions of modernity to a head, seemingly revealing the bankruptcy of the liberal order and the need for some other, better path. As democratic republics dithered and stumbled during the 1920s and 1930s, fascist and communist regimes seized control of their own destinies and appeared to offer compelling alternative models of modern political, economic, and social organization.

Over time, however, the problems with all these approaches became clear. Having discarded liberalism's insistence on personal and political freedom, both fascism and communism quickly descended into organized barbarism. The vision of the future they offered, as George Orwell noted, was "a boot stamping on a human face-forever." Yet classical liberalism also proved unpalatable, since it contained no rationale for activist government and thus had no answer to an economic crisis that left vast swaths of society destitute and despairing.

Fascism flamed out in a second, even more destructive world war. Communism lost its appeal as its tyrannical nature revealed itself, then ultimately collapsed under its own weight as its nonmarket economic system could not generate sustained growth. And liberalism's central principle of laissez faire was abandoned in the depths of the Depression.

What eventually emerged victorious from the wreckage was a hybrid system that combined political liberalism with a mixed economy. As the political scientist Sheri Berman has observed, "The postwar order represented something historically unusual: capitalism remained, but it was capitalism of a very different type from that which had existed before the war—one tempered and limited by the power of the democratic state and often made subservient to the goals of social stability and solidarity, rather than the other way around." Berman calls the mixture "social democracy." Other scholars use other terms: Jan-Werner Müller prefers "Christian Democracy," John Ruggie suggests "embedded liberalism," Karl Dietrich Bracher talks of "democratic liberalism." Francis Fukuyama wrote of "the end of History"; Daniel Bell and Seymour Martin Lipset saw it as "the end of ideology." All refer to essentially the same thing. As Bell put it in 1960:

Few serious minds believe any longer that one can set down "blueprints" and through "social engineering" bring about a new utopia of social harmony. At the same time, the older "counter-beliefs" have lost their intellectual force as well. Few "classic" liberals insist that the State should play no role in the economy, and few serious conservatives, at least in England and on the Continent, believe that the Welfare State is "the road to serfdom." In the Western world, therefore, there is today a rough consensus among intellectuals on political issues: the acceptance of a Welfare State; the desirability of decentralized power; a system of mixed economy and of political pluralism.

Reflecting the hangover of the interwar ideological binge, the system stressed not transcendence but compromise. It offered neither salvation nor utopia, only a framework within which citizens could pursue their personal betterment. It has never been as satisfying as the religions, sacred or secular, it replaced. And it remains a work in progress, requiring tinkering and modification as conditions and attitudes change. Yet its success has been manifest—and reflecting that, its basic framework has remained remarkably intact.

The Once and Future Order

The central question of modernity has been how to reconcile capitalism and mass democracy, and since the postwar order came up with a good answer, it has managed to weather all subsequent challenges. The upheavals of the late 1960s seemed poised to disrupt it. But despite what activists at the time thought, they had little to offer in terms of politics or economics, and so their lasting impact was on social life instead. This had the ironic effect of stabilizing the system rather than overturning it, helping it live up to its full potential by bringing previously subordinated or disenfranchised groups inside the castle walls. The neoliberal revolutionaries of the 1980s also had little luck, never managing to turn the clock back all that far.

All potential alternatives in the developing world, meanwhile, have proved to be either dead ends or temporary detours from the beaten path. The much-ballyhooed "rise of the rest" has involved not the discrediting of the postwar order of Western political economy but its reinforcement: the countries that have risen have done so by embracing global capitalism while keeping some of its destabilizing attributes in check, and have liberalized their polities and societies along the way (and will founder unless they continue to do so).

Although the structure still stands, however, it has seen better days. Poor management of public spending and fiscal policy has resulted in unsustainable levels of debt across the advanced industrial world, even as mature economies have found it difficult to generate dynamic growth and full employment in an ever more globalized environment. Lax regulation and oversight allowed reckless and predatory financial practices to drive leading economies to the brink of collapse. Economic inequality has increased as social mobility has declined. And a loss of broad-based social solidarity on both sides of the Atlantic has eroded public support for the active remedies needed to address these and other problems.

Renovating the structure will be a slow and difficult project, the cost and duration of which remain unclear, as do the contractors involved. Still, at root, this is not an ideological issue. The question is not what to do but how to do it—how, under twenty-first-century conditions, to rise to the challenge Laski described, making the modern political economy provide enough solid benefit to the mass of men that they see its continuation as a matter of urgency to themselves.

Critical Thinking

1. Is democracy too slow to respond to crises and too short to plan for the long term?
2. What is this so-called "political paralysis" that makes the governing challenges so complicated?
3. Do you agree with Gideon Rose that the post-war reconciliation of capitalism and liberal democracy had adapted to challenges in the past, and would so again?

Create Central

www.mhhe.com/createcentral

Internet References

The Reconciliation of Capitalism and Democracy
www.ihavenet.com/World-The-Reconciliation-of-Capitalism-and-Democracy-Foreign-Affairs.html

Capitalism and Democracy—On Point with Tom Ashbrook
http://onpoint.wbur.org/2012/01/17/capitalism-and-democracy
International Politics and Society—FES
www.fes.de/ipg/ONLINE2_2001/LESELISTEE.htm

GIDEON ROSE is editor of *Foreign Affairs,* and is a former National Security Council official.

Unit 3

UNIT

Prepared by: Caroline Shaffer Westerhof,
California National University for Advanced Studies

Participating in Politics: Acting within and out of Institutional Frameworks

This section builds upon diverse elements of political theory. It discusses payments to warlords in an area that bars journalists and is under United Nations sanctions. In contrast to this article, there is discussion of stability in the same region, but it is not considered a nation-state. Somaliland is not recognized as a country because of its breakaway status following the disintegration of Somalia in 1991. Somaliland seeks to be an example of free and fair elections based on inclusive citizenship to buttress political stability.

This brings us to the most widely used form of organizing citizen preferences and most common expression of citizen participation: voting. Voting is a requirement for citizenship in many countries; it is both an entitlement and a privilege. Given the significance of the vote outcome, who are the citizens that regularly exercise their voting privileges? Many studies note that the young tend to abstain from voting, with participation growing with age and peaking around those in their forties and fifties.

Why is it important to ensure that voting is the preferred choice of citizen participation? Consider this: If citizens are not voting, how do they express their policy preferences? Even in the United States, a common outlet of expression includes protesting, even bedding down in tents and the like in certain neighborhoods. A majority of protestors in Russia have more income, are better educated, and are likely to get their news from the Internet than the general public, and some are protesting in groups, risking jail. Street protests are taking place not only in a government that has been defined by top-down political control, but even in the United States where we speak of grassroots democracy.

If voters are not voting, their disenfranchisement may lead to the pursuit of extralegal means to access the political system or make demands on the government. With the increasing interconnectedness through cellphones, texting, and the Internet, the geographical and physical impediments to such extralegal means of participation means that they likely had negligible effect. Social networking and electronic access provide venues and the setting for raising awareness.

Importantly, social movements mobilized through these nontraditional contexts have grown in the face of possible government clampdown, in part because their large numbers provide anonymity and some insulation against adverse government repression and because such activism has led to a redefinition of civic associations and how they mobilize to improve political conditions and civil rights. Such use is seen in China, where technology is being used to mobilize netizens not only against the government but against other citizens. Such activity demonstrates that use of the Internet may lead to citizen vigilantism and campaigns of "harassment, mass intimidation, and public revenge."

It is to be noted that, while mass protests and demonstrations are useful, sole reliance on such mass demonstrations does not generally achieve the desired objectives. Is success based, if there is such, on regular or even institutionalized funding and organization to raise awareness, support, and defuse challenges to their agenda? Citizen participation and involvement are important, although they may be dangerous in a controlled political regime. Citizen participation is fundamental to political development and social stability; but such venues must not generate a negative political arena. There has to be purpose, organization, and funding. Actors in the system have to listen, understand, and provide the impetus for the new changes that will happen or there will be continued destruction as we are witnessing today.

Such is being questioned in Egypt, where the present rulers have $12 billion to spend. The reality of many theorists and practioners is that "No government erected on the ruins of Mohamed Morsi's regime will be deemed to be legitimate."

And yet within the Expat Focus, there are successful and fast growing economies. What makes the United Arab Emirates and Malaysian economy successful? The UAE has an open economy, and the government has increased spending on job creation and infrastructure. Malaysia has a flexible form of governance and welcomes foreign talent. Such, for both nations, encourages further growth, continued progress, and long-term challenges. The reality demonstrates that nation-states working with their citizens in an open society, and not against them, will encourage positive economic growth and political stability.

Article

Prepared by: Caroline Shaffer Westerhof,
California National University for Advanced Studies

After the Scottish Referendum: A Constitutional Chain Reaction Unfolds

CHARLIE JEFFERY

Learning Outcomes

After reading this article you will be able to:

Understand the constitutional chain reaction unfolding after the Scottish Referendum.

Understand why Prime Minister David Cameron was concerned about how Wales and Northern Ireland are governed.

Understand why the people in England are becoming concerned about the absence of institutional recognition of England in the UK political system.

What a twist in the tale. On 18th September 2014 the question was whether or not Scotland should be independent country, and on the morning of the 19th Prime Minister David Cameron announced he was looking for a decisive answer to the *English* question (and said we better also look again at how Wales and Northern Ireland are governed).

Cameron's announcement was the third step in a constitutional chain reaction that we now see unfolding before us. The first was the YouGov poll on 5 September which showed a 1%:49% Yes lead in referendum voting intention in Scotland. This, combined with other polls published in the next couple of days that also showed the race was neck and neck, sowed panic in the ranks of the No side.

Enter Gordon Brown. Speaking with the endorsement of the three pro-union party leaders, David Cameron, Nick Clegg, and Miliband, he set out on 8 September a breakneck timetable for delivering additional devolution to Scotland. This would see a new Scotland Bill debated in the House of Commons in March 2015 so that all three parties could pledge to enact that Bill in their manifestos for the May 2015 UK General Election.

Then on 16 September the three party leaders produced "The Vow," as recorded on the front page of Scotland's *Daily Record,* which reaffirmed the commitment to deliver additional devolution on Brown's timetable, and gave additional pledges on the NHS in Scotland and on the continuation of the Barnett formula that determines the funding available to the Scottish Parliament. The pledges on the NHS and Barnett were designed to head off the claims on the Yes side that the NHS was in danger of being privatized if Scotland remained in the UK and that current levels of funding for Scotland would be at risk if Scotland voted No.

All this smacked of last-minute panic. The pro-union parties had each produced proposals on additional devolution for Scotland in the event of a No vote months before, with clear areas of common ground in the fields of tax devolution and welfare powers. But they had failed to agree either common proposals or a clear timetable for action, allowing the Yes side to question the strength of their commitment to additional devolution. And they had had plenty of opportunity to offer the other pledges in "The Vow" and, more generally, to offer a more positive set of arguments about Scotland's place in the UK if Scots voted No. But the No side had continued to major on the negative themes of what many came to call its **Project Fear:** the risks and uncertainties of independence, especially the economic risks, especially the uncertainty about which currency an independent Scotland would use. There was a growing sense as the referendum approached that all the warnings about these risks

were getting tired, diminishing in their effectiveness and allowing Yes support in the polls to creep up as a result.

So that's why we saw a shift to a more positive agenda of
additional powers and guarantees for Scotland in the days
before the referendum. And, given the clear margin of the No
victory at 55.3% to 44.7% it seemed to work. But: that agenda
was unplanned, rapidly improvised, and as a consequence also
lacking in appreciation of the possible spillovers it might have
elsewhere in the UK.

Which is where the Prime Minister came in on the morn-
ing of 19 September with the third step in the chain reaction.
In the days after the Brown timetable was announced and the
"The Vow" was given, two sets of grumbles started to be heard.
The first was on the backbenches of the Conservative Party at
Westminster. Here the narrative was about how unfair it was to
England for Scotland to get additional powers, and in particular
for Scots MPs to continue to have a say on matters to do with
England in the House of Commons when English MPs had
no say in all the matters (with more now promised) that were
devolved to Scotland. What was needed was what has become
known as English votes on English laws at Westminster (or
EVEL, as its acronym has it), with Scottish (and, presumably,
Welsh and Northern Irish) MPs removed from at least some
parts of the legislative process on English matters.

The second set of grumbles was from Wales and had to do
with the pledge to maintain the Barnett formula as is. Wales
is widely felt to be underfunded relative to need through the
current Barnett arrangements (and Scotland funded generously
relative to its need). For some time now the mantra in Wales has
been one demanding "fair funding." Senior figures in both the
Labour Party and Plaid Cymru immediately cried foul about
the Barnett vow, echoing concerns raised earlier by Richard
Wyn Jones in a memorable contribution about the No side in
the Scottish debate "throwing Wales under the bus."

So a YouGov poll led to last-minute offers being made to
the Scots if they would vote No, and, when they did, we found
ourselves not just with a timetable for legislation on new powers for Scotland, but also a commitment to move to English
votes for English laws in the House of Commons, also on a
rapid timetable, and for action on further devolution in Wales
(Northern Ireland was also mentioned, though this seemed to
be for the sake of completeness rather than actually having any
ideas about what to do in Northern Ireland).

Since then we have seen two processes set up, one on additional powers in Scotland, the other exploring English votes for
English laws in the House of Commons (Wales and Northern
Ireland appear to be at the back of the queue and not deserving
of such urgency).

Both processes are fascinating, not least because of the party-
political dynamics they have opened up. In Scotland, Lord Smith

of Kelvin, fresh from his role in leading the organizing comm
tee of the Glasgow Commonwealth Games, is convening cro
party talks on more devolution focused on delivering Gord
Brown's timetable. That timetable is extraordinarily ambitio
The aim is to have a Command Paper published by the end
October 2014 setting out the parties' views on more devolutio
This then opens up a period of consultation designed to info
a White Paper published by the end of November, which w
set the parameters for a Bill to be introduced to the House
Commons by 25 January 2015, and that Bill to reach its se
ond reading—that is when the main principles of a Bill are fi
debated in plenary session in the House—by March.

That timetable will not allow for significant consultati
beyond the "usual suspects" in business, unions and the v
untary sector; rather sadly, given the vast public engageme
in Scotland with the referendum debate, there is no genui
opportunity to engage the public. It will be, essentially, a behi
closed doors compromise between the parties—or at least so
of them. Which ones is the interesting question.

Prior to the referendum Labour, the Conservatives and
Liberal Democrats each produced proposals for additio
devolution with a strong focus on tax and welfare devolutio
Labour's proposals are by far the most modest on tax dev
lution, betraying an unease in a centralist Westminster pa
about further devolution. Labour's proposals also envisag
the devolution of some welfare powers (housing benefit, atte
dance allowance and the work programme) and a strengtheni
of local government in Scotland. There is common ground he
with the Conservatives (on welfare) and the Liberal Democr
(on local government), but both these parties envisage signi
cantly more tax devolution than Labour, including full dev
lution of income tax and the possibility of assigning reven
generated in Scotland by other taxes (corporation tax for
LibDems and VAT for the Conservatives) to the Scottish Parl
ment's budget.

Perhaps the most interesting question is how the SNP w
engage with this process. It has signaled a commitment to
so, nominating a big-hitter, John Swinney, the Scottish Finar
Secretary, as its lead negotiator. And it has not suggested
would hold out for "devo-max," that is the devolution of eve
thing except defence and foreign affairs, but rather a num
of more pragmatic and potentially realisable objectives arou
job-creating powers and measures to tackle inequality.

Other ideas have bubbled up through SNP voices (e.g., po
ers to deviate from Westminster policies regulating frackir
or on a cross-party basis (on equalities policy and the Scott
franchise, following the successful experiment of extendi
the franchise to 16- to 17-year-olds in the referendum). O
ers still will be raised through consultation as "the usual s
pects" make their contributions. It remains to be seen whet

agenda of the Smith talks will open up in such ways to
tend beyond the pro-union parties' focus on tax and welfare
volution. The SNP's presence will certainly ensure pressure
that direction—and will put pressure on Labour in particular
move beyond its limited stance on further devolution. That
essure is made more acute by the geographical support for
s, which concentrated in areas of traditional Labour strength
and around Glasgow and in Dundee. Expect the SNP to try to
aintain the momentum at Labour's expense.

Labour is under pressure too in England. We know rather
s as yet about how William Hague's work on EVEL will
fold. The first to be engaged by Hague were restive Con-
vative backbenchers like Bernard Jenkin and John Redwood
a special meeting at Chequers, the Prime Minister's country
idence. There is a sizeable chunk of the Westminster party
t sees action on England as urgently needed, worries about
KIP draining support (and defector MPs) from the Conserva-
es on the issue, and needed to be reassured.

But while David Cameron's opening up of the English
estion was in part about internal party management and
e UKIP threat, it has also put Labour in a difficult place in
gland. While senior figures, including—fleetingly—Ed
liband, have flirted with the idea of developing a distinct
glish agenda and appeal for the Labour Party, this has been
d up with localism and city-regions rather than a solution at
estminster.

The reason is obvious enough. No one expects Labour to win
esounding majority in the next UK election, and it is quite
nceivable that a narrow Labour UK-wide majority could be
pendent on Labour's contingent of MPs from Scotland. So
s is not a good time for Labour to be confronted by the pros-
ct of MPs from Scotland being unable to vote on English
tters, which could remove its majority on such matters.

But there is also growing evidence that people in England
becoming concerned about the absence of institutional
ognition of England in the UK political system, think Scot-
h MPs voting on English matters is unfair, and see EVEL
the best of the various possible solutions. So Labour is in
nger of positioning itself as opposed to the expression of
neglected English voice in UK politics. Having realized

this, the Conservatives are now seeking to cause maximum
embarrassment.

Initially David Cameron proposed that the implementation of EVEL needed to proceed in lockstep with the Gordon
Brown timetable on additional devolution for Scotland. That
lockstep has now gone, with the Conservatives saying—rather
gleefully—that if Labour opposes progress on EVEL, they will
be happy to put the issue to English voters in next year's general election.

How ironic is it, that having left, through Gordon Brown, a
decisive mark on the constitutional chain reaction that is now
unfolding, Labour finds itself in such an exposed position vis-
à-vis the SNP in Scotland and the Conservatives in England?
How nostalgic the phrase "better together" must now sound.

Critical Thinking

1. Why did Prime Minister David Cameron offer a shift to a more positive agenda of additional powers and guarantees for Scotland in the days before the referendum?
2. Why does no one expect Labour to win a resounding majority in the next UK election?
3. Why was the world concerned that the referendum could be a close vote for either the "no" side or the "yes" side?

Internet References

Future of the UK and Scotland
www.futureukandscotland.ac.uk/about/people/charlie-jeffery

Scotland's future in Europe: Taming the paper tiger
www.opendemocracy.net/ourkingdom/alyn-smith/scotland's-future-in-europe-taming-paper-tiger

Scottish Independence
www.scotsman.com/scottish-independence/charlie-jeffery-scotlands-constitutional-future-from-both-sides

Welcome to Scotland's Futures Forum
www.scotlandfutureforum.org

CHARLIE JEFFERY is Professor of Politics at and Vice Principal, University of Edinburgh and Director of the ESRC Programme on The Future of The UK and Scotland.

Article

Prepared by: Caroline Shaffer Westerhof,
California National University for Advanced Studies

Recalibrating American Grand Strategy: Softening US Policies Toward Iran in Order to Contain China

Samir Tata

Learning Outcomes

After reading this article, you will be able to:

- Examine the premise that if U.S. policies toward Iran are softened, China can be contained.

- Examine the political and policy difficulties inherent in implementing strategy.

- Examine Clausewitz's philosophy on the influence of war and strategy.

Over the next decade, the United States will have to rethink its grand strategy as it addresses the challenge of maintaining its primacy as a global power in an increasingly multipolar world whose center of gravity has shifted to Asia. The task will be all the more daunting because significant fiscal and economic constraints imposed by a federal government debt that has mushroomed to nearly $16 trillion or about 100 percent of GDP, and a continuing economic slowdown that has been the deepest and longest since the Great Depression will force difficult tradeoffs as the United States seeks to realign and streamline vital national interests with limited resources.[1] The overarching national security objective of the United States must be crystal clear: to counterbalance and contain a rising China determined to be the dominant economic, political, and military power in Asia.

While China's rise will not be a straight line, its trajectory to great power status is obvious.[2] A twenty-first century version of a Greater East Asia Co-Prosperity Sphere with China at the epicenter is emerging.[3] China is the biggest economy in Asia, having surpassed Japan in 2010.[4] China is the largest trading partner of Japan, South Korea, Taiwan, Australia, India, and the ten countries of the Association of Southeast Asian Nations (ASEAN). Unquestionably, China is the economic engine of Asia, displacing both Japan and the United States. According to US government projections, China is expected to be the world's largest economy by 2019 in terms of purchasing power parity (which adjusts for cost of living) with a forecasted gross domestic product (GDP) of $17.2 trillion compared to an expected US GDP of $17 trillion.[5]

From a strategic perspective, the "Achilles heel" of China is its overwhelming dependence on Persian Gulf energy imports to fuel its rapidly growing economy. The sea lines of communication (SLOCs) over which these vital oil and gas imports are transported by tanker—from the Strait of Hormuz in the Persian Gulf to the Arabian Sea and Indian Ocean, continuing on to the Bay of Bengal and through the Malacca Straits into the South China Sea—is China's jugular vein. Virtually all Persian Gulf energy exports destined for China (as well as for Japan, South Korea, and Taiwan) flow through this route. Two important alternatives to the Malacca Straits are the Sunda and Lambok Straits in Indonesia linking the eastern Indian Ocean to the Java Sea which continues to the South China Sea. Another key energy route flows from Saudi ports on the Red Sea (principally the port of Yanbu) to the Bab el Mandab in the Gulf of Aden proceeding on to the Arabian Sea and the Indian Ocean and continuing to the Malacca Straits, or the Sunda and Lambok Straits. The five critical choke points—Hormuz, Bab el Mandab, Malacca, Sunda and Lambok—and the SLOCs linking them are controlled by the US Navy.

China's economic and military security is inextricably intertwined with its energy security. Since 2000, China has been a net importer of oil and gas, primarily from the Persian Gulf. China became the world's largest energy consumer in 2009, with 96.9 quadrillion British thermal units (BTU) of annual energy consumption compared to 94.8 quadrillion BTU for the United States.[6] By 2011, China surpassed the United States as the largest importer of Persian Gulf oil, importing 2.5 million barrels per day (bbls/d) from the region (representing about 26 percent of total Chinese oil consumption of 9.8 million bbls/d), overtaking the United States which imported 1.8 million bbls/d from the Persian Gulf (representing about 10 percent of total US oil consumption of 18.8 million bbls/d).[7] In fact, over half of US oil imports come from three countries in the Americas: Canada, Venezuela, and Mexico, with Canada being the single most important foreign supplier.[8]

The US Energy Information Administration (EIA) projects that by 2030 oil imports, mainly from the Persian Gulf, will represent 75 percent of total Chinese oil consumption. By contrast, US oil imports are expected to decline sharply and account for only 35 percent of total US oil consumption by 2030.[9] Clearly, Persian Gulf oil imports will be far more crucial to China than to the United States. Accordingly, for China, ensuring access to Persian Gulf oil and gas will loom large as a vital national interest. By contrast, for the United States, a key strategic priority will be denial of access to Persian Gulf energy resources to its adversaries.

China, of course, which has domestic oil reserves of about 20 billion barrels and domestic gas reserves of 107 trillion cubic feet (Tcf), is seeking oil and gas resources which it can effectively control in its own backyard.[10] In the East China Sea, low-end estimated oil reserves are 60 billion barrels, and in the South China Sea, low-end estimated oil reserves are 11 billion barrels.[11] Not surprisingly, the potential energy resources of these areas have generated intense rival claims involving China, Japan, South Korea, Vietnam, and the Philippines. However, the East and South China Seas have yet to be explored systematically, and their oil and gas resources are a long way from being developed and produced. By comparison, the proved oil reserves of Saudi Arabia alone amount to 263 billion barrels, and the combined proved oil reserves of Iran and Iraq are about 252 billion barrels.[12] Thus, from the Chinese viewpoint, the strategic importance of access to Persian Gulf oil and gas resources is not significantly changed even with Chinese control over access to oil and gas resources in the East and South China Seas.

If the United States is to counterbalance China successfully, it must be able to threaten China's energy security. Ideally, the United States should be in a position in which it can persuade the Persian Gulf oil producers, if necessary, to turn off the tap and decline to supply China with oil and gas. Furthermore, the United States must be able to put in place anti-access, area denial strategies (a) in the eastern Indian Ocean and Bay of Bengal to blockade the Malacca, Sunda and Lambok Straits; and (b) in the western Indian Ocean and the Arabian Sea to blockade the arc between the Bab el Mandab to the Strait of Hormuz. Indonesia, India, and Iran will be critical to the success of a recalibrated American grand strategy to contain China.

Notes

1. For total public debt outstanding, see US Department of the Treasury, Daily Treasury Statement, August 31, 2012, Table III-C, https://fms.treas.gov/fmsweb/viewDTSFiles?dir=a&f name=12083100.pdf For total GDP see Bureau of Economic Analysis (BEA), National Income and Product Accounts, August 29, 2012, http://www.bea.gov.

2. China is likely to face a pension and social security bomb by 2050. The combined impact of a low fertility rate (1.56) and skewed male to female ratio at birth (1.18 to 1) means that "Unlike the rest of the developed world, China will grow old before it gets rich." See "Demography: China's Achilles heel," The Economist, April 21, 2012, http://www.economist.com and "China's population: The most surprising demographic crisis," The Economist, May 5, 2011, http://www.economist.com.

3. Japan's original version of the Greater East-Asian Co-Prosperity Sphere was enunciated in August 1940 to serve as the rationale for the Japanese Empire being carved out by Japanese militarists. See Warren I. Cohen, East Asia at the Center: Four Thousand Years of Engagement with the World (New York: Columbia University Press, 2000), 352.

4. BBC News, "China overtakes Japan as world's second biggest economy," 14 February 2011, http://www.bbc.co.uk.

5. US Energy Information Administration (EIA), "World gross domestic product (GDP) by region expressed in purchasing power parity, Reference case," International Energy Outlook 2011, http://www.eia.gov.

6. US Energy Information Administration, Table A1 "World total primary energy consumption by region, Reference case," in International Energy Outlook 2011, http://www.eia.gov.

7. For total Chinese oil consumption and imports, see US Energy Information Administration (EIA), China: Country Analysis Brief, September 4, 2012, http://www.eia.gov; for total US oil consumption and imports see EIA, "Energy in Brief: How dependent are we on foreign oil?" July 13, 2012, http://www .eia.gov; and EIA, "Petroleum and Other Liquids: US Net Imports by Country," August 30, 2012, http://www.eia.gov.

8. Ibid. In particular see "Energy in Brief: How dependent are we on foreign oil?"

9. Ibid. For further details regarding the forecasted dramatic drop in US oil imports, see figure 114 "US net imports of petroleum and other liquids fall in the Reference case" in EIA, Annual Energy Outlook 2012," June 25, 2012, http://www.eia.gov.

10. US Energy Information Administration, China: Country Analysis Brief, September 4, 2012, http://www.eia.gov.

11. EIA, East China Sea: Analysis Brief, September 12, 2012, http://www.eia.gov; South China Sea: Analysis Brief, February 7, 2013, http://www.eia.gov.

12. "2011 World Proved Reserves," http://www.eia.gov.

Critical Thinking

1. Can the U.S. contain a rising China that is determined to become the economic, political, and military power in Asia?

2. Can the U.S. rethink its strategy in order to maintain its primacy as a global power?

3. Will the U.S. be successful in pursuing a policy of containment toward China?

Create Central

www.mhhe.com/createcentral

Internet References

Carl Von Clausewitz on War; Sun Tzu, The Art of War and Strategy

www.sonshi.com/clausewitz.html

Demography: China's Achille's Heel
www.economist.com/node/21553056

Samir Tata—Journal of International Affairs
jia.sipa.columbia.edu/authors-listing/author/samir-tata

NATO: Time to Refocus and Streamline /ISN
www.isn.ethz.ch/Digital-Library/Articles/Detail/?id=167376

Parameters—Strategic Studies Institute–U.S. Army
www.strategicstudiesinstitute.army.mil/pubs/parameters

SAMIR TATA is a foreign policy analyst. He served as an analyst with the National Geospatial-Intelligence Agency, researcher with Middle East Institute, Atlantic Council, & National Defense University. He has a B.A. in Foreign Affairs & History from the University of Virginia, and an M.A. in International Affairs from George Washington University.

Article

Prepared by: Caroline Shaffer Westerhof,
California National University for Advanced Studies

This Fracking Zeal Overshadows the Perfect Energy Solution—Solar

The government ignores the drawbacks to shale gas, while its erratic policies around solar frustrate budding entrepreneurs.

LEONIE GREENE

Learning Outcomes

After reading this article, you will be able to:

Understand why public support for fracking is falling.

Understand the global politics of fracking.

The government's consultation on the rights of fracking companies to drill under your home was published the day after the local and European elections, hours after the polls closed. Perhaps that was a wise move given that public support for fracking seems to be falling. It hardly needs former Conservative energy secretary Lord Howell to warn that fracking "could prove extremely dangerous politically." The careful timing on the latest announcement shows he may not be the only one who thinks so.

The British Geological Survey has said there could be 4.4bn barrels of oil in the shale rocks of southern England. As a result, the announcement proposes a 12-week consultation on a law that would bypass the law of trespass when it comes to work carried out 300 meters or more below ground, and payments to affected communities of £20,000 for each well drilled.

The government's enthusiasm for fracking sits in stark contrast to its erratic rhetoric and actions on solar energy. The solar industry has recently been ambushed by a fourth review in less than three years. Constant policy upheaval makes investment to reduce costs difficult, and the latest review is particularly ill considered. Usually governments offer a grace period to investors if they are going to change financial arrangements, but this one

offers almost none—which means many emerging solar companies that invested in good faith are set for a financial hit. For all the rhetoric about a shift to rooftop solar, the government's own policy framework actually limits this important market.

Poor solar farms have attracted negative local press, as they should do. Certainly, real concerns such as displacing food production must be addressed by the industry and planners. But a great many more good quality solar farms have been established invisibly, screened with trees and hedges, and they have been welcomed by local communities and by major conservation groups like the RSPB (because of the haven they can offer wildlife), and by farmers hit by weather extremes as the climate changes.

Solar farms can be installed in weeks and then nothing really happens for decades: no noise, no smell, no waste. Yet benign solar farms have been labeled "monstrous" by ministers who have nothing to say about fracking's "whiff of diesel" or its "thump of compressors that can be sensed up to two miles away" (Lord Howell again). Not to mention the regular heavy truck traffic or intensive water consumption, or the strict regulatory controls needed to prevent methane leaks on which its carbon-saving case depends.

The double standards here are rather extraordinary. The bias is hard to fathom when solar has delivered beyond the expectations of even its greatest advocates. Costs in the UK have dropped 30% in 18 months and large-scale solar is now our second cheapest major renewable energy source. But ministers must understand that they can't wait for solar energy costs to fall, because most of the costs are not the technology—they are grid connections, infrastructure, planning, skilled staff, and other "soft" costs.

Reaching the cheapest solar possible in the UK means sustained investment by British SMEs, not just waiting for fair international prices. In the US, the land of shale gas, the White House's SunShot initiative is on track to drive solar below the cost of gas by 2020. That gives them massive international competitive advantage. As Jonathon Porritt said, if you think solar is just part of the solution, you've missed the plot. Far from constraining the British solar industry, the government should be doing everything it can to strengthen the UK's position in a soaring international solar market.

What we need politicians to do is to champion good quality solar farms and to liberate the huge potential of the UK's rooftop market. If the government can provide a steady framework, the solar industry can definitely be the cheapest low-carbon technology by around 2018, and ready to take on fossil fuels with no public subsidies at all soon after that.

It is time politicians listened a lot less to big polluting international energy companies, and a lot more to British entrepreneurs who are creating real competition and delivering a clean energy revolution through this extraordinarily benign and accessible technology.

They should also listen to the public. The Department of Energy and Climate Change's own opinion poll tracker shows solar enjoys its highest approval ratings ever at 85%. It seems the country is firmly behind solar. Westminster must catch up.

Critical Thinking

1. Why are there such political double standards and controversy over fracking?
2. Why, as yet, are there not strict regulatory controls for some fracking conditions?
3. Do the positive aspects and the negative issues in fracking balance out?

Internet References

It's all a conspiracy: Nato claims Russia behind ant-fracki environmentalist
www.politics.ie/forum/current-affairs/227209-its-all-conspiracy-na claims-russia-behind-ant-fracking-environmentalist.html

The Politics of Fracking
www.forbes.com/sites/christopherskroupa/2014/02/19/fracking-politics

This fracking zeal overshadows the perfect energy solution—so
www.theguardian.com/commentisfree/2014/may/25/fracking-ener solution-solar-shale-gas

Vinson & Elkins Shale & Fracking Tracker: Shale Developm in Germany
www.fracking.velaw.com/shale-development-in-germany

LEONIE GREENE of the Solar Trade Association accuses the gove ment of using solar as the fall guy for its clean energy budget woes.

Greene, Leonie, *This Fracking Zeal Overshadows The Perfect Energy Solution–Solar,* The Guardian, May 2014. Copyright Guardian News & Media Ltd 2014.

Article

Prepared by: Caroline Shaffer Westerhof,
California National University for Advanced Studies

The Protesters and the Public

Putinism Under Siege

DENIS VOLKOV

Learning Outcomes

After reading this article, you will be able to:

- Explain how citizens' demands in Russia were handled by a government that has been defined by top-down political control.

- Define the handling of Putin's slogan and its importance in 2011: "Stability and Order."

- Explain the social mobilization movement in Russia.

The mass protests that shook Russia in December 2011 and March 2012 (with more in May) caught both domestic and international observers by surprise. Yet there were warning signs, including internal conflict in Russia's political system and growing civic activism.

Since the global economic crisis began to hit Russia in 2008, Russians have had a growing sense of uncertainty about the future, coupled with a feeling that the country is moving in the wrong direction. Indicators of public optimism have declined, as has approval for Vladimir Putin, Dmitri Medvedev, and their ruling United Russia party.[1]

This mood of uncertainty and vulnerability has touched all socioeconomic groups, including those living in comparatively prosperous regions such as Moscow. Russians universally lament the arbitrariness of government and its security agencies, the inability to protect one's rights, and the impossibility of directly impacting the broader state of affairs in the country. For Russia's "privileged minority," the confluence of material privilege with political impotence and defenselessness is highly irritating.

Isolated protests have occurred in recent years, and independent civic initiatives including protest committees, labor unions, and ecological organizations have appeared, but the participants form only a tiny percentage of the total population. Inevitably, these groups have run into the corrupt practices of Russia's government elite and business interests, and have become politicized in the process. This increased public activism has naturally led to conflict, which is compounded by the inability of citizens to address Russia's systemic corruption through legislative or judicial means.

Open conflict has increasingly become a regular feature of Russia's political system. The system of top-down control favored by Putin's regime is designed to block rather than ease systemic change. Authorities tend to ignore problems until citizens' frustrations spill over into (not necessarily peaceful) protest, at which point officials adopt some mixture of repression plus halfhearted measures to redress grievances, hoping that unrest will subside and the public mood will improve. Thus protest is a given, even if saying exactly where, when, and how the next one will break out is difficult in a partly closed society such as Russia's, where civic problems and social stresses are not openly discussed.

In December 2011, civic mobilization took place in two phases: first, in the form of a protest vote during the December State Duma elections, and second, during the post-election street protests in Moscow and in Russia's larger regional capitals. The number of participants far exceeded past opposition protests, bringing hundreds of thousands of Russians out into the street for the first time in several years.

Although any number of factors fed the protest vote during the State Duma elections, prominent irritants included the September 2011 maneuver by which Medvedev ceded the United Russia presidential nomination to Putin, as well as the fraud and abuses of power which characterized that party's conduct of the parliamentary campaign. All this happened, moreover, against a backdrop of anxiety and uncertainty caused by the global economic crisis.

The fraud hardly came as a surprise. Civic groups in major urban areas made known their dissatisfaction with both the campaign environment and the election results. Their complaints reached the general public and shaped public discussion in the weeks following the election. For those who united around the election-monitoring organizations GOLOS and Citizen Observer, and who followed Russia's independent press—which gathered information from thousands of activists on election day—the arbitrary repression that the government carried out was unacceptable. Herein lies the primary difference between Russia's civil society and the "patient majority." Civil society will publicly and repeatedly defend itself and its positions, thus defining the civic nature of the

2011 and 2012 protests. Going forward, the difficulties in reconciling the interests of these disparate groups may intensify. Studying the causes of instability in developing countries for a book first published in 1968, Samuel P. Huntington noted that during the modernization process "all groups, old as well as new, traditional as well as modern, become increasingly aware of themselves as groups and of their interests and claims in relation to other groups."[2]

The Demographics of Protest

The Levada Center's public-opinion polls allow us to examine the protests at their peak.[3] Those who witnessed the initial December 2011 protests in Moscow noted the preponderance of youth in attendance, as well as their mobility and aptitude for using online social networks to aid in organization and recruiting. Quickly, however, the demographics of the protests began to broaden, incorporating people of all ages. By February 2012, participants in the 18-to-24 age bracket were accounting for just a fifth of all participants, roughly the same number as those aged 55 and older. Most protesters were middle-aged. Thus, what began as a youth protest did not stay that way.

A majority of those participating in the protests identified themselves as "democrats" or "liberals" (between 60 and 70 percent). Practically all participants expressed dissatisfaction with Putin. The principal motivations of those participating included "dissatisfaction with the current situation in Russia" (73 percent), "indignation over electoral fraud" (73 percent), "dissatisfaction that key decisions were being made by politicians without citizen input" (52 percent), and disillusionment with President Medvedev's promises of modernization (42 percent). Few expressed solidarity with opposition parties (15 percent) or individual protest organizers (13 percent).

Protest participants differed from the general population in more than just their political sympathies. They were atypical of Russians in general, and even of Moscow residents. About 80 percent had at least some post-secondary education; only 30 percent of all Russians can claim that much schooling. Almost two-thirds were male, while Russia's general population is mostly female. As key sources of information, protesters cited the Internet (70 percent), radio (about 45 percent), friends and acquaintances (about 30 percent), television (17 to 18 percent), and newspapers (15 to 18 percent). By contrast, 81 percent of Russians in general receive the bulk of their news from television, while just 13 percent read news online. Finally, around 70 percent of protesters reported themselves as relatively well off while only half of all Muscovites and a quarter of all Russians did so.

The Levada Center's polls captured the key differences between the political demands of the protesters and those of the Russian public in general. For example, 97 percent of protesters called for the removal of Vladimir Churov, the head of Russia's Central Election Commission, while just 39 percent of Russians felt similarly. Almost 85 percent of protesters called for the release of political prisoners; only 35 percent of

Russians shared a similar sentiment. Ninety-five percent of protesters called for new parliamentary elections; only 29 percent of Russians agreed. Eighty-nine percent of protesters liked the slogan "Not one vote for Vladimir Putin!"; only 24 percent of Russians agreed.

The gap between Russia's privileged, protest-friendly minority and its patient majority was clearly evident during and after the elections. The bulk of Russia's people live in relative poverty away from major cities, get much of their income from the state in the form of pensions, and rely on state-run television for news. Among this portion of the populace, there is widespread passivity and a Soviet-holdover tendency to regard repressive government as normal. Most of the changes that these Russians have lived through have only made things worse for them. In surveys, the public says it mainly believes that people come to pro-Putin rallies in order to oppose "dangerous ongoing changes in the nation."

The majority, fearing change, meant to vote for the devil it knew. Given this intention, and given a political scene deliberately stripped of alternatives by official bans on certain parties, by state control of the major television channels, and by systematic regime efforts to discredit opponents, it is small wonder that the voting's outcome seemed predetermined.

Yet it must be said that the active minority has been sadly inactive when it comes to bridging the gap between itself and the passive majority. The opposition parties that appeared in the 1990s ignored average Russians and consisted of members of the ranks of the old Soviet elite. Nor did the Russian public, having few political skills and beset by a sea of changes, demand involvement.

To the extent that various social groups in Russia are gradually beginning to identify their own political interests and to attempt to protect them when possible, existing parties may become impediments to the development of grassroots political change as long as they remain elite networks that exclude these new civic initiatives.

Today, more than half of Russians think that a political opposition is needed. Moreover, approximately 25 to 30 percent affirm that they would not mind seeing opposition figures such as Grigory Yavlinsky, Vladimir Ryzhkov, Garry Kasparov, Mikhail Kasyanov, and Eduard Limonov in parliament. Despite this support, Russians have consistently refused to vote for opposition politicians or their parties. In the eyes of Russian voters, liberal parties and their leaders who took part in the organization of the 2011 and 2012 protests do not represent a sufficiently broad cross-section of Russian society. Thus in mid-2011, just 5 percent of Russians believed that the liberal-democratic party Yabloko represented the interests of the whole population. By comparison, polling data for United Russia shows that roughly 20 percent of the general population feels that this party of the Putin regime represents the collective interest. In the eyes of a huge 74 percent majority, moreover, United Russia is the only real political power in the country—no other party comes close. The Levada Center's polling data tend to reinforce the common criticism of the opposition parties as groups that "just talk and do nothing."

It is noteworthy that the general public, in surveys, more than adequately identified the protesters' motives. Many agreed that the protesters were motivated by their discontent with the current political system (37 percent), their indignation with electoral fraud (25 percent), and the ruling party's refusal to consider their opinions (22 percent). Meanwhile, the active minority, or what some observers call Russia's "liberal society," does not seem to have reciprocated. Its members still show little or no sign that they understand the motives of the majority that fears change. Until the protest movement learns to take the majority's concerns seriously and to address them with concrete stands on real issues, it will remain in minority status and find its aspirations harder to achieve than they might otherwise be.

The Putin regime, meanwhile, faces grave troubles of its own. In order to match the protests, it has spurred countermobilizations and staged mass demonstrations by its own supporters. But since the regime, as Lev Gudkov has pointed out, leans so heavily on the suppression of independent political activities of any kind,[4] *any* mobilization is risky for it and threatens to undermine its grip on power. By drawing Russians into politics, the regime may be writing its own death warrant.

The rise of protest and the emancipation of social groups currently being witnessed in Russia are byproducts of the absence of any real mechanisms for aggregating public preferences: This absence leaves a vacuum into which public outrage flows. Yet outrage alone may not be enough to force constructive change toward more systematically inclusive (that is, more democratic) forms of decision making. In Russia, the links between wealth and government are such that the short-term preservation of wealth and power always trumps the need for systemic adaptation. We could be witnessing a case of what Shmuel Eisenstadt called "modernization breakdown."

Civic Choices

The Levada Center's polling shows that civic organizations working on concrete social issues are far more popular than opposition political parties or abstract political movements. Assisting children, protecting the greater Moscow area's Khimki Forest from highway development, and even battling with Kremlin officials over the flashing blue lights that they use to drive recklessly and with impunity around the capital all attract higher support than opposition parties or movements backing more abstract causes.

Václav Havel called such bottom-up civic activities "parallel structures," and noted how they address "the vital needs of specific people."[5] Spontaneously arising around specific problems, these structures tend to be open, self-governing, and inclined to raise their own funds. For a time, they are able to exist "alongside" the political system or at least on its edges. Politicization always beckons, however, and in Russia can take place quickly. This may not be a bad thing, since civic leaders who become active in politics may be key to the reform

and humanization (in Havel's sense) of Russian politics. Those representing the interests of specific groups must seek to draw the broadest possible public support, with a focus on finding new partners.

To its credit, the Russian opposition was able to quickly tie the problem of electoral fraud to the current structure of the Russian political system, and speedily organized large protest rallies in response. Yet more needs to be done. The interests of different social groups need to be articulated and aggregated.

The protests of 2011 and 2012 have shown that significant numbers of Russian citizens are not content to be indifferent. Perhaps the mass protests finally forced many Russians to think about their country's political system and the possibility of taking part in politics. Many Muscovites, including some under the age of 25, decided to participate in the Moscow municipal elections, and they helped to elect independent candidates to slightly more than a fourth of the seats in Moscow's municipal assemblies. Among these newly elected deputies are a number of well-known civic activists, who are already attempting to unite independent deputies and coordinate their efforts.

Thanks to the protests, new civic activists have become prominent beyond Moscow. The upcoming mayoral elections in Russia's larger cities and the 2014 Moscow City Duma elections will show if the current level of civic activism can be maintained and if it can actually affect the course of Russian politics. It remains to be seen how the direct election of governors and the new political-parties law will affect the situation.

If there are more mass protests ahead, the form they take and their ability to impact established parties and the state will depend on the internal organization of Russia's civic sphere. If the disparate groups and individuals who first linked up during the 2011 and 2012 protests prove able to maintain and develop their work together, the prospects for democratic change in Russia will greatly improve.

Notes

1. Except where noted otherwise, the results presented throughout this paper come from nationwide public-opinion polls conducted by the Moscow-based Levada Center with a sample size of N = 1,600 respondents ages 18 and older, and a statistical error of 3.4 percent. The results of the Levada Center's polls are available at www.levada.ru.

2. Samuel P. Huntington, *Political Order in Changing Societies* (New Haven: Yale University Press, 2006), 37.

3. Based on two Levada Center polls: 1) poll carried out by the Committee for Fair Elections of participants in the 24 December 2011 protest on Sakharova Prospekt in Moscow (791 respondents, 4.8 percent margin of error), www.levada.ru/26-12-2011/opros-na-prospekte-sakharova-24-dekkabrya; 2) poll carried out on behalf of *Novaya Gazeta* of participants at the 4 February 2012 Yakimanka Street and Bolotnaya Square demonstrations in Moscow (1,346 respondents,

5.2 percent margin of error), www.levada.ru/13-02-2012/opros-na-mitinge-4-fevralya.

4. Lev Gudkov, "The Nature of 'Putinism,'" *Russian Public Opinion Herald,* no. 3, 2009, 11.

5. Havel borrowed this concept of "parallel structures" from Václav Benda. See Havel's discussion of it in his 1978 essay "The Power of the Powerless," section XVIII, available at http://vaclavhavel.cz/showtrans.php?cat5clanky&val572_aj_clanky.html&typ5HTML.

Critical Thinking

1. How does social mobilization arise in a tightly controlled political system?

2. How can such protests be developed "from the bottom-up"?

3. What has the Law of Treason, passed in 2012, accomplished todate?

Create Central

www.mhhe.com/createcentral

Internet References

After a Year of Protest, a Different Russia Beckons
http://articles.washingtonpost.com/2012-12-04/world/35624360_1_anti-putin-boris-dubin-levada-center

New Report: The Protest Movement in Russia 2011 – 2012
http://hro.rightsinrussia.info/archive/right-of-assembly-1/levada/report

Opposition Figures Walk Out of Putin's Protest Fines Debate
http://en.ria.ru/russia/20120524/173651905.html

Critics Say New Russia Treason Law Is 'Broad' and 'Dangerous'
www.foxnews.com/world/2012/11/14/controversial-treason-law-takes-effect-in-russia-despite-putin-promise-to/

Accountable Only to Putin, Russia's Top Cop Sets Sights on Protest Movement
www.foxnews.com/world/2013/03/28/accountable-only-to-vladimir-putin-russia-top-cop-sets-sights-on-protest/

DENIS VOLKOV is a researcher at the Yuri Levada Center, an independent Moscow-based organization devoted to the analysis of Russian public life. He comments frequently on politics in the Russian media and studies youth political engagement, the sources and limits of democratization, and the role of digital media in social and political change. This essay was translated from the Russian by Patrick Walsh.

From *Journal of Democracy,* July 2012, pp. 55–62. Copyright © 2012 by National Endowment for Democracy and The Johns Hopkins University Press. Reprinted with permission of The Johns Hopkins University Press.

Article

Prepared by: Caroline Shaffer Westerhof,
California National University for Advanced Studies

Message delivered by Ms. Sahle Zewde on behalf of the Secretary General to the United Nations Seminar on Assistance to Palestine

BAN KI-MOON

Learning Outcomes

After reading this article, you will be able to:

Discuss the tensions and volatile situations on the ground that presently make it impossible to negotiate an Israeli-Palestinian settlement.

Understand the difficulties inherent in creating and accepting a two-state solution between Israel and Palestine.

It is my pleasure to send greetings to the participants in the United Nations Seminar on Assistance to the Palestinian People. I thank the Committee on the Exercise of the Inalienable Rights of the Palestinian People for keeping the international community's attention focused on this important subject.

Within weeks after political efforts toward a negotiated two-state solution reached an impasse, the situation on the ground grew more fragile. I condemn in the strongest terms the murder of the three Israeli teenagers abducted on 12 June in the West Bank. There can be no justification for the deliberate killing of civilians. I sincerely hope that Israeli and Palestinian authorities will work together to bring the perpetrators swiftly to justice, and I extend my deepest sympathy to the families of the victims. I call on all parties to abide by their obligations under international law and to refrain from any actions that could further escalate this highly tense situation.

I reiterate my call for both sides to resume meaningful negotiations with international engagement and support, and to address the much needed political horizon in order to avert further instability on the ground and to revive work toward achieving a durable peace. For the two-State solution to be salvaged, both parties must honor their commitment to resolve all permanent status issues, in accordance with Security Council resolutions, the Madrid principles, the Road Map, the 2002 Arab Peace initiative and existing agreements between the parties. They must also refrain from unilateral acts that diminish the prospects for a resumption of negotiations.

I am also concerned about persisting negative trends in the West Bank, including the recent killings of Palestinians, and the negative repercussions on the civilian population due to ongoing operations. I am extremely concerned about Israel's continuing settlement activity in the occupied West Bank, including East Jerusalem, which is illegal under international law and contradicts Israel's Road Map obligations. Demolitions of Palestinian homes and property in East Jerusalem and Area C also contravene Israel's obligation to protect the civilian population under its occupation.

The calm in Gaza has been shattered with resumed rocket firing on a near daily basis and Israeli retaliatory operations. I continue to condemn indiscriminate rocket firing and call on all parties to avoid any loss of civilian life. The persisting dire economic and humanitarian situation in Gaza remains of serious concern. I repeat my call for immediate steps to improve conditions and ensure a full opening of crossings into Gaza, including Rafah, to allow legitimate trade and movements of people, which is essential for creating economic opportunities for Palestinians.

Strengthening Palestinian institutions and improving governance is key to stimulating investment and development in the occupied Palestinian territory. Going forward, it will be important to shore up support for the Palestinian National Development Plan 2014–2016.

As we face an increasingly volatile situation on the ground and in the wider region, the message is clear: negotiations and compromise are essential to achieve a viable long-term settlement to the Israeli-Palestinian conflict. Without a credible political horizon, the Oslo paradigm is in real jeopardy. The international community must help and urge the parties to reshape parameters around the globally agreed goal—an end of the occupation that began in 1967; making way for an independent, sovereign, viable and prosperous Palestinian State, living side by side in peace with Israel within secure and recognized borders; and a just, lasting and comprehensive peace in the Middle East.

In this spirit, please accept my best wishes for a successful event.

Critical Thinking

1. Can the Palestinian and Israeli authorities work together without negative repercussions within the next decade?
2. Does the Israeli-Palestinian conflict increase regional devastation in the Middle East?

Internet References

Global Issues—Palestine and Israel
www.globalissues.org/issue/111/palestine-and-israel

How the pope triumphed over the Israeli-Palestinian conflict
www.timesofisrael.com/how-the-pope-triumphed-over-the-israel-palestinian-conflict/#!

Islamic Hatred: The Foundation of the Palestinian/Israeli Conflict
www.americanthinker.com/2014/06/islamic_hatred_the_foundation_of_the_palestinianisraeli_conflict.html

Israel and Palestine Articles
www.israelandpalestine.org/israel-and-palestine-articles

The Times of Israel—Israeli-Palestinian Conflict
www.timesofisrael.com/topic/israeli-palestinian-conflict/#!

BAN KI-MOON is the Secretary-General of the United Nations. The message was delivered by Ms. Sahle-Work Zewde, Director-General of the United Nations Office at Nairobi.

Prepared by: Caroline Shaffer Westerhof,
California National University for Advanced Studies

Article

The New Jihad

A new generation of Islamist extremists battle-hardened in Iraq and Syria sees the old guard of al Qaeda as too passive.

MARGARET COKER

Learning Outcomes

After reading this article, you will be able to:

Understand the development in the rise of a self-declared caliph that exposes a theological battle between al Qaeda and its competing affiliate in Iraq.

Discuss why the "new Jihad" sees the old guard leadership as "too politically passive and restrained in the use of violence."

Last week, a self-described heir to the Prophet Muhammad declared himself the supreme leader of a new Islamic state stretching from eastern Syria to northern Iraq. How did Abu Bakr al-Baghdadi, the nom de guerre of a mediocre Iraqi religious scholar in his mid-40s, outmaneuver al Qaeda as the new vanguard of jihadist ideology? How did he and his followers—armed with Kalashnikovs, smart phones and their ominous black banner—so suddenly take over the campaign to rid the Muslim world of Western and secular influence?

The rise of Mr. Baghdadi and his newly proclaimed "caliphate" highlights what had been a closely held secret of the Sunni jihadist movement: a split in the ranks that had been festering for years. It pits a new generation of shock troops hardened by battle in Iraq and Syria against al Qaeda veterans who had built the movement but were increasingly seen as too passive, both politically and theologically.

Mr. Baghdadi's proclamation was stunningly brazen. The leader of a faction of puritanical Sunni militants who have plagued Iraq with suicide bombings and beheadings, he was long considered a relatively inconsequential cog in the larger al Qaeda machine. Few people outside jihadist circles had heard of him, let alone seen him, before last month, when his followers in the militia known as the Islamic State of Iraq and al-Sham, or ISIS, rolled across northern Iraq, conquering Mosul, one of the largest cities in the country. Then on July 4, Mr. Baghdadi emerged at Mosul's al-Nuri Grand Mosque, promising to restore to his Sunni brethren their "dignity, might, rights, and leadership," according to a video of the sermon distributed by his group.

Mr. Baghdadi's military offensive has startled the United States and its Middle Eastern allies, who fear that it portends prolonged regional instability and terrorist attacks far afield from Iraq. Yet for the man leading what he now calls simply the Islamic State, the latest campaign has meant more than territorial conquest. Mr. Baghdadi's victories also mark the crescendo of a 10-year theological battle between veterans of al Qaeda, the core organization started by Osama bin Laden in the 1980s and now led by the Egyptian-born extremist Ayman al-Zawahiri, and its rebellious affiliate in Iraq, which Mr. Baghdadi took over in 2010. The prize: purported leadership of the world's estimated 1 billion Sunni Muslims and of a jihad supposedly waged in their name.

The rupture between Mr. Zawahiri's old guard and Mr. Baghdadi's new guard escalated last year, when Mr. Baghdadi refused Mr. Zawahiri's demand to formally declare his obedience and instead called the al Qaeda leader's rulings antithetical to God's commands. It was an audacious snub within the puritanical circles of al Qaeda and its fellow travelers. It was also the start of a slow-moving coup against the established jihadist hierarchy.

Today's strains flow from decades of wrangling over Islamist doctrines of religious and political revolution. In the 1940s and 1950s, during heady days of nationalism and rebellion in the Middle East, the Egyptian writer Sayyid Qutb—widely considered the father of contemporary jihadist thought—merged Quranic verses, Islamic prophecies, and Third World revolutionary fervor to produce a seminal tract advocating Islamist political violence.

The early jihadist intelligentsia that adopted Qutb's views included a young Saudi named Osama bin Laden and other members of a fringe movement called Salafism, which holds that Muslim society should adopt a governing and religious framework that adheres to Muslim practices from the early days of Islam's founding in the seventh century. Those who espouse using violence to achieve such a puritanical state are known as Salafi jihadists.

Among the followers of this creed, the battle between Mr. Zawahiri and Mr. Baghdadi is a pivotal development. "Like the old saying goes: The revolution devours its own," says Jérôme Drevon, a fellow at the Swiss National Science Foundation who specializes in Islamist movements. "What we are seeing is a generational split between older jihadis who have learned pragmatic lessons [of overreach] . . . and a younger, more brutal generation who don't believe in or haven't lived long enough to learn those lessons."

Al Qaeda (which is Arabic for "the base") had significant though limited ideological appeal and recruiting power throughout the 1980s and 1990s. Its charismatic leader, bin Laden, recruited Arab radicals and others to fight the Soviet occupation of Afghanistan. He also turned his sights on what he considered impure and impious Arab tyrannies—above all in his native Saudi Arabia, home of Islam's two holiest cities, Mecca and Medina.

Bin Laden also broadened his scope to target the United States and the West, which al Qaeda came to call "the far enemy" for propping up Israel and Arab autocrats such as the Saudi royal family and Egypt's Hosni Mubarak. Al Qaeda's allure was strengthened by its spectacular September 11, 2001, terrorist attacks and by satellite television and Internet technology that spread its message across the globe.

The group's brain trust had always relied on a division of power between the ideologues—such as Mr. Zawahiri, an Egyptian physician who grew up in the 1940s and 1950s alongside Qutb and his followers—and the executives like bin Laden and his military chiefs, who secured the money, inspired the recruits and perfected the bombs and the battle tactics.

Mr. Zawahiri honed al Qaeda's basic tenets. He declared that the world, including most Muslim societies, languished in a state of impurity and that it was al Qaeda's religious duty to cleanse it. The main culprits, according to Mr. Zawahiri's teachings, were the secular West and its Arab allies, both marked as primary targets in al Qaeda's holy war.

After 9/11, the United States and its partners drove al Qaeda out of its haven in Taliban-ruled Afghanistan and weakened its

operational abilities. Mr. Zawahiri also became vulnerable criticism from an even more fanatical end of the jihadist spe trum over a doctrinal issue that lies at the core of the Sal quest to build a pure Islamist state.

The dispute centers on Mr. Zawahiri's belief that caliphate—a state that can demand allegiance from all M lims and declare jihad against the enemies of the faith—c emerge only after the wider Muslim world has been purifie Mr. Zawahiri hopes to bring Muslims out of their unredeem state of *jahiliyya*—the type of spiritual ignorance that exist before the Prophet—by excising all contact with corrupti Western influences and placing governing institutions in t hands of administrators who share this vision and can prom gate it to the mass of Muslims.

This religious interpretation was shared by the Talib leader Mullah Mohammad Omar—which is why al Qae didn't declare a caliphate when the Taliban seized control Afghanistan in the 1990s, according to Hassan Abu Hani a Jordanian scholar and former Salafi who is an independe expert in Islamist groups. "A caliphate has to be based on t consent of the public," Mr. Abu Hanieh said. "Afghan soci was at war, and thus, according to [al Qaeda's] religious und standing, the time was not right for this desired goal."

But Mr. Baghdadi and his followers reject this doctri of an evolving religious and social consensus. They belie instead that a pure Islamic regime can be more swiftly impos by force. This basic split has existed for a decade between Qaeda and its one-time offshoot in Iraq, which formed af the United States invaded in 2003 and helped establish the fi Shiite government in Iraq in centuries.

The doctrinal dispute first came to light in the mid-2000s a set of letters that bin Laden and Mr. Zawahiri wrote to A Musab al-Zarqawi, the infamous founder of al Qaeda in Iraq a Jordanian responsible for a wave of beheadings, bombir and kidnappings. Bin Laden, in hiding after fleeing Afgha stan after 9/11, scolded Zarqawi for attacks that targeted Ira majority Shiites and shed Sunni blood as well. Such tacti he argued, divided Muslims, alienated many Iraqi Sunnis a diverted efforts away from al Qaeda's focus on killing Ame cans and toppling heretical Arab regimes.

But to Zarqawi and his followers, killing anyone w rejected their puritanical views—including Shiites or even d senting Sunnis—was a step toward purity. They chafed at Laden's reprimand, but they didn't break ranks. Zarqawi f mally pledged *bay'a*—or obedience—to bin Laden, effectiv papering over the ideological division.

By the late 2000s, however, U.S. forces had killed Zarqa and the Iraqi offshoots of al Qaeda had gone through seve incarnations. By then, Mr. Baghdadi had appeared on the sce After years of imprisonment by the United States, he joir hat was then known as the Islamic State of Iraq, or ISI. The roup had published a pamphlet titled "The Birth of the Islamic tate Declaration," reasserting its belief that Muslims had a oly duty to create—by force if necessary—the conditions that ould allow a caliphate to re-emerge.

In many ways, the doctrinal differences among Salafi jihadt factions mirror the dispute that raged among Russian comunist factions at the start of the 20th century. The two major ctions—the Mensheviks and the Bolsheviks, led by Lenin—lit over the basic question of the party's role. Should it work develop the social consciousness that would move humanity ward a perfect workers' state, or should it try to bring about ch change immediately through violent revolution?

"Every radical movement has its wings, its pragmatists and s puritanical firebrands," said Haras Rafiq, a counterterrorism dviser for the U.K. government and a scholar at London's Quilam Foundation, which seeks to counter Islamist extremism.

Lenin supported the path of aggressive force and outflanked s Menshevik opponents politically after 1903. By 1918, he ad solidified his rule over the communist movement by leadg it to victory over Czar Nicholas II's dying empire.

Mr. Baghdadi's rise to power mirrors Lenin's in its efficiency ad brutality. By 2010, Mr. Baghdadi—whose main success until that time was winning a doctorate in religious studs from a mediocre Iraqi university—had taken over ISI. After .S. forces killed bin Laden in May 2011, Mr. Baghdadi gave any pretense of unity with al Qaeda. His followers swore legiance to their own leader, not to Mr. Zawahiri, bin Laden's ccessor and longtime deputy—a stinging show of defiance.

Mr. Baghdadi spent the next few years locked in ideological attles with Mr. Zawahiri, especially after 2011, when Sunni nadists began to join the worsening civil war in Syria. Tenon mounted in September 2013, when Mr. Zawahiri issued a amphlet called "General Guidelines of the Work of a Jihadist," odifying al Qaeda-approved rules of warfare. It circumscribed ligiously sanctioned killings.

But followers of Mr. Baghdadi continued to insist that any-ae who disagreed with their movement's harsh interpreta-on of Islam could be labeled an apostate—a practice used to stify the group's decade long practice of killing Shiites and llow Sunnis who rejected its views. As the struggle against rian President Bashar al-Assad—the leader of a dictatorship ominated by Alawites, a small sect descended from Shiite lam—grew bloodier, Mr. Baghdadi rebuffed Mr. Zawahiri's eatise as incompatible with the war he was fighting in Syria d across the border in Iraq.

The power struggle finally came to a head on April 9, 2013, hen Mr. Baghdadi launched his first outright rebellion against Qaeda. In an audio recording released online, he declared hostile takeover of the Nusra Front, a Syrian jihadist rebel militia linked to al Qaeda whose leader had pledged allegiance to Mr. Zawahiri. Mr. Baghdadi declared that the two groups would merge under a single name: the Islamic State of Iraq and al-Sham, or ISIS.

Sunni jihadists were jolted by the move. The Nusra Front immediately rejected Mr. Baghdadi's takeover bid and refused to swear allegiance to him. In June, Mr. Zawahiri released a three-page letter intended to extinguish "the fire of sedition" ignited by Mr. Baghdadi. In the missive, Mr. Zawahiri ordered Mr. Baghdadi to retreat from Syria while retaining control of the jihadist project in Iraq. But in a reply disseminated through the Internet, Mr. Baghdadi not only refused to retreat but also said he had "chosen the command of God over the command in the letter [by Mr. Zawahiri] that contradicts it."

Al Qaeda's old guard was outraged at this affront to their gray-bearded leader. For months, several elders of the movement had tried to reconcile Mr. Baghdadi to the larger al Qaeda group—to no avail. On February 3, Mr. Zawahiri formally disowned ISIS, and later that month, Mr. Zawahiri's personal emissary to mediate the Syrian struggle was killed by a suicide bomber. Syrian rebels accuse ISIS of the murder, a charge that the splinter group denies.

By spring, Mr. Baghdadi was in full ascent, sweeping aside al Qaeda's sanctimoniousness with tangible military gains. His forces solidified control of a swath of Iraqi territory, and he prepared to launch a high-profile operation to recruit others to his doctrinal and political views. His forces stunned the region by conquering Mosul and marching south toward Baghdad.

Mr. Baghdadi's expanding empire, which includes control over some of Iraq's prime oil facilities, has put al Qaeda on the back foot—and left the United States and its allies worrying about the security threats that could emerge from this new, virulent form of jihadism. The chunk of territory that Mr. Baghdadi's followers have carved out of Iraq and Syria affords them a haven in which to train and plot—one that, unlike pre-9/11 Afghanistan, lies at the heart of the Arab world and close to Europe and Israel.

Some intelligence officials fear that this new competitor to al Qaeda could redouble its attempts to launch a spectacular terrorism attack in Western Europe or the U.S. On Tuesday, Attorney General Eric Holder warned that the danger that radicalized Westerners could return home from Syria's civil war to plot terrorist attacks now amounts to "a global crisis."

Meanwhile, the aftershocks from the jihadist rupture are still reverberating. Since Mr. Baghdadi's sermon last week declaring himself caliph, al Qaeda affiliates in Yemen have denounced him. So too has the mainstream Sunni religious establishment, including Cairo's al-Azhar seminary, which has always opposed al Qaeda's actions, and Yussuf al-Qaradawi, an Egyptian cleric widely seen as the spiritual leader of the Muslim Brotherhood.

But it is still unclear what effect, if any, such censure will have on the audience that Mr. Baghdadi has shown himself adroit at cultivating: the younger Islamist radicals, including dozens of European Muslims, who have been flocking to him.

"There is a wellspring of disillusioned Muslims in Western Europe vulnerable to radicalization" by the Islamic State, says Richard Barrett, the former head of counterterrorism for MI6, the U.K.'s foreign spy agency, and now an adviser at the Soufan Group, a private counterterrorism consulting firm. "They are looking for a leader who doesn't sit back and cogitate but who acts on his beliefs, who understands their feelings of marginalization"—a leader who offers "promises of greatness."

Critical Thinking

1. What is this "new Jihadist" ideology?
2. Is there a wellspring of disillusioned Muslims in Western Europe vulnerable to radicalization?
3. Can you project the potential existence of an Islamic State of Iraq and al-Sham known as ISIS?

Internet References

Iraq's ISIS Is Eclipsing al-Qaeda, Especially with Young Jihadists
www.newsweek.com/2014/07/18/iraqs-isis-eclipsing-al-qaeda-especial young-jihadists-257402.html

ISIS declares creation of Islamic state in Middle East, "new era international jihad"
www.rt.com/news/169256-isis-create-islamic-state

ISIS Leader Allegedly Appears on Video Urging "Jihad" a Support for "Caliphate" at Mosque
www.theblaze.com/stories/2014/07/05/isis-leader-allegedly-appears-video-urging-jihad-and-support-for-caliphate-at-mosque

The New Jihad—Wall Street Journal
www.online.wsj.com/articles/why-the-new-jihadists-in-iraq-and-syr see-al-qaeda-as-too-passive-1405096590

MARGARET COKER is a senior reporter for *The Wall Street Journa* For the last 10 years she has reported on the Middle East.

Article

Prepared by: Caroline Shaffer Westerhof,
California National University for Advanced Studies

The Famous Dutch (In)Tolerance

"Variations of Geert Wilders's xenophobic message are shared by the majority of the political parties represented in the Dutch parliament."

JAN ERK

Learning Outcomes

After reading this article, you will be able to:

- Understand the concept of the "tyranny of the majority."
- Examine why the Party of Freedom in the Netherlands has made discrimination acceptable.
- Explain the concept of xenophobia.

The Dutch have long enjoyed a reputation for tolerance, and they are indeed a tolerant people: They are tolerant of the anti-immigrant sentiment that has engulfed their country's politics over the past decade. Part of the political partnership running the Netherlands today is a party whose agenda includes ethnic registration, a tax on Muslim headscarves, repatriation of Dutch criminals of immigrant origin, a blanket ban on the construction of mosques, and outlawing the Koran.

To a large extent, this situation is a side effect of the fact that anti-Muslim discourse has encountered growing acceptance in recent years. Such discourse has allowed anti-immigrant sentiment—in the Dutch case, sentiment against the people of Moroccan and Turkish derivation who constitute a majority of the country's immigrants—to become palatable to mainstream sensibilities.

In fact, the far-right Party of Freedom (PVV) could never have gained inclusion in the political coalition governing the nation had it continued using the race-based rhetoric associated with xenophobic parties of the past. Instead, the PVV employs anti-Islam rhetoric. The words do not carry the same anti-immigrant overtones as race-based rhetoric, but they have the same effect.

In June 2010, national elections resulted in a major electoral success for the upstart PVV, which had been formed only four years before by Geert Wilders. Afterwards the PVV became a coalition partner of the Christian Democrat Appeal (CDA, a Christian Democrat party) and the People's Party for Freedom and Democracy (VVD, a right-liberal party). Leaders of the three parties unveiled a new coalition program on September 30, a cabinet was put together in the following weeks (though the PVV gained no ministerial portfolio), and the government was sworn in on October 14.

Not long before this, Wilders had tried to take his party's message to the United States, joining in the opposition to the planned construction of a Muslim community center near the former site of the World Trade Center in New York City, but he failed to attract much media interest in North America. Wilders managed to create more interest in Australia, where in an interview he called Islam a "retarded and violent" religion.

The PVV's membership in the governing coalition will likely help Wilders increase his international profile beyond Europe, where he is already well known. But how did his party, in a country renowned for its progressive politics, become a governing partner?

The Anti-Islam Norm

A simple but misleading narrative seems to dominate media reporting on the rise of the xeno-phobic right in the Netherlands. According to this narrative, a single party led by the colorful populist Wilders broke ranks with The Hague–based Dutch political establishment and stood up to the left-liberal media, thereby shaking the country's progressive foundations. This picture is clear and compelling. It is very kind to the Dutch political establishment. It is also incorrect.

Wilders's peroxide blond hair, his offensive outbursts, and his clownish antics comport with the image that the media have painted for him, that of the outsider. But in fact, variations of Geert Wilders's xenophobic message are shared by the majority of the political parties represented in the Dutch parliament. Put simply, Wilders is a product of the Dutch political system and his message is not confined to the fringes of the political spectrum. His message is disguised in anti-Islam language, which makes it more palatable than is naked xenophobia to mainstream sensibilities.

Although no member of the PVV holds a ministerial portfolio, the party's influence over the formation of the cabinet last year was recently exposed when it became clear that certain posts—including that of the minister of integration—had had to be vetted by Wilders.

Moreover, the governing coalition's program includes a number of priorities that defined the PVV's 2010 electoral campaign. The government proposes to ban the face-covering Islamic burqa. Residence without a permit is to be made a criminal act, and arranging family unification for immigrants will become harder. The governing coalition plans to halve the number of people allowed to immigrate to the Netherlands from so-called non-Western countries, and to require those who are allowed in to participate in stricter and more expensive integration courses.

Some of the PVV's anti-Islam positions are concealed in ambiguous wording. One example is the rather bizarre goal of cutting unemployment and social security benefits to those "whose clothing is not suitable for finding work"—which potentially could become a means for denying benefits to Muslims who wear traditional garb.

To be sure, not all components of the government's program necessarily represent realistic proposals. For example, this author has never seen anyone in the Netherlands wearing a burqa, so the ban against it is more a coded message to supporters than a piece of public policy. Yet this only accentuates the fact that the coalition program, while highlighting symbolic issues, has failed to address many pressing problems in the economic realm. The government has made a few selective cuts in public spending, but it has proposed no structural reform of the economy, no reform of the housing market, and no relaxation of the country's rigid labor market.

Meanwhile, immigration has become the top political issue in a country that—compared to other nations across the Western world—does not have a very large immigrant population. The four biggest immigrant communities in the Netherlands are Turks, Moroccans, Antilleans, and Surinamese; together they total just under 1 million people, in a country of 17 million. Yet these Dutch citizens now find themselves living under a coalition government that has adopted specific policies targeting them.

Margin to the Middle

This picture of Dutch politics probably clashes with the impression of the Netherlands that most foreign visitors to Amsterdam take home with them. The Netherlands is of course bigger than the old city center of the capital, and the rest of the country has always been more socially conservative than its biggest city, which among its tourist attractions offers (sanitized) vice.

In any case, Dutch people's tolerance of soft drugs, pornography, and prostitution is not the same as social permissiveness. The Dutch word that refers to the decriminalized provision of vice, *gedogen,* merely suggests that those who infringe against collective morality will be tolerated and granted tacit immunity from prosecution. Such tolerance implies no endorsement, and this is nothing new.

What is new is the acceptance of a far-right xenophobic party as a bona fide governing partner. Parties with similar agendas have appeared on the Dutch landscape in the past. These, however, not only were politically marginalized—they were pursued by magistrates for promoting discrimination.

For example, the far-right Dutch People's Union entered the parliament in 1977, but immediately became a target of prosecutors, and was banned the following year (although a

complicated legal process followed). The Center Party (CP) was another such party, entering parliament in 1982. Internal splits spawned offshoots such as the Center Democrats (CD), the Center Party '86 (CP'86), the New National Party (NNP), and the Dutch Bloc. CP'86 was banned in 1996 and was dissolved by magistrates the following year for advocating discrimination and endangering public order. The same year the veteran leader of the CD (who had started his career in the CP) was found guilty of inciting racial hatred.

It is important to recall that these far-right outfits operated on the margins of Dutch mainstream politics. Yet now the two largest center-right parties in the parliament maintain a political partnership with Wilders—and they do so even though, coincident with the formation of the coalition government, Wilders was the subject of a court case that involved inciting racial hatred against Muslims. (Prosecutors themselves, who had brought the case to court partly because they had come under criticism from antiracism activists for doing too little regarding Wilders, declared their opinion that he was not guilty.)

The PVV's status as the third-largest party in the parliament might not appear to justify all the attention it has received—but the Dutch electoral system is based on the principle of proportional representation, and it lacks the nationwide vote threshold that is a feature of most other proportional systems. In Germany, for example, political parties must gain at least 5 percent of the nationwide vote to gain seats based on their proportion of the votes cast.

The absence of such a threshold in the Netherlands means that the Dutch parliament is composed of a multitude of parties ranging from the Party for Animals, with 2 seats, to the right-liberal VVD, with 31. In this context, the PVV's 24 seats give Wilders major clout within the ruling partnership. By themselves, the CDA with its 21 seats and the VVD with its 31 seats would have fallen short of a governing majority in the 150-seat parliament. With the PVV included, a parliamentary majority was achieved.

Word Games

So what explains the acceptance of the xeno-phobic PVV in mainstream Dutch politics? First, Wilders's position on Islam is shared by the majority of Dutch parties in the parliament—there is nothing preposterous or marginal about his message in the contemporary Netherlands. Wilders's immoderate language and attention-seeking antics might annoy some of his political partners, but his party's message is not alien to mainstream Dutch politics.

Second, while the xenophobic far-right parties of the past explicitly targeted immigrants, which created problems for them, Wilders's PVV has found a way around this by targeting a religion, Islam, instead of immigrants themselves. Voters need not feel they are targeting their Muslim immigrant compatriots; they are just manning the barricades to protect Western freedoms from onslaught by an intolerant, backward, Eastern culture. Of course, anti-Islam language need not in every national context equal anti-immigrant xenophobia—but the majority of Dutch immigrants are Muslims, and the connection is obvious.

The Dutch media, and Wilders himself for that matter, prefer as a descriptive prefix for his party the term "anti-Islam" (and not "anti-Muslim"). "Anti-Islam" suggests that the PVV opposes the values and teachings of the religion at an abstract, ideological level. The term attempts to obscure the fact that, in the Netherlands, the targets of anti-Islam sentiment are bound to be individual followers of Islam—that is, Dutch Muslims. The difference between "anti-Islam" and "anti-Muslim" might at first glance seem minor and semantic, but this choice in labeling has played a key role in bringing anti-immigrant sentiment into the mainstream, acceptably cloaked.

The Dutch public was already receptive to such a message. A 2005 survey by Pew Global Attitudes found that 51 percent of respondents in the Netherlands held an unfavorable opinion of Muslims living in their country—a number much higher than in other Western nations. (In the United States the number was 22 percent; in Britain it was 14 percent.)

Among younger Dutch people, the anti-Islam current is particularly pronounced. The 2009 International Civic and Citizenship Education Study, which reported on attitudes among secondary-school pupils in 39 countries, found that Dutch students (and Dutch-speaking Flemings in Belgium) held the most negative views regarding immigrants. Dutch students tended more than others to oppose the idea of granting equal rights to immigrants.

Meanwhile, labor market statistics show tendencies indicating immigrant marginalization. The analyst Peter Kee's findings on native-immigrant wage differentials (published in *Oxford Economic Papers*) reveal structural discrimination: The average nonimmigrant Dutch worker earns 35 percent more than the average Antillean-Dutch, 41 percent more than Surinamese-Dutch, 54 percent more than Turkish-Dutch, and 44 percent more than Moroccan-Dutch.

The pervasiveness of anti-Muslim sentiment goes a long way toward explaining how political parties, to varying degrees, have adopted into their programs anti-Islam views, the somewhat more intellectually acceptable sibling of anti-Muslim sentiment. But it is not clear what a Dutch political party can expect to achieve by adopting such a position. Unless Muslims somehow convert *en masse* to Christianity, demonizing Islam can only increase Muslim isolation from Dutch society while intensifying Muslims' solidarity. Worse, it could fan Islamic fundamentalism.

Unless Muslims somehow convert en masse to Christianity, demonizing Islam can only increase Muslim isolation and solidarity.

Political discussions about Islam in the Netherlands tend to lump all Muslims into one category. There are no secular or religious Muslims; no left or right; no radicals or moderates; no working class or middle class; no Shiites or Sunnis; no Turks, no Arabs, no Albanians, no Indonesians, no Iranians— just Muslims. One immediate outcome of lumping all Muslims

together has been to achieve precisely that: Muslims in the Netherlands have become more unified.

Secular, liberal Muslims, especially among the Turkish-Dutch, have been pushed toward finding common cause with their conservative coreligionists. Different ethnic communities have been brought closer together. An example is the Moroccan-Dutch and Turkish-Dutch, who had remained separate from one another since their arrival in the Netherlands. Today they are accepting the one-size-fits-all Islamic label.

It should have been self-evident that painting an entire religion as oppressive and its followers as backward could only exacerbate the ghettoization of Dutch Muslims. Then again, measures announced by the coalition government to facilitate the integration of immigrants were perhaps designed as disincentives for Muslims to remain in the Netherlands. Such measures, however, are unlikely even to bring about that outcome.

Measures to facilitate the integration of immigrants were perhaps designed as disincentives for Muslims to remain in the Netherlands.

The segments of Moroccan-Dutch and Turkish-Dutch populations that have not already integrated into Dutch culture and language will likely continue to live, mentally and physically, in ethnic ghettos. The well-integrated and aspirational segments of these two communities, on the other hand, are more likely than those in the ghetto to feel increasingly unwanted. If younger, educated, and better-integrated individuals start leaving the country, the Netherlands will be left with those who lack that option, thereby ensuring the perpetuation of a marginalized and disenchanted minority.

On January 10, 2010, leading figures of the Turkish-Dutch community published an open letter in the daily *Volkskrant* on precisely this issue, voicing their concerns about the increasing isolation of the young. As the educated start showing tendencies to leave, discrimination is making the remainder particularly susceptible to radical Islam.

It's Murder

Wilders did not create the anti-Islam sentiment that now pervades the ranks of the majority of the political parties and their voters—including some on the left. That trail was blazed by other, mainstream Dutch politicians before him. In fact, Wilders's success marks the culmination of a pattern evident since the late 1990s.

The first mainstream politician to court the anti-immigrant vote was a senior member of the VVD, Frits Bolkestein. The author Ian Buruma, in his 2006 book *Murder in Amsterdam: The Death of Theo van Gogh and the Limits of Tolerance,* recounts that Bolkestein told him: "One must never underestimate the degree of hatred that Dutch feel for Moroccan and Turkish immigrants. My political success is based on the fact that I was prepared to listen to such people."

Bolkestein was later appointed a commissioner of the European Union. In that post, he was able to take his anti-Islam crusade to the European level, warning against the Islamization of Europe and celebrating what he believed was a Christian, European victory against Muslim Turks in Vienna in 1683. (Bolkestein perhaps did not know that the Ottoman army then besieging Vienna included Hungarians under the prince of Transylvania, Imre Thököly; the Moldovan army under Prince George Dusak; and Romanian and Bulgarian units, as well as a number of smaller Christian contingents. His historically creative narrative in any case fit the mood of the times.)

While Bolkestein was reminiscing about medieval battles, dour mainstream politics in the Netherlands was shaken by the appearance of a flamboyant and charismatic character who challenged the very foundations of the Dutch political establishment. Pim Fortuyn suddenly emerged in the early 2000s with a style and message that contrasted markedly with the cliquish political culture of The Hague. His main message entailed criticism of Islam and calls for tighter restrictions on immigration. But Fortuyn was more than a one-dimensional, anti-immigrant politician; he held a broadly libertarian collection of views on all aspects of politics.

Fortuyn was murdered by an animal-rights activist in 2002. This, the first political murder in the history of the Kingdom of the Netherlands, produced a nationwide shock wave. Collective disbelief and outrage reached a new high with the murder of Theo van Gogh, a contrarian author/actor/director and equal-opportunity offender whose controversial missives had targeted both Jews and Muslims. He was stabbed to death by a Moroccan-Dutch man in 2004. A note left by the murderer warned Ayaan Hirsi Ali, van Gogh's high-profile collaborator and a former Labor politician who had by then joined the VVD, that she was next in line.

Hirsi Ali, an enterprising young female Dutch politician of Somali origin, played perhaps the key role, due to her Muslim origins, in bringing anti-Islam xenophobia into the mainstream. Hirsi Ali and her carefully crafted personal story eased the lingering discomfort some felt about the targeting of Muslim immigrants: If this Muslim immigrant woman of color herself warns us about the dangers of Islam and its practitioners, it surely cannot be xenophobia; this is instead a clash between (our) democratic freedoms and (their) backward and oppressive religion.

Ruthless, Incompetent

The ranks of the VVD included another such enterprising politician, Rita Verdonk, who had raised her profile in national politics by becoming a vocal proponent of the anti-Islam viewpoint. Verdonk, who had to compete for media attention with other VVD members like Bolkestein, Hirsi Ali, and Wilders (who used to be a VVD member), managed the astonishing feat of becoming—despite being an anti-immigrant politician—the minister of immigration and integration. This allowed her to peddle her message to a bigger audience.

One of Verdonk's suggestions, as part of her 2006 proposal for a "national code of conduct," was to outlaw on the streets the use of languages other than Dutch. Also that year she managed to add her name to the "Hall of Shame" of the

international monitoring group Human Rights Watch, when she tried to deport homosexual Iranian asylum seekers back to Iran.

Verdonk's anti-immigrant campaign was not an unadulterated success. In a 2006 poll, her parliamentary colleagues voted her the nation's worst politician, one who somehow managed to combine ruthlessness and incompetence. Nonetheless, her anti-Islam message resonated well with the public.

In the 2006 election she received the highest number of preference votes, surpassing VVD party leader Mark Rutte. Verdonk then tried to unseat Rutte from the party leadership. Failing to achieve that goal, she established her own party, Proud of the Netherlands, in 2008. Verdonk's popularity has not matched her ambitions, however, and her party has failed to enter parliament.

In the meantime, Rutte has shown that he can continue disseminating anti-Muslim ideas in the VVD without Verdonk and Wilders. In a 2008 interview, Rutte stated that Islam has nothing valuable to bring to the Netherlands—other than couscous. If we assume Rutte is aware that the Koran does not include recipes involving semolina granules, we can reason that his comment was not meant to attack Islam as a religion, ideology, or culture, as he might claim, but instead to attack the Muslim citizens of the Netherlands.

As Islamophobia took hold in the political mainstream, Muslim Dutch fled other parties and ended up bolstering the performance of the Dutch Labor Party in 2007 local elections. This, however, was not a welcome development as far as the Labor leader Wouter Bos was concerned. Following the election, Bos in an interview expressed unease about having immigrant representatives among municipal councilors because he viewed Muslim political culture as incompatible with Dutch values. Trying to distance his party from its growing Muslim support, Bos declared that the election results did not mean that Labor had become the party of immigrants.

Bos's message was taken up as well by the leader of the Labor party in the Amsterdam municipal council, Hannah Belliot. In an interview she sent a message to immigrants: "At home you can say whatever you want. . . . But as an economic migrant you must work, make as little use of welfare as possible, and keep quiet."

The chair of the Labor Party organization, Lilianne Ploumen, offered further support for Bos. In language that would have been unthinkable a few years before, Ploumen led calls to do away with what she saw as the failed model of tolerance. In a position paper for the Labor Party in 2008 Ploumen stated that "the criticism of cultures and religions should not be held back due to concerns about tolerance. . . . Government strategy should bring our values into confrontation with people who think otherwise." The Labor Party chair then told "newcomers to avoid self-designated victimization."

To the left of the Labor Party sits the Dutch Socialist Party (SP), which itself has not been impervious to the growing anti-immigrant mood in the Netherlands. The SP did not join the anti-Islam currents right away, but following the Bulgarian and Romanian accession to the European Union in 2007—a time when the Dutch working class was worried about a potential influx of migrants from Eastern Europe—the Socialists flirted with anti-immigrant sentiment by opposing the free movement of labor within the EU. (To be fair, some of the SP's positions can be traced to the early 1980s, when the party opposed immigration as a capitalist ploy to break working-class solidarity and bring down pay.)

Few Dissenters

Widespread Dutch acceptance of an anti-Muslim message is a little surprising in a country that not so long ago was an unwitting accessory in the massacre of around 8,000 Bosnian Muslim men and boys. In the summer of 1995, Dutch troops transferred control of the United Nations safe haven of Srebrenica to a Bosnian Serb militia besieging the town. Dutch troops then helped the Serbs separate fightingage males from the others. Women and children were moved to a nearby town, while over the following days the militia organized the systematic execution of the males. The incident was Europe's worst mass killing since World War II. The fact that the Bosnian Serb militia claimed it was protecting Christendom against Islam shows the sinister potential of such language.

Some of Wilders's ideas would be comical, on account of their bizarre reasoning and internal inconsistency, were the political stakes of his message lower. Wilders claims to stand for freedom of expression, but he wants to ban the Koran. He believes Islam and its holy book have no place in Europe—or in Western civilization—because the Koran is a fascist work identical to *Mein Kampf.* Maybe Wilders himself has not read these two books and cannot remember which region of the world spawned fascism, but of course it is not the veracity of his claims that matters. The PVV, as a far-right party seeking to expand its appeal, must make sure to disown the heritage of European fascism.

During a December 2010 official visit to Israel, Wilders called for that country to annex and settle the West Bank. He of course is not the only far-right European politician to court Israel. Filip de Winter of the Belgian party Vlaams Belang and Heinz-Christian Strache of Austria's Freedom Party have also taken their anti-Islam message there. Their professed pro-Israel views do not please all Israelis, however. Following Wilders's visit, the daily *Haaretz* portrayed these European visitors as extremists "who after trading in their Jewish demon-enemy for the Muslim criminal-immigrant model are singing in unison that Samaria is Jewish ground."

Indeed, the far right's frequent invocations of the need to defend Judeo-Christian Europe against Islam, its declarations of support for Israel, and its habit of associating Islam with fascism are tools for severing the visible links between the far right of today and that of yesterday. This helps make such parties appear more acceptable as political partners (and potentially helps restrict international criticism).

The far right's declarations of support for Israel and its habit of associating Islam with fascism are tools for severing the visible links between the far right of today and that of yesterday.

One would have expected Wilders's ideas to be scrutinized and criticized by mainstream Dutch politicians, but the majority seems either to be on the same wavelength or simply to tolerate his views. One important exception is a small minority within the CDA. The first sign of party dissent regarding partnership with the PVV was the resignation of the deputy coalition negotiator, who also quit his parliamentary seat.

More CDA unease was exposed when the new coalition program was presented to the party congress for approval. During this process, it became clear that the deputy negotiator was not the only Christian Democrat with reservations about joining forces with the far right. While there was no sign of large-scale, open dissent, 32 percent of CDA members—including some senior members—voted against the coalition agreement (while the VVD supported the agreement unanimously).

A particularly interesting split exists now within the liberal political family: While the VVD assumed the lead in bringing about the new political partnership with Wilders, the left-liberal Democrats 66 party (D66) has not shied away from voicing its dislike of Wilders and its disapproval of the governing partnership. Preceding the announcement of the new coalition program, a couple of VVD members switched allegiance to their left-liberal siblings.

While the right-liberal VVD and the left-liberal D66 share roots in the continental European liberal heritage and see eye to eye on many issues such as support for a liberal market economy, a small state, and individual rights and freedoms, it is on the issue of Islamophobia that these two liberal parties have adopted opposite positions. Meanwhile, D66's lone ally in combating anti-Muslim sentiment has been the Green-Left party, which has moved from being a single-issue environmentalist party to one that leans toward left-liberal positions on other issues.

Questioning Loyalty

Of course, no guarantee exists that the partnership among the CDA, the VVD, and Wilders's PVV will be a smooth one, or that it will last. The early days of the governing coalition were shaken by revelations that six PVV members of parliament had concealed their criminal records—including violent, sexual, and financial offenses ranging from improper relations with subordinates in the military to head-butting critics to abusing the social insurance system. These have taken some credibility away from the PVV's strong law-and-order message.

Anti-Islam sentiment might be the lowest common denominator among these parties, but in a time of economic difficulties, the parties over the coming months will have to negotiate a complex political minefield. An early example of this has been a hapless effort by Prime Minister Rutte to contain criticism of the appointment of a minister of dual Dutch-Swedish citizenship to the new cabinet. Opposition to dual citizenship has been a longstanding PVV position; Wilders had objected to the inclusion of Turkish-Dutch and Moroccan-Dutch members of parliament in the previous cabinet, stating that "even if [the Moroccan-born junior minister of social affairs] had a blond mop and a Swedish passport, I would still want to see him go."

A March 2007 parliamentary motion by the PVV that questioned the loyalty of ministers with dual citizenship was supported by the right-liberal VVD. But following the swearing-in of the new cabinet in October 2010, the media reported on the dual citizenship of the new junior health minister. Rutte's response was that the Swedish citizenship of the minister was not a problem; however, it would have been different had the minister held Turkish citizenship.

The fact that Wilders himself has Indonesian immigrant roots and that he dyes his hair blond might be interesting avenues for studying the underlying psychological reasons for his xenophobic proclivities, but that is beyond the scope of this essay. What the preceding discussion shows is how changes in political discourse can make traditional xenophobia appear to be a bona fide point of view about clashing civilizations, cultures, and values.

Wilders is not the populist voice of the disen-franchised, questioning the elitist political establishment. He is part of the mainstream politics of the Netherlands, a mainstream in which the majority of the parties use the same anti-Islam language that he uses. And no matter how they try to obscure the reality, the inevitable targets of anti-Islam sentiment are individual Muslim immigrants. The message is not in fact anti-Islam. It is anti-Muslim.

Critical Thinking

1. How can discrimination be acceptable in The Netherlands, which is a country that permits interracial relationships?

2. Is The Netherlands a positive influence in Europe, having paid all its World War II debts?

3. Why are many in The Netherlands capitalizing on anti-immigration issues?

Create Central

www.mhhe.com/createcentral

Internet References

Migration Information Source
www.migrationinformation.org

Erk, Dr. JG—Social and Behavioural Sciences—Leiden University
http://socialsciences.leiden.edu/politicalscience/organisation/faculty/erk-dr-jg.html

On the (In)Famous Dutch (In)Tolerance: Anti-Immigrant Fringe Becomes Mainstream
http://citation.allacademic.com/meta/p_mla_apa_research_citation/4/8/5/3/5/p485354_index.html

JAN ERK is senior lecturer at Leiden University, The Netherlands.

Unit 4

Prepared by: Caroline Shaffer Westerhof,
California National University for Advanced Studies

UNIT

The Executive: Accountability and Responsiveness at the Top

Responsiveness at the top: Accountability. How does the CEO of a nation-state, and his or her associates, balance responsiveness and accountability within the different institutions of government. How is policymaking handled? Does decision making depend on the behavior, integrity, public service of the actors? Is policymaking always effective at the top? Is it biased, depending on the actors, individually and collectively? How does their performance as institutions and in policymaking fare in the midst of the nation's political development? The institutions are the executive, the legislature, and the unelected officers of the judiciary, the military, and the bureaucracy. We address the political questions of when, why, how, and what regarding executives and their cohorts in policy and decision making.

We begin with the question, "Why executives?" The explanation may be found in theories of government, articulated by venerated political theorists such as John Locke, John Stuart Mill, Jean-Jacques Rousseau, and the framers of the U.S. Constitution: to achieve efficient and efficacious policymaking. Even if a community is small enough to allow everyone to partake in policymaking and implementation, it is inefficient to do so. Think about a community the size of a country and it becomes clear that it is prohibitive to have everyone partake in policymaking. Thus, citizens choose a representative government to make those policies on their behalf. The paradox is that the more diverse the society, the larger and more diverse the representative government becomes. That, in turn, progressively works against efficient policymaking. On the other hand, in a democratic, political system it makes for more people participating in the process.

CEOs and executives in political system tie the various units of the organization together, which can ease the burden of disagreement as well as enhance such, as we saw in October 2013 in the United States "budget shutdown." Depending on the political system, power, tyranny, decision making, consensus, and accommodation are all part of the process.

We witness how Hungary's former Prime Minister and the ruling Fidesz Party obtained a strong majority in the legislature and proceeded to rewrite the constitution; thus the new constitution redefined that states' institutional structures. Among the controls on the executive that are compromised is the significant restriction of the Constitutional Court's review of laws, giving the executive strong and institutionalizing power well into the future.

What does this mean? On the one hand, the political damage cannot be ignored when (1) the checks and balances to the executive are compromised or (2) checks fail to work. In Chile, the middle-class is disabusing the government of the notion that economic achievements will keep the citizenry happy and the government in office. Instead, the middle-class is making demands of the government to untie historic relations with businesses—all political parties are seen to have such ties—in order to provide stronger social programs in education, the environment, and other consumer rights. Likewise, in Singapore—where the ruling party has been in political power since 1969—citizens are clamoring for new constitutional counterweights to the authority of the government that may turn a largely ceremonial presidential position into one with more constitutional authority. As a supporter for one of the presidential candidates points out, "We are the people. Listen to us."

The lessons from Chile and Singapore are particularly instructive for other transitioning or less-democratic countries, such as Russia and China. In both countries, there is an adherence to the "letter" of democratic development but not its spirit. Until recently, it appeared that strong policy performance—particularly in terms of the economy—is a sufficient mark of executive excellence and enough to keep the executive in office. However, increasingly, it is clear that policy performance alone is not enough; as a country transitions economically, its people also transition politically. Given that economic performance is predictably unpredictable, political leaders have to do more to stay in office: They have to embrace and promote "social diversity" rather than choke it in order to demonstrate to the voters that they are responsive and accountable.

It becomes apparent that political choice is just that: "Conflict Is a Choice, Not a Necessity." When one recognizes the reality of such policy thought processes one recognizes that such is a reality determination, if one truly wishes to seek a global peace for both the West and the East. It is important, that for some executives, it becomes a power and character issue. Can leaders be blinded by cronyism, corruption, moral manipulation, and divisive policies? If they are, a horrendous backlash can occur by other nation-states. Yet we are witnessing the political networking of Chinese economic leaders in meetings with members of the Washington, D.C. political establishment. Thus, it is possible to avoid conflict, as we anticipate that the economic playing field will be leveled because of the decisions of particular senior management in diverse political systems.

Further, how do we define executive leadership in a dictatorial nation? Does one person control the entire arena, whether it be public policy, execution of individuals, or other issues? Is the Supreme Leader truly such? How do world leaders confront such individuals and situations? Is conflict a choice or a necessity? Who determines?

Article

Prepared by: Caroline Shaffer Westerhof,
California National University for Advanced Studies

The Future of U.S.-Chinese Relations

Conflict Is a Choice, Not a Necessity

HENRY A. KISSINGER

Learning Outcomes

After reading this article, you will be able to:

- Understand how the United States can be friendly with a country that sells nuclear weapons to some of our deep-seated antagonists.

- Understand the economy of China and why some 500,000 Americans are dependent upon their jobs in China.

- Understand the cultural and economic reasons why United States and China must have a postive relationship.

Dealing with the New China

(A) reason for Chinese restraint in at least the medium term is the domestic adaptation the country faces. The gap in Chinese society between the largely developed coastal regions and the undeveloped western regions has made Hu's objective of a "harmonious society" both compelling and elusive. Cultural changes compound the challenge. The next decades will witness, for the first time, the full impact of one-child families on adult Chinese society. This is bound to modify cultural patterns in a society in which large families have traditionally taken care of the aged and the handicapped. When four grandparents compete for the attention of one child and invest him with the aspirations heretofore spread across many offspring, a new pattern of insistent achievement and vast, perhaps unfulfillable, expectations may arise.

All these developments will further complicate the challenges of China's governmental transition starting in 2012, in which the presidency; the vice-presidency; the considerable majority of the positions in China's Politburo, State Council, and Central Military Commission; and thousands of other key national and provincial posts will be staffed with new appointees. The new leadership group will consist, for the most part, of members of the first Chinese generation in a century and a half to have lived all their lives in a country at peace. Its primary challenge will be finding a way to deal with a society revolutionized by changing economic conditions, unprecedented and rapidly expanding technologies of communication, a tenuous global economy, and the migration of hundreds of millions of people from China's countryside to its cities. The model of government that emerges will likely be a synthesis of modern ideas and traditional Chinese political and cultural concepts, and the quest for that synthesis will provide the ongoing drama of China's evolution.

These social and political transformations are bound to be followed with interest and hope in the United States. Direct American intervention would be neither wise nor productive. The United States will, as it should, continue to make its views known on human rights issues and individual cases. And its day-to-day conduct will express its national preference for democratic principles. But a systematic project to transform China's institutions by diplomatic pressure and economic sanctions is likely to backfire and isolate the very liberals it is intended to assist. In China, it would be interpreted by a considerable majority through the lens of nationalism, recalling earlier eras of foreign intervention.

What this situation calls for is not an abandonment of American values but a distinction between the realizable and the absolute. The U.S.-Chinese relationship should not be considered as a zero-sum game, nor can the emergence of a prosperous and powerful China be assumed in itself to be an American strategic defeat.

A cooperative approach challenges preconceptions on both sides. The United States has few precedents in its national experience of relating to a country of comparable size, self-confidence, economic achievement, and international scope and yet with such a different culture and political system. Nor does history supply China with precedents for how to relate to a fellow great power with a permanent presence in Asia, a vision of universal ideals not geared toward Chinese conceptions, and alliances with several of China's neighbors. Prior to the United States, all countries establishing such a position did so as a prelude to an attempt to dominate China.

The simplest approach to strategy is to insist on overwhelming potential adversaries with superior resources and materiel. But in the contemporary world, this is only rarely feasible. China and the United States will inevitably continue as enduring realities for each other. Neither can entrust its security to the other—no great power does, for long—and each will continue to pursue its own interests, sometimes at the relative expense of the other. But both have the responsibility to take into account the other's nightmares, and both would do well to recognize that their rhetoric, as much as their actual policies, can feed into the other's suspicions.

China's greatest strategic fear is that an outside power or powers will establish military deployments around China's periphery capable of encroaching on China's territory or meddling in its domestic institutions. When China deemed that it faced such a threat in the past, it went to war rather than risk the outcome of what it saw as gathering trends—in Korea in 1950, against India in 1962, along the northern border with the Soviet Union in 1969, and against Vietnam in 1979.

The United States' fear, sometimes only indirectly expressed, is of being pushed out of Asia by an exclusionary bloc. The United States fought a world war against Germany and Japan to prevent such an outcome and exercised some of its most forceful Cold War diplomacy under administrations of both political parties to this end against the Soviet Union. In both enterprises, it is worth noting, substantial joint U.S.-Chinese efforts were directed against the perceived threat of hegemony.

Other Asian countries will insist on their prerogatives to develop their capacities for their own national reasons, not as part of a contest between outside powers. They will not willingly consign themselves to a revived tributary order. Nor do they regard themselves as elements in an American containment policy or an American project to alter China's domestic institutions. They aspire to good relations with both China and the United States and will resist any pressure to choose between the two.

Can the fear of hegemony and the nightmare of military encirclement be reconciled? Is it possible to find a space in which both sides can achieve their ultimate objectives without militarizing their strategies? For great nations with global capabilities and divergent, even partly conflicting aspirations, what is the margin between conflict and abdication?

That China will have a major influence in the regions surrounding it is inherent in its geography, values, and history. The limits of that influence, however, will be shaped by circumstance and policy decisions. These will determine whether an inevitable quest for influence turns into a drive to negate or exclude other independent sources of power.

For nearly two generations, American strategy relied on local regional defense by American ground forces—largely to avoid the catastrophic consequences of a general nuclear war. In recent decades, congressional and public opinion have impelled an end to such commitments in Vietnam, Iraq, and Afghanistan Now, fiscal considerations further limit the range of such an approach. American strategy has been redirected from defending territory to threatening unacceptable punishment against potential aggressors. This requires forces capable of rapid intervention and global reach, but not bases ringing China's frontiers. What Washington must not do is combine a defense policy based on budgetary restraints with a diplomacy based on unlimited ideological aims.

Just as Chinese influence in surrounding countries may spur fears of dominance, so efforts to pursue traditional American national interests can be perceived as a form of military encirclement. Both sides must understand the nuances by which apparently traditional and apparently reasonable courses can evoke the deepest worries of the other. They should seek together to define the sphere in which their peaceful competition is circumscribed. If that is managed wisely, both military confrontation and domination can be avoided; if not, escalating tension is inevitable. It is the task of diplomacy to discover this space, to expand it if possible, and to prevent the relationship from being overwhelmed by tactical and domestic imperatives.

Community or Conflict

The current world order was built largely without Chinese participation, and hence China sometimes feels less bound than others by its rules. Where the order does not suit Chinese preferences, Beijing has set up alternative arrangements, such as in the separate currency channels being established with Brazil and Japan and other countries. If the pattern becomes routine and spreads into many spheres of activity, competing world orders could evolve. Absent common goals coupled with agreed rules of restraint, institutionalized rivalry is likely to escalate beyond the calculations and intentions of its advocates. In an era in which unprecedented offensive capabilities and intrusive technologies multiply, the penalties of such a course could be drastic and perhaps irrevocable.

Crisis management will not be enough to sustain a relationship so global and beset by so many differing pressures within and between both countries, which is why I have argued for the concept of a Pacific Community and expressed the hope that China and the United States can generate a sense of common purpose on at least some issues of general concern. But the goal of such a community cannot be reached if either side conceives of the enterprise as primarily a more effective way to defeat or undermine the other. Neither China nor the United States can be systematically challenged without its noticing, and if such a challenge is noted, it will be resisted. Both need to commit themselves to genuine cooperation and find a way to communicate and relate their visions to each other and to the world.

Some tentative steps in that direction have already been undertaken. For example, the United States has joined several other countries in beginning negotiations on the Trans-Pacific Partnership (TPP), a free-trade pact linking the Americas with Asia. Such an arrangement could be a step toward a Pacific Community because it would lower trade barriers among the world's most productive, dynamic, and resource-rich economies and link the two sides of the ocean in shared projects.

Obama has invited China to join the TPP. However, the terms of accession as presented by American briefers and commentators have sometimes seemed to require fundamental changes in China's domestic structure. To the extent that is the case, the TPP could be regarded in Beijing as part of a strategy to isolate China. For its part, China has put forward comparable alternative arrangements. It has negotiated a trade pact with the Association of Southeast Asian Nations and has broached a Northeast Asian trade pact with Japan and South Korea.

Important domestic political considerations are involved for all parties. But if China and the United States come to regard each other's trade-pact efforts as elements in a strategy of isolation, the Asia-Pacific region could devolve into competing adversarial power blocs. Ironically, this would be a particular challenge if China meets frequent American calls to shift from an export-led to a consumption-driven economy, as its most recent five-year plan contemplates. Such a development could reduce China's stake in the United States as an export market even as it encourages other Asian countries to further orient their economies toward China.

The key decision facing both Beijing and Washington is whether to move toward a genuine effort at cooperation or fall into a new version of historic patterns of international rivalry. Both countries have adopted the rhetoric of community. They have even established a high-level forum for it, the Strategic and Economic Dialogue, which meets twice a year. It has been productive on immediate issues, but it is still in the foothills of its ultimate assignment to produce a truly global economic and political order. And if a global order does not emerge in the economic field, barriers to progress on more emotional and less positive-sum issues, such as territory and security, may grow insurmountable.

The Risks of Rhetoric

As they pursue this process, both sides need to recognize the impact of rhetoric on perceptions and calculations. American leaders occasionally launch broadsides against China, including specific proposals for adversarial policies, as domestic political necessities. This occurs even—perhaps especially—when a moderate policy is the ultimate intention. The issue is not specific complaints, which should be dealt with on the merits of the issue, but attacks on the basic motivations of Chinese policy, such as declaring China a strategic adversary. The target of these attacks is bound to ask whether domestic imperatives requiring affirmations of hostility will sooner or later require hostile actions. By the same token, threatening Chinese statements, including those in the semiofficial press, are likely to be interpreted in terms of the actions they imply, whatever the domestic pressures or the intent that generated them.

The American debate, on both sides of the political divide, often describes China as a "rising power" that will need to "mature" and learn how to exercise responsibility on the world stage. China, however, sees itself not as a rising power but as a returning one, predominant in its region for two millennia and temporarily displaced by colonial exploiters taking advantage of Chinese domestic strife and decay. It views the prospect of a strong China exercising influence in economic, cultural, political, and military affairs not as an unnatural challenge to world order but rather as a return to normality. Americans need not agree with every aspect of the Chinese analysis to understand that lecturing a country with a history of millennia about its need to "grow up" and behave "responsibly" can be needlessly grating.

On the Chinese side, proclamations at the governmental and the informal level that China intends to "revive the Chinese nation" to its traditional eminence carry different implications inside China and abroad. China is rightly proud of its recent strides in restoring its sense of national purpose following what it sees as a century of humiliation. Yet few other countries in Asia are nostalgic for an era when they were subject to Chinese suzerainty. As recent veterans of anti-colonial struggles, most Asian countries are extremely sensitive to maintaining their independence and freedom of action vis-à-vis any outside power, whether Western or Asian. They seek to be involved in as many overlapping spheres of economic and political activity as possible; they invite an American role in the region but seek equilibrium, not a crusade or confrontation.

The rise of China is less the result of its increased military strength than of the United States' own declining competitive position, driven by factors such as obsolescent infrastructure, inadequate attention to research and development, and a seemingly dysfunctional governmental process. The United States should address these issues with ingenuity and determination instead of blaming a putative adversary. It must take care not to repeat in its China policy the pattern of conflicts entered with vast public support and broad goals but ended when the American political process insisted on a strategy of extrication that amounted to an abandonment, if not a complete reversal, of the country's proclaimed objectives.

China can find reassurance in its own record of endurance and in the fact that no U.S. administration has ever sought to alter the reality of China as one of the world's major states, economies, and civilizations. Americans would do well to remember that even when China's GDP is equal to that of the United States, it will need to be distributed over a population that is four times as large, aging, and engaged in complex domestic transformations occasioned by China's growth and urbanization. The practical consequence is that a great deal of China's energy will still be devoted to domestic needs. . . .

Critical Thinking

1. Why are U.S. relations with China a complex combination of cooperation and contention?
2. How have the atrocities of the World Trade Center and the Pentagon devastation changed relations between the United States and China?
3. Why does Dr. Kissinger believe that "Conflict Is a Choice, Not a Necessity"?

Create Central

www.mhhe.com/createcentral

Internet References

The Future of U.S.-Chinese relations—Opinion—Al Jazeera English
www.aljazeera.com/indepth/opinion/2012/06/
201263143517185405.html

Henry Kissinger Addresses Yale Students on U.S.-China Relations and American Diplomacy

http://jackson.yale.edu/henry-kissinger-addresses-yale-students-us-china-relations-and-american-diplomacy

The Future of U.S.-China Relations — All Things Nuclear

allthingsnuclear.org/the-future-of-u-s-china-relations

Kissinger reflects on U.S.-China Relations Columbia Daily Spectator

www.columbiaspectator.com/2012/04/17/kissinger-reflects-us-china-relations

HENRY A. KISSINGER is Chair of Kissinger Associates and a former U.S. Secretary of State and National Security Adviser. This essay is adapted from the afterword to the forthcoming paperback edition of his latest book, *On China* (Penguin, 2012).

Article

Prepared by: Caroline Shaffer Westerhof,
California National University for Advanced Studies

Chile's Middle Class Flexes Its Muscles

Patricio Navia

Learning Outcomes

After reading this article, you will be able to:

- Understand how Chile's middle class is pressuring successfully for greater economic security.
- Understand the concept of democracy in Chile.
- Understand the success and *debits of* what is referred to as a social market economy.

Chileans can live their entire lives without much interaction with a state institution. A middle class woman, born in a private clinic paid for by her parents' private health insurance, will attend a (government-subsidized) private voucher school. She will graduate from a private university paid for with government-subsidized student loans. If the young professional joins the mining sector, she likely will work for one of the private companies that control 70 percent of Chile's copper production. Her mandatory retirement contributions will be sent directly from her employer to the private retirement management fund of her choice. In all likelihood she will have private health insurance. She will send her children to private school. She'll pay her utilities to private companies, obtain a mortgage from a private bank, and even drive on privately operated highways in the capital city of Santiago.

Since the end of the Augusto Pinochet dictatorship in 1990, Chile has grown robustly and steadily. For 20 years, a center-left coalition, Concertación, led an impressive period of development. Poverty declined from 40 percent of the population in 1990 to 15 percent in 2009. Child obesity has replaced malnutrition as a leading public health concern. Primary and secondary education is now universal. And almost 60 percent of college-aged Chileans are enrolled in higher education institutions. More than 70 percent of them are first-generation college students.

Having regained their rights as citizens in 1990, Chileans increasingly are exercising their rights as consumers. Larger and more diverse, the middle class is testing its political muscle as it demands that social policies be redesigned to fit its needs. Indeed, Chile's new middle class has developed a sense of vertigo, fearing vulnerability and at the same time seeking to fly even higher. The social safety net, designed to aid those at the lowest 40 percent of the income ladder, is set too low for the next 40 percent. The high-flying middle class wants a safe place to land in case times get rough. But because the tax structure is not sufficiently progressive, the government lacks resources to fund programs for the middle class. Many Chileans thus want tax reforms to fund the expansion of government assistance, especially in higher education.

After the Protests

The student protests that rocked Chile in 2011 fueled claims that the country's market-friendly model is crumbling. However, opinion surveys show that Chileans remain optimistic that their middle-class expectations will materialize. Chileans do not want to make a left turn in the elections scheduled for next year. They want to continue moving forward, faster and more securely.

The recent social mobilizations in favor of education, the environment, gay rights, consumer rights, and other post-materialist demands, far from suggesting political decay, show a vibrant civil society committed to democracy. After remaining steadily in the middle of the 50 percent range for about a decade, support for democracy among Chileans surpassed 60 percent in recent years, according to a Latinobarómetro poll. In a recent Diego Portales University survey, 78 percent of respondents said they believe future economic conditions will improve for their families. Education (32 percent) and crime (29 percent) rank atop the main national problems. Employment (8 percent) and inflation (2 percent) are at the bottom of the list.

However, Chileans increasingly worry that opportunities are insufficient and the playing field is not level. Historically low levels of trust in political institutions (10 percent trust political parties and the legislature) are now affecting the government generally (down from 33 percent in 2010 to 21 percent in 2011), according to Latinobarómetro. Even trust in the Catholic Church has declined—from 43 percent to 24 percent from 2010 to 2011—as a result of pedophilia scandals. Trust in private companies declined from 20 percent to 16 percent in the same period.

In 2009, a conservative businessman, Sebastián Piñera, won the presidential election on a message of change in the context of continuity. He promised to more efficiently lead Chile into the promised land of development. The social protests and active student movement of 2011 highlighted the caveats of Chile's successful experience of economic development. The protests also sunk Piñera's approval ratings to the lowest observed since democracy was restored. Some critics of the market-friendly model have prematurely declared the end of Chile's social market experiment. A more reasonable assessment suggests the need for increased effort to foster social inclusion and expand opportunities.

Two problems stand out. First, inadequate regulation and government oversight tilt the balance in favor of providers against consumers. Business concentration is high in several sectors of the economy. Private companies that provide formerly public services—utilities, health insurance, education, and private roads—often abuse their position and impose excessively high fees and penalties on consumers who miss payments. In some cases they even abuse consumers who pay on time.

Chileans want government institutions to step up their involvement and provide better consumer protection. Several of the grievances behind last year's student protests have to do with the government's inability—or unwillingness—to adopt stricter regulations to guarantee quality education and control skyrocketing university tuition costs. Chileans perceive that political parties side with business interests, and that democratic institutions do not represent people's interests well. Still, when asked about their political identification, a majority identify themselves as moderates. Chileans do not want to throw out the democracy- and market-friendly baby with the bath water.

> **Chileans do not want to throw out the democracy- and market-friendly baby with the bath water.**

The second problem is an insufficient safety net. Successive center-left governments focused on earmarking social programs and subsidies to the poorest 40 percent, leaving the middle class unprotected. Because the safety net is inadequately funded, expanding existing programs to the middle class would not suffice. The public sector tax take is slightly over 20 percent of GDP. Without a more progressive tax code, little progress can be made to strengthen the safety net and expand opportunities for the middle class.

As a candidate, Piñera campaigned on leveling the playing field for the middle class. Though he has lost favor with the public, his initial message remains popular. Meanwhile, the Concertación opposition is divided among those who defend their 20-year government legacy of moderation and pragmatism and those who seek to follow the leftist populist model found elsewhere in Latin America. If the Concertación stays in the middle, calling for moderate reforms that will strengthen individual rights for citizens and consumers, it will likely retake power in 2013.

Rising Expectations

Twenty days after his inauguration, Piñera bluntly encouraged higher expectations when he declared—mocking previous Concertación governments—that "what others failed to do in

20 years, we already did in 20 days." The spectacular rescue of 33 trapped miners in October 2010 underlined the message of efficacy. If Piñera could successfully rescue the miners, he could also address education, health care, and other pending—and admittedly difficult—challenges that Concertación governments failed to tackle.

Piñera's clumsy handling of the 2011 student protests has distracted attention from progress on other issues—including social programs; maternity leave reform; and electoral reform to make registration automatic, which will incorporate millions of previously excluded Chileans into the voting rolls. When he took office, Piñera successfully freed the right of its Pinochet authoritarian legacy and seized the social market economic model from the Concertación. Moderation, gradualism, and pragmatism are no longer Concertación trademarks. The center-right will remain electorally competitive if it sticks to Piñera's centrist policies. Even if he achieves little else, Piñera already has transformed the Chilean political landscape.

Last year's student protests tested his ability to deliver on his promise of expanding opportunities for the middle class. But the protests also showed that the middle class, having consolidated its electoral dominance, seeks to transform the social market economy into a more inclusive market-friendly model.

Critical Thinking

1. Why is the center-right coalition government responding to the demands of a reformed social market economy?
2. Why is the Chilean government responding to the middle class demands?
3. Is Chile on the road to sustaining a political system that we identify as a "democracy"?

Create Central

www.mhhe.com/createcentral

Internet References

Chile: Protest for the "Promised Land"
www.opendemocracy.net/patricio-navia/chile-protest-for-%E2%80%9Cpromised-land%E2%80%9D

Chile Seeks Developed Status, Meets Soaring Energy Costs
www.bloomberg.com/news/2013-01-15/chile-seeks-developed-status-meets-soaring-energy-costs.html

Chile after the Elections
clas.uchicago.edu/page/chile-after-elections

Do Segregated Schools in Chile's Capital Stunt Mobility?
http://santiagotimes.cl/do-segregated-schools-in-chiles-capital-stunt-mobility

PATRICIO NAVIA teaches at the Center for Latin American and Caribbean Studies at New York University and is a professor of political science at Diego Portales University in Santiago.

From *Current History*, February 2012, pp. 75–76. Copyright © 2012 by Current History, Inc. Reprinted by permission.

Article

Prepared by: Caroline Shaffer Westerhof,
California National University for Advanced Studies

U.S., China Hopeful of BIT after Talks Reignited

CHEN WEIHUA

Learning Outcomes

After reading this article, you will be able to:

- Understand why the Bilateral Investment Treaty is considered a priority for United States and China.

- Understand how the China-United States BIT will affect the global economy.

- Examine the effects if the BIT talks between China and United States were disrupted.

If Chinese and United States leaders hammer out and agree on their long-discussed investment treaty, Chinese officials and observers believe the deal will further encourage Chinese outbound investment in the US.

With Chinese outbound direct investment rising dramatically, leaders from both nations reignited negotiations on the Bilateral Investment Treaty at the just-concluded China-US Strategic and Economic Dialogue in Washington.

"The two sides agreed to enter a more substantive stage of negotiation as soon as possible," said Chinese Minister of Commerce Gao Hucheng on Thursday in Washington.

Talks on a BIT have gone through nine rounds of preliminary discussions between the two countries, drawing a great deal of attention from business communities in both China and the US. Gao described the previous talks on a BIT as "technical negotiations" that laid a foundation for more substantive talks.

China was the world's third-largest outbound investor last year. Its direct investment into the US reached $20 billion, compared to $70 billion in US direct investment within China. In recent years, Chinese outbound investment has been rapidly growing.

"This requires us to establish a better legal framework with our partners that will better protect the interests of Chinese investors," Gao said.

He predicted that in the next three to five years, the amount of Chinese outbound investments will exceed US investments into China.

Gao said leaders stepped up negotiations on a BIT as a result of the consensus reached a month ago by Chinese President Xi Jinping and US President Barack Obama in Sunnylands, California.

He said investment is an important part of the China-US economic and trade relationship.

"It requires creative thinking to build a cooperative and mutually beneficial environment," he said.

A senior official from the US Treasury Department hailed the discussion on the BIT at the S&ED, applauding some of the concessions from China, especially involving the service sector.

"A high-standard US-China BIT is a priority for the US and would work to level the playing field for American workers and businesses by opening markets for fair competition," said US Treasury Secretary Jack Lew in a statement on Thursday afternoon.

Orville Schell, director of the Center on US-China Relations at the Asia Society, said if the two countries are serious about cementing better relations, it is essential that Chinese FDI in the US be explicitly welcomed.

"By helping the US to capture more of the significant new investment capital now starting to seek exit from China, a US-China BIT would serve a critical purpose. One can only hope the treaty will find early agreement and lead to a more cooperative atmosphere that enables other more intractable, but even more important, bilateral issues to resolutions," Schell said.

While the US claims it offers the most open environment for foreign investors, many Chinese feel that Chinese FDI within the US has been unjustly targeted.

Besides a possible BIT, a wide range of economic and trade issues were discussed over the two-day S&ED. China raised its concerns over US restrictions on high-tech exports to China and the US' review process of Chinese FDI into the US. Both sides also discussed trade protectionism.

Critical Thinking

1. How will the success of the BIT benefit global economic issues?
2. Why is China media calling for "de-Americanising" after U.S. shutdown?
3. Would BIT talks be affected because China's September 2013 growth is slower?

Create Central

www.mhhe.com/createcentral

Internet References

China, US Explore New Treaty
   usa.chinadaily.com.cn/epaper/2013-07/12/content_16767835.htm

Change Drives China-US Talks
   http://usa.chinadaily.com.cn/business/2013-07/17/content_16789180.htm
Economy—*China daily US Edition*
   usa.chinadaily.com.cn/business/economy_9.html
World Trade Online
   insidetrade.com
Shanghai Daily
   www.shanghaidaily.com

CHEN WEIHUA is the Chief Washington Correspondent of *China Daily* and Deputy Editor of *China Daily USA*.

Prepared by: Caroline Shaffer Westerhof,
California National University for Advanced Studies

Article

Africa's Turn: A Conversation with Macky Sall

Stuart Reid

Learning Outcomes

After reading this article, you will be able to:

- Explain how Senegal has been a bastion of stability and democracy within the African continent.

- Explain the personality, power, and complexion of the nation-state Senegal under President Macky Sall.

- Explain why Senegal offers stability and growth to foreign investors.

Since it gained independence from France in 1960, the West African country of Senegal has been a bastion of stability and democracy on a continent that has seen relatively little of either. During the presidency of Abdoulaye Wade (2000–2012), however, the Senegalese exception seemed under threat. The elderly Wade grew increasingly authoritarian and corrupt, and he managed to run for a third term even though the constitution prohibited him from doing so. But in March 2012, Senegalese voters dealt Wade a decisive defeat, electing the reformist candidate Macky Sall instead. Trained in France as a geological engineer, Sall had served in a number of government posts under Wade, including prime minister, before publicly breaking with him in 2007. In opposition, Sall created a new political party; served a second term as mayor of his hometown, Fatick; and organized an anti-Wade coalition. Sall spoke with *Foreign Affairs* senior editor Stuart Reid in Dakar in June, days before U.S. President Barack Obama's arrival in Senegal for a state visit.

Since independence, most African countries have suffered from coups and civil wars. But Senegal has enjoyed over five decades of stability and multiparty competition. What's your secret?

It stems from a long historical process. Senegal's first revolution came at the same time as America's. In 1776, there was a revolution in the north of Senegal—what we call the Torodbe revolution—that set out new guidelines for governance. There

was colonization afterward. But even during the colonial era, beginning in 1848, people could vote for the colonial authorities. In 1914, we elected the first black member of the French National Assembly, Mr. Blaise Diagne, a Senegalese. So before independence, there was already electoral competition.

Another secret can be found in the Senegalese constitution. We have a semi-presidential regime, which means that the government is responsible not only to the president but also to the parliament. There is one chief executive, in contrast with some countries that have two—something that creates tensions that can end in coups. Senegal's flexible and robust constitution has protected us from coups for 53 years since independence.

We also have stable institutions. Only seven days elapsed between the election of March 25, 2012, and my swearing-in. In the meantime, the legal system issued a ruling, and democratic institutions prepared the transfer. The army and the police complied with the results of the election. A country that does not have stable institutions and a clear constitution cannot be successful.

Senegal is also something of a regional exception in that 90 percent of the population is Muslim, yet the state is secular.

Actually, 95 percent are Muslim. In Senegal, the state has the duty to protect people of all religions—Muslim, Christian, animist. People have the freedom to believe in what they want. That is a fundamental element of our constitution. This does not mean that the majority or the minority cannot express themselves; rather, the state is there to respect the freedom of each citizen to believe in what he or she wants to believe in.

Why did voters choose you instead of Wade? What did your victory represent?

My victory certainly meant that the Senegalese people chose change. The country was divided. The partisans of the former regime were committed to a path where the term of office was no longer limited, even though the constitution of 2001 was clear that no one could have more than two five-year terms. Then, the people came together to stand up against a proposed bill that would have allowed a president to be elected with 25 percent of the vote.

A great deal of hope is what put me in power. I'm quite aware of that. So my role is to strengthen this democratic choice. That's what I'm trying to do through the institutional reform commission that I set up, which must work to strengthen democracy and not to bring about a new regime.

You promised to crack down on corruption. What have you done, and what do you have left to do?

It's important that everyone, including those in government now, realize that the era of impunity is over. And we have done a lot in one year. I revived the anticorruption court, which was created by President Abdou Diouf in 1981 but eventually stopped functioning; it was there, but you couldn't nominate the attorneys and magistrates. I nominated magistrates who agreed to work according to the procedure of the court, which hasn't been changed. I have submitted a bill on budget transparency. From now on, the government has to make its accounts public on a quarterly basis. The law will also require budgetary officials to declare their assets publicly before they take office.

I also created OFNAC, which is an office to combat fraud. When there are allegations of corruption against current officials, that office has the power to conduct an investigation and refer the case directly to the justice system. These are new measures to increase transparency and good governance, which are important for guaranteeing investment.

Isn't it true that all politicians, including you, benefited from corruption under Wade?

As far as I am concerned, we benefited from privileges related to our position—prime minister or president of the national assembly—which is completely normal. It has nothing to do with embezzlement or corruption. When you can prove that your assets are in line with your income, there's no problem. That's not what is being challenged. What is being challenged is the accumulation of resources that has nothing to do with legal and justifiable sources of income, including mine when I was with President Wade.

Senegal's neighbor Mali has had a difficult year, with a coup d'état, the Tuareg rebellion, the Islamist takeover of the north, and French intervention. What can Senegal do to improve the prospects for Malian democracy?

First of all, we would like to recognize the role played by the international community, without which Mali would have lost its territorial integrity and independence. This is why we have commended the efforts made by the United Nations, which voted for a resolution that permitted France, along with African forces from ECOWAS [the Economic Community of West African States] and Chad, to stop the jihadist terrorists and reclaim Malian territory.

Today, we are in the final stages of consolidating the peace. The agreement that was just signed in Ouagadougou [Burkina Faso] will help organize elections for July 28 across the country—including in Kidal, a Tuareg stronghold. I believe that Senegal's role is to continue to side with Mali, to support it in its reconciliation policy as well as in its development policy. We share a long border, more than 400 kilometers [about 250 miles], which must be watched closely. Our fates are linked. What is happening in Mali could happen in any of our countries.

What role should countries such as Senegal play in regional security compared with outside actors such as the United States and France?

We cooperate with France, which is an ally and a friend. It is of course a former colonial power. But France understands the stakes in and the sociology of our countries. The United States also has a security policy in the region, and it is our partner through AFRICOM [the U.S. Africa Command] and everything that it does in terms of military cooperation with various countries.

It is clear that terrorism is a plague in our countries. It compounds our development problems. We have to ensure the security of our populations, the inviolability of our borders, and the stability of our states so that we can focus on such issues as development and poverty.

Senegal, like most members of ECOWAS, can be considered a pivotal country, because it has a military that can intervene at home just as it can abroad. Senegal has more than 2,000 soldiers in operations across Africa. We are present in Cote d'Ivoire, Guinea-Bissau, Darfur, the Democratic Republic of the Congo, and other countries. There could be better-thought-out cooperation that would enable Africa, in case of a challenge like the one we experienced recently in Mali, to have special forces capable of reacting first to stop the danger and neutralize the threat and, afterward, to cooperate economically and strategically.

So can Africa take care of its own problems now?

No. Africa cannot handle its own problems, because we are not yet at the point where we have the logistical capabilities to deploy troops in case of emergency. It's simply a matter of means, not a matter of men. Remember, when our troops intervened in Mali, they deployed over land. Today, Senegalese troops are in Gao, which is 2,400 kilometers [almost 1,500 miles] away. They had to travel there in convoys of trucks and four-by-four vehicles. That's a problem. So as long as the logistics are not sorted out, we will always be lagging behind. But we are handling matters with our community organizations, with our respective countries, and particularly with our partners, such as the United States, France, and the European Union, among others.

After much delay under the previous administration, the former dictator of Chad, Hissène Habré, will now be tried for crimes against humanity by a Senegalese court, not by a court in Europe. Does this represent a new model for African justice?

Yes. The world has changed, and in 2013, it's not acceptable for us to still be expelling African leaders to European countries. Africa should have the means to try people who have been accused of crimes. In the case of Mr. Habré, an African Union resolution demanded that Senegal, where he has lived in asylum for the past 20-plus years, organize his trial. Under my predecessor, the Senegalese government accepted this mandate. This mandate must be enforced, and that's what we're in the process of doing.

If Habré is convicted, will you go after his assets?

It is not our duty as a state to make a decision. It's the duty of the justice system to do what it has to do. We cannot interfere with his personal affairs or his assets. The justice system will shed some light on it and decide what must be done.

If Senegal is committed to justice for Habré, then why is your current prime minister Habré's former banker?
I did not appoint my prime minister because of the Habré case. Now, if it comes out that he is truly linked to the Habré case, or if he is charged with anything, then I will make a decision. But for the moment, there's no reason to doubt him or take measures against him so long as a ruling has not been made.

What did the election of Obama mean to Africans?
Africans took a lot of pride in the election of Obama, because it proved wrong those who believed in racist assumptions, that a black man could not live up to a white man. Of course, President Obama is the president of the United States, not the president of Africa, so he stands up for the interests of America. But his election broke down barriers.

Some say that Obama has done less than President George W. Bush and President Bill Clinton in terms of promoting trade with Africa or assisting with public health efforts there.
You cannot ask President Obama to do something that he can't do. He came to power in a time of historic difficulties in the United States. The economy was on the brink, there was a war in Afghanistan and a war in Iraq, there was the subprime mortgage crisis. All these crises led him to take care of his country first, to put an end to the wars in Iraq and Afghanistan.

I think he can be judged at the end of his tenure. None of his predecessors could do anything real during their first terms. It's in the second term that they enjoyed more freedom and could take the initiative. I do hope that he's going to do something that will be important. There's no doubt about it. That's the feeling I have.

Much of the budget of the Senegalese government, 20 percent, still comes from foreign aid. What can African countries do to wean themselves off international assistance?
Aid indeed represents 20 percent of our budget. But there was a time when it was 60 percent. We need that aid for development, but more than aid, we need investment. We are working today to establish public-private partnerships and attract private investment. That development will trigger productivity that will enable us to have a balanced budget and eventually no longer need aid, which is not easy to raise. African countries also have high levels of debt compared to elsewhere, and we cannot develop infrastructure without getting out of debt. Africa needs help.

Senegal's rate of economic growth is lower than those of its neighbors. Why does it remain so low?
Well, what accounts for Senegal's slow growth—in 2013, it will be 4.3 percent—is that we are handicapped by the energy sector, which is making the economy less competitive. We have initiated bold measures to provide for a sustainable response to the energy crisis. We also have another handicap: our agricultural sector, which should be the engine of growth, remains traditional, with low yields and the inefficient use of land. So

we have decided to modernize the agricultural system, while protecting the family nature of some holdings, with seed capital to increase yields and productivity through mechanization.

What about reducing the role of the state in the economy?
I'm a liberal, so I believe the economy is not something that the state creates. It is business, it is competitiveness, it is productivity that does that. But the state has a fundamental role: to secure an environment conducive to business. Thus, it is necessary to have the rule of law and make sure that private investment is protected. Above all, we have to fight against factors that limit investment—in particular, corruption and red tape. I have launched major initiatives to fight corruption and illegal enrichment, as well as to remove administrative constraints. Very soon, you will see our reforms aimed at speeding up the time it takes to start a business. Our single-window system gathers together in the same place—in APIX, which is the agency to promote investment—all the services that foreign or national investors need, to save time, in terms of procedures.

What about human capital? In Senegal, over 60 percent of women over the age of 15 are illiterate. Many people suffer from malaria or malnutrition. Sixty percent of the population lives on less than $2 a day. What are you doing about these problems?
Most of Senegal's population is young, as is characteristic of Africa. We have a high population growth rate, around 2.5 percent, so if the economic growth rate is not three times that, it is very difficult to create wealth. As a result of this very fast-growing population, we have youth unemployment. We need to educate young people, ensure their health, and make sure that they are required to attend school at least until they turn 16. There are more than 300,000 youths who enroll in primary school each year, so we need enough classrooms and teachers. Senegal made major progress in education before I even came to power, and we are continuing it, because we are deeply convinced that it is human capital that will make the difference. And then there are our major efforts in higher education, which we are continuing to pursue despite some difficulties. But we have no choice. We have to invest in vocational training in order to ensure the full development of our people through employment. And even if they do not get a job here, they can emigrate with their skills. Many countries need doctors, engineers, and technicians; Senegal can provide them.

Women's rights are correlated with economic growth; what are you doing regarding girls in school?
We have a law on gender parity for elected positions. It's really an extraordinary leap forward made by Senegal. We also have basic incentives so that young girls stay in school as long as possible. We are pleased to see the quality of training for girls in school; more and more, in secondary school and at university, they earn better grades than boys. Increasingly, women are getting trained in all areas. Initially, they studied literature and the law; now, they are in all fields—scientific, medical, everything. But we must persevere. In cities, there isn't a problem. But we want to see the same improvement in a rural areas, where there are still battles to be fought. But given our high rate

of universal access to education, this is a fight we have almost won here in Senegal.

China has ramped up its investment in Africa. Some fear this is not good for the prospects of African democracy. Are they right?

Well, I can't see why the development of Chinese investment would constitute a danger for democracy. The cooperation with China is much more direct and faster than the cooperation we have with Western countries—the United States, European countries, and other bilateral donors. There are a lot of criteria on governance, on this and that, and a lot of procedures. That's one of the obstacles to effective cooperation: too many procedures. Each partner has its own list of these procedures, and so countries spend a lot of time dealing with procedures. I'm not saying that what China is doing is better, but at least it's faster. And we need speed.

Are you optimistic about the fate of Africa?

I am very optimistic, because I am aware that Africa today has every chance to catch up. Africa has a young population, natural resources, and, now, democracy. Africa is stable, democratic, and secure, and its natural resources are better managed thanks to transparency in the extractive industries. For investors, Africa provides a faster and more exciting return on investment, because everything remains to be done—infrastructure, energy, and development. Development has gone around the world, to Europe, to America, to Asia. It's Africa's turn now.

Critical Thinking

1. How has the state of Senegal remained secular in a country where 90% of the population is Muslim?

2. What makes Senegal president Macky Sall an icon of stability on a continent where such is not the norm?

3. What has been accomplished and achieved through the years since Senegal gained its independence in 1960?

Create Central

www.mhhe.com/createcentral

Internet References

Macky Sall News—Bloomberg
http://topics.bloomberg.com/macky-sall

Senegal Cheers Its President for Standing Up to Obama on Same-Sex Marriage—*New York Times*
www.nytimes.com/2013/06/29/world/africa/senegal-cheers-its-president-for-standing-up-to-obama-on-same-sex-marriage.html

World Leaders Forum
www.youtube.com/watch?v=lONU82c0yjA

Africa's Turn—*Foreign Affairs*
www.foreignaffairs.com/discussions/interviews/africas-turn

Macky Sall | euronews
www.euronews.com/tag/macky-sall/

STUART REID is Senior Editor, *Foreign Affairs.*

Unit 5

UNIT

Prepared by: Caroline Shaffer Westerhof,
California National University for Advanced Studies

The Legislature: Is Representation Also Representative?

The concept of representation focuses on legislatures' role in the political process: how they balance democratic responsiveness and accountability with effective policymaking; how continuous reelection, serving some 20 or more terms is effective representation; and how their performance as institutions and in policymaking may run up against political development. To that effect, we systematically address the questions of "why, what, and how" regarding the legislature. Legislatures demonstrate and capture representation of their constituents in government and serve to check against the excesses of executives or they may become the stronghold of representation for autocratic leaders. It is possible that where the executive imposes the "discipline" of a single policymaker in lawmaking, the legislature aims at representing the range of citizens' responses and needs in policy and legislation making while balancing the tyranny of the single executive decision-maker. Ideally, the legislature may be a small replica of the citizenry in all its diversity. One of the most important tasks of legislators is to represent. In an authoritarian regime the legislature becomes the "mouthpiece" for the tyrannical leader.

How important is it that the legislature performs as a representative institution? One way to answer that question is to consider the alternative: what happens when legislatures fail to represent. Such can lead to "tyranny of the majority;" which is not measured in numbers, but the concept of majority is registered as "Who holds the power?" The Party of Freedom (PVV) in The Netherlands makes it clear that the only real guard against widespread negative stereotypical views against minorities and xenophobia is to ensure that legislatures truly represent that concept.

In Israel we witness the power and control of Israel's minority ultra-religious groups, being now challenged by new electoral rules. Of course, even when the role is embraced by legislators, realization of representation is often not so easy. Underrepresentation of minorities tends to be the norm, because countries often embrace electoral systems that privilege the majority. Why? Part of the problem may be the electoral system. For example, most countries embrace the single-member district electoral system. In the single member district, candidates with the most votes often win the seat as legislative representative. In practice, single-member district electoral systems also skew, rather than ensure, representativeness.

In parts of India we see political party dissension coming to the forefront as voters try to push for changes through their elected representatives. Such changes include a demand for separate statehood. In the United States, also, one must go through Congress to change state boundaries or create a new state. Political party dissension and voting results have come to the forefront in polls in certain parts of India as in the United States. Pakistan is in crisis. Can Pakistan be stabilized through changing personalities and political party representation in its legislature?

Specifically, with increased representation, the legislature strengthens as a representative institution and, hence, provides more stability through representation. However, with increased representation, the legislature also becomes more competitive, as parties—large and small—gain seats into the legislature. With such a broad array of parties, the ability to unify and guard against the excesses of the president as executive is concurrently reduced while the ability of the prime minister and cabinet as executive to formulate policies and implement them is also reduced. Institutionally, the executive is structured in one of three ways: as president in a presidential system; as prime minister and cabinet in a parliamentary system; as president and prime minister in a presidential-parliamentary hybrid system. In a presidential system, the executive—the president—is independently elected to office. Many voters, particularly in the United States, may independently vote for the president from one party and elect representatives from another party. Such can make for negotiations between the president and the representative body in trying to develop legislation. In a parliamentary system, the executive—generally a reference to the prime minster, but more accurately applied to the entire cabinet—is chosen by the elected legislature or parliament. In parliamentary systems, there is no independent election for the executive. In a presidential-parliamentary hybrid system, also known as the semi-presidential system or mixed system, the president is elected independently, while the prime minister and cabinet are chosen by the legislature. The mixed system is becoming the political system of choice in emerging democracies: at last count in 2002, there were 25 nations with mixed systems, up from only three in 1946.[1]

The mixed systems maximize efficiency in policymaking but provide some guard against executive authority.[2]

Of course, this means that the representational and institutional roles of the legislature remain at the fore in emergent democracies. In this regard, representation must be measured by more than physical symbol. To truly represent a constituency, a legislator must achieve successful policymaking, not populist appeals. Indeed, the legislator's role is to actively avoid such populist appeals, since these provide springboards for individual political careers but do nothing in terms of the enhancing the political or economic infrastructure that will improve the people's lives.

It is important to note that legislators do not have to initiate policies in order to support or oppose them. What legislatures must do in order to demonstrate representation in policymaking is to pass or decline legislation, which entails the essential tasks of discussing, examining, and debating the policies introduced, doing so with an eye on the big picture of economic and political development in the country. In principle, the aggregation of all legislators' input ensures that proposed legislation captures or is amended in the end product to contain the diversity of citizens' responses and needs or the affirmation of the autocratic leader.

This brings us full circle to the importance of citizens' participation, particularly at the polls. Lack of participation at the polls, regardless of whether in emergent or mature democracies, undermines the political process and its development. Insofar as the lack of representativeness affects participation, many of the potential barriers to representation from electoral systems may be relatively easy to remedy. For instance, transparent campaign finance laws have helped address the disadvantages faced by minority or women candidates. What is clear is that the representativeness of legislature is not merely a political principle but a means to ensuring political stability or to affirming the decisions of the dictatorial leader, whether acknowledged or not.

Notes

1. See José Antonio Cheibub and Svitlana Chernykh. 2008. "Constitutions and Democratic Performance in Semi-Presidential Democracy." *Japanese Journal of Political Science* vol. 9 no 3: 269–303.

2. See Michael Sodaro, *Comparative Politics: A Global Introduction* (*3rd edition*). New York: McGraw-Hill (2007).

Article

Prepared by: Caroline Shaffer Westerhof,
California National University for Advanced Studies

Israel's Unity Government: A Bid to Represent the Majority

For decades, Israel's system of representation gave tiny parties an outsized voice, particularly on the issue of settlements. The unity government now has a chance to prioritize majority views.

JOSHUA MITNICK

Learning Outcomes

After reading this article, you will be able to:

• Examine the concept of majority rule as it affects those who hold the power but also are in the minority in numbers.

• Examine the clashes between the Jewish ultra-religious groups and secular Jews.

• Examine the degree and spirit of democracy within the political system in Israel.

Benjamin Netanyahu's new unity government arrives with the implication that there is something even more fundamental and pressing for Israel than peace with its Arab neighbors: fixing an electoral system responsible for political instability and outsized influence of minority groups like ultra-religious Jews.

Electoral reform was one of the four key goals that Mr. Netanyahu and his rival-turned-ally, Kadima leader Shaul Mofaz, in explaining their stunning 11th hour agreement to join forces in a unity coalition that averted near finalized plans for an election in September.

Symptoms of electoral dysfunction include a decades-old exemption allowing ultra-religious men to opt out of army service, and the inability of the government to evacuate settlement outposts built on property which even the government admits is on Palestinian land.

The culprit is Israel's system of proportional representation. Experts say it has given rise to a tyranny of the minority that rewards narrow-interest parties representing ultra-Orthodox Jews, Israeli settlers, or Russian immigrants with veto on policy by threatening to implode coalition governments.

"This means that the majority is under-represented in government and the minority is over-represented," says Amnon Rubenstein, a law professor and former Justice Minister for the left-wing Meretz Party who is pushing a plan to reform Israel's system. "This causes cynicism and loss of belief in democracy."

Seven Elections in 20 Years

The power of the smaller parties has created notoriously unstable governments. In the past 20 years, Israel has been forced to hold seven general elections. And the last time an Israeli government finished out its term was in 1988. At the same time, support for mainstream big tent parties like Netanyahu's Likud Party and the Labor Party have suffered a drop-off in support, and are more vulnerable to pressure.

That has created a situation in which Israeli prime ministers are more involved in the politicking necessary to keep their coalitions together rather than policy making or strategic planning.

"Government needs to be able to implement policy in a much more vigorous manner. An American president knows he's going to be in power for four years, he doesn't have to waste enormous energies the whole time on simply staying in power," says Jonathan Rynhold, a political scientist at Bar Ilan University. "[Israeli] Politicians spend much too much time going to bar mitzvahs. They spend too much time on politics than policy. The public thinks they're being cynical, but there's no other way to govern."

Israel uses a form of extreme democracy, giving parties with as little as 2 percent of the general vote seats in the parliament.

The upside to the system is that gives expression to the country's mosaic of ethnic, religious, and ideological groups in the parliament, and then forces them to govern via coalition.

In practice, however, Israel's parliament has become a jumble of small and medium size parties representing small population segments which have become the coalition kingmakers in the rivalries between bigger mainstream parties.

Ultra-Orthodox Priorities

That's how the ultra-Orthodox, or Haredi, parties have been able to get government money to keep kids in religious seminaries and out of the compulsory draft or the work force. They've also been able to get government funding for autonomous school systems which have smaller class sizes and follow an independent curriculum that omits core subjects.

"The wholesale exemption of the Haredim [from military service] is a consequence of Israel's distorted electoral system. The two issues are intertwined," says Yossi Klein Halevy, a fellow at the Shalom Hartman Institute in Jerusalem. "It's our dysfunctional coalition system that allows a separatist minority to dictate policy to the mainstream. These are the issues that have to be unlocked."

There are a myriad of proposals floating around to reform Israel's electoral system. In the 1990s, Israel experimented with instituting a direct vote for prime minister alongside the contest between the parties to make the chief executive less dependent on small parties. But the number and diversity of small parties grew anyway. The system was eventually scrapped.

"We have to find measures for minority groups to be represented in larger political vehicles," says Ofer Kenig, a fellow at the Israel Democracy Institute, a think tank which has also called for reform. "In the UK you don't have a Pakistani immigrant party, they find their way to the Labor or Conservative party, and this is because of the electoral system that doesn't make it possible for them to compete independently."

If Israeli politicians and experts find the right formula, experts say, it should encourage a more inclusionary brand of politics that will result in policies to better integrate the ultra-Orthodox and Israeli Arabs into the mainstream through programs like national service.

Implications for Palestinians

It should also weaken the ability of the Jewish settlers in the West Bank to block steps toward a political settlement with the Palestinians.

"They would still have power, but it would be lessened," says Mr. Rynhold. "You would cease to see new settlements popping up every Wednesday and Friday."

As a result the reaction has been mixed to Prime Minister Benjamin Netanyahu's mammoth unity coalition with more than three fourths of the parliamentary deputies. Some see it as more cynical coalition politics to survive for a year and a half. Others hope that not having to rely on the small parties will enable him to push through big reforms.

"Israel has a stable government with an enormous secular majority . . . we finally have a government that represents the Israeli majority which no sectoral party can extort," wrote Ari Shavit in the liberal Haaretz newspaper. But "if this was the maneuver of the decade to win one more year in the Prime Minister's residence, it's all over for him. The public will not forgive or forget."

Critical Thinking

1. *What is the realism of President Netanyahu's speech* in the United Nations attacking the language of the Iranian president, Hassan Rouhani, at the last United Nation General Assembly meeting (October 1, 2013)?

2. How is the ultra-religious right taking control of the political order within Isrel?

3. If there are clashes between the ultra right religious groups and secular Jews, how can there be political unity in Israel?

Create Central

www.mhhe.com/createcentral

Internet References

How Netanyahu's 'Unity' Government May Affect Palestinians, Iran
www.csmonitor.com/World/Middle-East/2012/0508/How-Netanyahu-s-unity-government-may-affect-Palestinians-Iran

Israel's Ultra-Orthodox Soldiers under Fire
http://online.wsj.com/news/articles/SB10001424127887324522502504579000660630783386

Ithaca College
urpasheville.org/proceedings/ncur2011/

U.N. Peacekeeping Unit to Exit Israeli Border Area
http://online.wsj.com/news/articles/SB100014241278873238448045785288341246464470

JOSHUA MITNICK is a correspondent, Christian Science Monitor.

Article

Prepared by: Caroline Shaffer Westerhof,
California National University for Advanced Studies

The Quality of South Africa's Electoral Accountability, 1994–2014: Freedom, Flaws, and Food Parcels

Victoria Graham

Learning Outcomes

After reading this article, you will be able to:

- Discuss the implications of the quality of electoral accountability in South Africa over its 20 years as a democracy.

- Understand that although the South Africa Constitution and legislation provide for public broadcasting to be fair and representative, why it is evident that the media has failed in this responsibility.

1 Introduction

In April 1994 South Africa's first non-racial multiparty election took place. It marked an official end to the country's segregationist and authoritarian past and ushered in a new democracy, delivering not only the universal franchise but also formal equality before the law, avenues for citizen participation in governance and statutory institutions buttressing democracy (Muthien, Khosa and Magubane 2000). Twenty years later, on the 7th May 2014, South Africa fully consolidated its status as a young democracy when it witnessed its fifth national and provincial elections. All elections thus far have been declared 'free and fair' by a host of international and national election observers,[1] but does this label necessarily reflect substantive electoral accountability in the country? In other words, to what degree have elections been free and fair and to what extent has the electoral system supported the deepening of democracy in South Africa over the past 20 years?

Electoral accountability, expressed through the act of free and fair elections and the contribution of political parties to the electoral process, is innate in a representative democracy. So important are elections that, as Lindberg (2006, 1) notes "Every modern definition of representative democracy includes participatory and contested elections perceived as the legitimate procedure for translation of rule by the people into workable executive and legislative power." After all, "it is through the ability of citizens, at regular elections, to retain or dismiss their elected representatives . . . that the principle of popular control is made flesh" (Beetham, Byrne, Ngan and Weir 2002, 85). Through elections, citizens can make demands on the leaders which in turn implies the obligation that elected political leaders have to behave properly and lawfully or answer to the voters for their political decisions (Diamond and Morlino 2005). Political parties simplify the choices the public has to make by offering broad policies and different sets of politicians

---

[1] The Commonwealth; Electoral Institute for Sustainable Democracy in Africa (EISA); the African Union (AU); the Southern African Development Community (SADC) Parliamentary Forum; the SADC Electoral Commission; the SADC Electoral Support Network; the African Alliance for Peace; the Association of African Electoral Authorities; the National Democratic Institute; the European Union; the South African Civil Society Election Coalition; and the Election Monitoring Network. See, for example, the EISA Election Observer Mission Report (2004); the South African Civil Society Election Coalition (2009), Business Unity South Africa (2009), and the AU Observer Mission (2009).

[2] See O'Donnell (2005); Diamond and Morlino (2005); and Diamond and Gunther (2001).

choose between and in this way strengthen electoral accountability (Beetham et al. 2002).

However, it has also been noted that the holding of elections does not necessarily translate into good quality democracy. That is, while electoral democracies might be classified as democratic by virtue of the existence of elections, this does not guarantee that all traditional attributes of democracy are being adhered to (Bratton and van de Walle 1997). They may, in truth, be lacking in respect of a number of societal freedoms, such as poor civil liberties regimes, limited societal toleration, corruption, crime, and violence.

In light of this scholars have increasingly turned their attention to ascertaining how well countries are sustaining their democracies by assessing the *quality* of their democracy (see, for example, Altman and Perez-Linan 2002, 85–100; Morlino 2011). Questions of degree are asked as to the various strengths and weaknesses that exist with the goal of determining how democracies can be improved and deepened (Beetham 2004; Beetham, Carvalho, Landman and Weir 2008). That is, to what degree are state democratic procedures experienced and the essential democratic principles realized? (Baker 1999, 273–274). For example, *to what degree* is the government committed to democratic values or *to what extent* do women and minorities participate in the politics of the state? This element of "degree" helps to capture the overall quality of democracy within a state.

The Quality of South Africa's Electoral Accountability

In examining the quality of South Africa's electoral accountability, this article examines the *extent* to which elections are held in a regular, universal, free, and fair manner as well as the *extent* to which the existing party system is able to assist in the working of democracy. The criteria for assessment are derived from the International Institute for Democracy and Electoral Assistance's State of Democracy Framework (International IDEA 2010) and Leonardo Morlino's Tool for Empirical Research on Democratic Qualities (Morlino 2011). In pursuit of the first consideration the following indicators are examined: a comprehensive and constitutional legal framework as a foundation for free and fair elections; the efficiency, accountability, transparency, and impartiality of the electoral management body (EMB); the degree to which the electoral climate is free from political violence and intimidation; electoral participation and the transparency and timeliness of registration and voting procedures; voting day issues; the degree of acceptance of the result by the government and the electorate; and media coverage of elections throughout the election phase. With regard to the second consideration, the democratic role of political parties,

three aspects are discussed: the transparency of party financing and regulations that govern such financing; the prevalence of a stable and competitive multiparty system and the degree of alternation in government; and the proportionality of the electoral system.

2.1 A Comprehensive and Constitutional Legal Framework as a Foundation for Free and Fair Elections

Over the decades few have been able to agree on what constitutes standardized assessment criteria for a "free and fair" election for several reasons not least of which is the difficulty of distinguishing between the concepts "freedom" and "fairness" (see Elklit and Reynolds 2005, 147–162). Nevertheless, this label is still used widely as an overall description and/or evaluation of elections to determine whether the playing field is level (Fakir and Holland 2010). Moreover, to address this "vagueness" the Principles for Election Management, Monitoring, and Observation (PEMMO) in the Southern African Development Community (SADC) region were introduced in 2003 as guidelines for election observers (EISA 2004).

As a member of the SADC, South Africa is committed to upholding these electoral principles as well as those of the SADC Electoral Commissions Forum (ECF), African Union (AU), the EISA, the SADC Electoral Support Network, and the SADC Parliamentary Forum, namely:

- The need for a comprehensive and constitutional legal framework;
- The importance of transparent and accessible pre-election procedures (including the delimitation process, voter registration, and candidate nomination);
- The equitable use of the media and public resources and issues of political party finance;
- The organization and management of the election phase, including the location of polling stations, their layout, and access to them; the secrecy of the ballot, and the counting process;
- The post-election phase, including the settlement of election disputes and ways of ensuring that results are acceptable; and
- The requirements for unhindered, credible, professional, and impartial monitoring and observation of the electoral process.

As per the guidelines, it is essential that the necessary legal and institutional frameworks are in place to serve as the "basis for the conduct and delivery of free, fair, credible, and legitimate elections" (EISA 2004, 7). In South Africa, three Acts came into being prior to the first elections to govern the conduct and implementation of the national and provincial elections: the

1993 Electoral Act (amended in the Electoral Act No. 73 of 1998), the 1993 Independent Electoral Commission Act and the Constitution of the Republic of South Africa Act of 1993. In accordance with the Constitution, elections are held every five years using the proportional representation electoral model. The Municipal Electoral Act No. 27 of 2000 defines the legal framework for local or municipal government elections.

2.2 The Efficiency, Accountability, Transparency, and Impartiality of the Electoral Management Body

The Electoral Commission, more commonly known as the Independent Electoral Commission (IEC), was established through the aforementioned IEC Act of 1993. The IEC is South Africa's EMB responsible for facilitating and overseeing the entire voting process and ensuring that the elections are free and fair. Mandated to be "impartial" and to "exercise its powers and perform its functions without fear, favor, or prejudice" in Chapter 2 of the Electoral Commission Act No. 51 of 1996, the IEC is accountable to the National Assembly and must report on its activities and performance annually (section 181(5) of the Constitution). Apart from the duties prescribed in the Constitution and noted above, section 5(1) of the Electoral Commission Act lists numerous additional responsibilities for the IEC including the compilation and maintenance of a voters' roll, the promotion of voter education and the adjudication of administrative disputes that may arise from the organization, administration or conducting of elections.

Critical Thinking

1. How would you define *democracy* in South Africa?
2. To what degree does the concept of "free and fair" elections in South Africa reflect substantive electoral accountability in the country?
3. To what degree does a nation-state determine that its electoral processes serve as the "basis for the conduct and delivery of free, fair, credible, and legitimate elections"?

Internet References

A big election win for South Africa's ANC, but results suggest future challenges
www.rawstory.com/rs/2014/05/a-big-election-win-for-south-africas-anc-but-results-suggest-future-challenges

Akufo-Addo meets South Africa's Independent Electoral Commission
www.gbcghana.com/1.1732616

Election "selfies" could land voters in jail
www.techcentral.co.za/election-selfies-could-land-voters-in-jail/47951

Fifth Consecutive Electoral Victory for ANC
www.voanews.com/content/south-africas-ruling-anc-party-wins-5-consecutive-election-/1911905.html

South Africa's election free and fair: AU
www.southafrica.info/news/elections-090514c.htm

VICTORIA GRAHAM is a senior lecturer in International Studies Monash, South Africa, in Johannesburg. Her research interests include the quality of democracy, comparative politics, and diplomacy.

Article

Prepared by: Caroline Shaffer Westerhof,
California National University for Advanced Studies

Pakistan 2020

A Vision for Building a Better Future

Hassan Abbas

Learning Outcomes

After reading this article, you will be able to:

- Identify the strength and the means of Pakistan's power structure.

- Examine and identify the continuing crisis within Pakistan.

- Examine the violence in Pakistan that hinders the nation's stability.

Executive Summary

In recent years, Pakistan has stumbled from one crisis to another. A number of political and socioeconomic challenges threaten to further destabilize a country that already is reeling from insurgencies along its northwestern border. Pakistan's newest democratic government is struggling to maintain control over parts of its territory where militant religious groups are intent on challenging its authority and legitimacy. The country's conflict with India over Kashmir, now in its seventh decade, appears as intractable as ever, and the war in neighboring Afghanistan has deepened instability throughout Pakistan. The transition from a near-decade-long rule under a military dictatorship is slow and complicated, as rampant corruption and politicization of the bureaucracy present huge obstacles to the state-building process.

Although Pakistan's vibrant civil society, relatively open media, and the rise of an independent higher judiciary provide some glimmers of hope, poor economic and development indicators coupled with worrying demographic trends pose serious challenges to the well-being of millions of Pakistanis. Energy shortages have worsened in recent years, and the destruction caused by the floods of 2010 has exacerbated the country's many strains. In short, how Pakistan manages these challenges in the coming years will have great consequences for its future prospects.

While recent reform efforts in the higher judiciary and constitutional amendments to strengthen democratic institutions and expand provincial autonomy signal a positive trajectory for the country, sustaining democratic governance is complicated by radicalization and violence perpetrated by an intolerant and extremist minority in the country. Terrorist attacks on respected and cherished Sufi shrines throughout Pakistan and high-profile assassinations—including the January 2011 killing of Salman Taseer, the governor of Punjab, and the assassination of Shahbaz Bhatti, Pakistan's only Christian cabinet minister, in March 2011—illustrate the lengths to which religious extremists in Pakistan will go to silence opposition voices in the country. And rather than condemning these acts of vigilante justice as un-Islamic, the government's slow and timid response to the violence has allowed voices of intolerance to gather strength.

Preventing Pakistan from further deterioration will require a sustained, long-term commitment from the government of Pakistan, the United States, and other international stakeholders to promote genuine reform in the coming decade. This commitment must be enshrined in a comprehensive package of policies aimed at promoting sustainable constitutional democracy, credible and effective rule of law and law enforcement, a significant expansion and improvement of the education and health sectors, and a peaceful resolution of the conflict with India. Economic growth and foreign investment in Pakistan arguably will follow such progress.

In Pakistan, there is a growing consensus about the need for reform, but the resources and will that are required to plan, support, and implement such an agenda remain elusive. In this context, the role of private and public sector media in preparing Pakistani society and the state for competition in the global economy and in creating a culture of innovation cannot be overlooked.

For this report, the Asia Society Pakistan 2020 Study Group focused on seven core issues that are essential to realizing a sound future for the country by 2020: (1) strengthening democratic institutions; (2) strengthening the rule of law; (3) improving human development and social services, especially in health and education; (4) developing the energy infrastructure; (5) assisting the victims of the 2010 flood in their recovery; (6) improving internal security; and (7) advancing the peace process with India. This report is not meant to represent a consensus among all the members of the Pakistan 2020 Study Group. Rather, it presents the findings and conclusions reached by the project director and the report's principal author, Hassan Abbas, through consultations with Study Group members. While individual members may disagree with parts of the report, the Group broadly supports the overall set of recommendations.

Civil-Military Relations and Democracy

The democratic leadership of Pakistan is struggling to consolidate and strengthen civilian-led democratic institutions in a country that has been ruled by military generals for half of its existence as an independent state. In this context, one of the most important challenges facing Pakistan is the military's dominance of the country's fiscal priorities and strategic calculus. For civilian institutions to take root and flourish over the next decade, the process of democratization must continue. The following course of action should be pursued to strengthen democratic governance in the country:

- A strict adherence to term appointments for armed forces personnel by the civilian leadership will support the professionalization of the Pakistani military.
- Making the expenditures of the Pakistani military more transparent is critical and will require enacting parliamentary legislation through a legislative process similar to those followed by many governments worldwide.
- Civilian supremacy in the Pakistani army can be established through the development of internal mechanisms, for example, by emphasizing democracy in military academies, making the Pakistani military's budget transparent, and involving civilians in strategic decision-making processes.
- The interests of the United States and other important allies of Pakistan will be better served by giving priority to strengthening relations with the democratic leadership and institutions of the country.
- Achieving stability in Pakistan and strengthening democratic traditions in the coming decade will require all major Pakistani political parties to hold regular elections and enact term limits for their leaders, limit the areas where candidates can contest an election to their home constituencies, and establish a transparent mechanism by which funding can be provided to low-income candidates.

Rule of Law and the Judiciary

The weaknesses of Pakistan's judicial system not only pose a serious challenge to access to justice, but also hinder the fight against terrorist groups. In the most basic sense, the rule of law in Pakistan must aim to protect the rights of citizens from arbitrary and abusive use of government power. A functioning judiciary is a fundamental element of any society's rule of law. Expanding reform efforts from higher to lower judicial levels of the system will be critical for Pakistan in the coming years.

The following measures should be carried out to strengthen the rule of law in Pakistan over the coming decade:

- The 2002 Bangalore Principles of Judicial Conduct—which stipulate that, in addition to independence, the values of impartiality, integrity, propriety, competence, diligence, and equal treatment of all before the courts are essential to proper judicial conduct—must be followed.
- Respecting the separation of powers enshrined in the constitution, as well as placing reasonable limits on the Supreme Court's use of *suo moto* powers, will contribute greatly to the enhancement of the rule of law in Pakistan.
- Security for judges, especially for those in lower courts hearing sensitive cases such as those concerning blasphemy and terrorism, must be enhanced.
- The United Nations Convention on the Elimination of All Forms of Discrimination Against Women needs to be ratified without delay.
- The National Judicial Policy should be implemented, with an emphasis on provisions calling for oversight, disciplining corrupt and inefficient judicial officers, setting a timeline and establishing special benches for prioritizing cases that can be fast-tracked, and funding courtroom construction and the hiring of judicial officers and administrative staff.
- In the Federally Administered Tribal Areas, the Pakistan government and Supreme Court must establish as a matter of priority a functioning judicial system with civil and criminal courts and a reformed legal code to replace the outdated and irrelevant Frontier Crimes Regulation.

Human Development

Poor governance and weak institutions have eroded the Pakistani public's confidence in the government's capacity to address their everyday needs. Pakistan currently ranks 125th (out of 169 countries) on the United Nations Development Programme's Human Development Index. The government is investing little in socioeconomic development, which also is hindering the growth potential of Pakistan's economy and depriving people of opportunities to live a satisfying life.

Education

Given the dire crisis in education in Pakistan today, the country will not achieve universal primary education by 2015, as set forth in the United Nations Millennium Development Goals. The focus should be on getting as close to the goal as possible by 2015, with a renewed commitment to achieve universal primary education by 2020. As a first step, Pakistan must immediately raise its public expenditures on education from less than 1.5% to at least 4% of gross domestic product, and by 2020, the expenditures should be set to at least 6%. Without making this minimal commitment, a reversal of the worrying trends in the education sector is unlikely to occur. An immediate increase in public expenditures on education to at least 4% of gross domestic product should target the following priority areas:

- Devising and implementing an accountable and predictable system of teacher recruitment, hiring, payment, retention, and training, as well as promotion based on merit, achievement, and outcomes will greatly improve the quality of education and teacher performance in Pakistan.
- The introduction of curriculum reform focusing on a life-skills-based approach to education will promote real-world applications of creative thinking and analytical reasoning.
- Developing a robust central regulatory system will contribute to the maintenance of standards and the collection of timely data on service delivery, operations, infrastructure availability, fiscal flows, learning achievements, teacher performance, and school outcomes in the education sector.
- A dynamic set of institutionalized relationships should be established between the central regulatory mechanism and the autonomous and independent subnational government units responsible for service delivery.
- Separating the higher education function completely from the primary education function and enacting legislation to provide specialized management and authority over higher education institutions will ensure greater regulatory control.
- Madrasa reform can be achieved through strategies for curricular improvement. Public school curricula should be devised, designed, and monitored by provincial governments and combine religious and secular education.
- The government of Pakistan can fulfill its education reform plans if foreign donors and international agencies focus their aid efforts on establishing a single coherent approach to providing significant budget support in this sector.

Health

Pakistan is in need of deep-rooted reform in its health care system, which must include systems of governance outside the public health sector that affect the performance of health systems. While universal access to basic public health facilities is an ambitious goal that many Pakistanis desire, investments now must begin to build a strong infrastructure by 2020 to make this goal attainable. Immediate action in the following priority areas should begin to address health needs in Pakistan:

- Proactive steps to improve health governance will be greatly enhanced by the development of a national consensus on a health reform agenda.
- In addition to devolving service delivery responsibilities from the federal level to the provincial and district levels, capacity building at the provincial level will allow for the planning, evaluation and implementation of alternative service delivery and financing mechanisms.

Key national functions for health should be retained by the federal structure.

- Collecting, analyzing, and swiftly scaling up successful best practices from existing examples of public service delivery reengineering at the primary health care and hospital levels will contribute greatly to health sector improvement in Pakistan.
- Separating policy-making, implementation, and regulatory functions in the health sector, as well as adopting market-harnessing regulatory approaches, will lead to an improvement in service delivery.
- Concrete steps for increasing public financing in health must begin alongside measures to improve utilization and limit pilferage. Strengthening essential services, enhancing social protection for the informally employed, and pooling insurance for the unemployed are priority areas for any increase in revenues in the health sector.
- An innovative system of private–public, employer- and sponsor-subsidized, and pooled group health insurance can be introduced nationwide, especially for low-income groups.
- Investments must be made to leverage the full potential of health information technology in mobile health systems, with the aim of improving transparency in procurements, increasing philanthropic subsidies, enhancing quality assurance, and promoting access to medical education. Technology such as telemedicine can help bridge the gap between rural and urban access to quality health care.
- Collecting, analyzing, and disseminating health information for shaping policy and planning at the decision-making level can be achieved through the development of an apex institutional arrangement.
- By adopting market-harnessing regulatory approaches, the first point of contact in primary health care will be broadened while enabling equitable access and the purchase of health care for many Pakistanis.
- Strengthening government oversight and regulations in private sector health care delivery will prevent and check problems such as malpractice and facilitate public–private collaborations in health delivery.

Energy Infrastructure

Pakistan faces chronic infrastructure challenges when it comes to energy sources. In addition to nurturing social and political instability, Pakistan's poor energy infrastructure imposes enormous economic costs in the form of unemployment and loss of revenue. An uninterrupted supply of energy to fuel the nation's economy should be the highest priority for Pakistan's economic managers. To meet its current and future energy demands, the government of Pakistan should invest a minimum of $5 billion in energy production by 2020. Additionally, the following measures in the energy sector should be implemented:

- Pakistan must enhance its capacity to cultivate more power from renewable energy sources, particularly by improving its ability to harness wind energy along its southern coast and by making use of solar power.

- Along with proper upkeep and maintenance of existing hydropower dams, more dams are needed to meet current and future energy requirements in Pakistan. This can be achieved by directing investments toward the construction of a very small number of large dams (Kalabagh dam is one project that has been stalled) or a larger number of small reservoirs. At the same time, these plans must be integrated into a broader strategy to improve water resources management throughout the country. Additionally, Pakistan can dispel the impression that big dam projects will benefit only larger provinces by exploring ways to reach a consensus among all the provinces on its water infrastructure and providing provinces with legally binding guarantees.
- Energy efficiency in Pakistan can be improved if government-owned power generation infrastructure is refurbished technologically and power infrastructure is upgraded with a modern efficient grid.
- Foreign donors can play a key role in building Pakistan's energy capacity by providing expert advice to the public and private sectors in Pakistan on energy development and management. The United States, in particular, should explore investing in a large energy infrastructure project in Pakistan, which will not only deepen strategic ties with Pakistan but also create goodwill in the country.

The Floods of 2010

The massive floods in Pakistan during the summer of 2010 set back all development indicators in the country. The enormity of the humanitarian crisis caused by the floods requires concerted planning and a seamless transition to the rehabilitation and reconstruction phase. Securing resources for the post-relief phase continues to be a challenge, but every effort should be made in the next two to three years to ensure that reconstruction in Pakistan proceeds effectively. The following steps should be taken to ensure that Pakistan fully recovers from the flood and is adequately prepared for future disasters:

- Pakistan's vulnerability to disasters can be addressed by immediately implementing sound building regulations, starting land rehabilitation, de-silting canals and waterways, and constructing dikes.
- Integrating climate change scenarios into the Pakistan government's annual development plans will help develop a well-coordinated strategy to address the impacts of global climate change in the country while ensuring progress toward meeting the Millennium Development Goals targets for poverty reduction.
- Regional as well as global support for reconstruction in flood-hit areas is critical. To improve its credibility and potentially attract more funds for reconstruction, Pakistan must be fully transparent about the use of international funds.
- Stabilizing and improving access to steady, affordable, and nutritious food supplies in Pakistan is essential, especially for the 6 million people most affected by the floods.

- Enhancing access to health services and medicines for flood-affected areas has to be a government priority, in addition to evaluating and addressing the health risks caused by the flood, including the spread of waterborne diseases.
- The losses incurred by displacement, migration, or damage to income-generating assets as a result of the floods highlight the need for introducing alternative mechanisms for flood survivors to reestablish their source of livelihood, especially for those whose primary source of income has been obliterated. Future asset-protection mechanisms need to be introduced concurrently—for example, through livestock insurance and weather-indexed crop insurance.
- Developing a comprehensive management framework for disaster prevention and mitigation in all aspects of national planning will help reduce Pakistan's vulnerability to natural calamities. The National Disaster Management Authority needs to be strengthened and properly resourced to function as a national focal point. In this context, Pakistan must follow the Kyoto Convention's recommendations on disaster prevention and management diligently.

Internal Security

Achieving internal security is of paramount importance to ensuring a stable and prosperous future in Pakistan. The significant rise in terrorist activity throughout the country, besides being a serious threat and demoralizing fact for its people, has dampened economic growth in Pakistan. At the core of internal security is the creation of a capable, well-resourced, structurally coherent, and institutionally autonomous police and law enforcement infrastructure. At the same time, any strategy must include measures that tackle the root causes of insurgency and violence in the first place, such as poverty, illiteracy, a sense of injustice, and a widely held perception that "external forces" are attacking Pakistan.

The following steps should be taken to ensure internal security in Pakistan:

- De-radicalization programs and the effective use of law enforcement backed by military force must be enhanced to reduce religious militancy.
- The Pakistan government will have to confront the multiple insurgent and terrorist groups operating simultaneously in the country and prevent these groups from establishing a sanctuary.
- Establishing an efficient, professional, and accountable law enforcement infrastructure will require fully implementing the 2002 Police Order to reorganize the police into a politically neutral force and discarding the controversial amendments made in 2004. Police safety commissions—already provided for under the new law—should be empowered to monitor police performance. An efficient police force can be created by devising and implementing procedures and policies aimed at improving conditions for police officers,

establishing citizen–police liaison committees, and enhancing police and intelligence services cooperation.

- Military and civilian intelligence agencies must follow guidelines provided by law when gathering information and conducting interrogations. Human rights violations, especially in Baluchistan, where reports of abductions of political activists by security forces are common, must end.

- A robust witness protection program that also protects investigators, prosecutors, and judges—particularly in major criminal and terrorism cases—can be created through amendments in the Criminal Procedure Code.

- Rigid and impartial enforcement of the law will help ameliorate ethnic strife and sectarian killings in cities, especially in Karachi. This strategy will require revising the curriculum in public schools, as well as in madrasa networks, in ways that encourage pluralism and deter any dissemination of intolerance.

- Curricular improvement in Pakistan along scientific lines can be modeled on similar efforts in Indonesia and other countries. In this context, progressive religious scholars who challenge violent extremists must be provided full security as well as state support for their independent research work and publications.

- Internal security can be achieved if the international community directly targets its assistance toward helping Pakistan in this area. Half of U.S. funding allocated for counterterrorism and counterinsurgency support in Pakistan, for example, can be directed toward supporting scientific investigations and enhancing forensic capabilities in law enforcement. Additionally, the rules of engagement of coalition forces and policies on drone attacks should be reassessed.

Relations with India and Neighbors

Pakistan's development is almost impossible without regional cooperation, and China and India play a very important role in this context. An optimistic scenario in the next 10 years would be for Pakistan's economy to grow at a rate of approximately 5% annually, which would provide a cushion so that the country could begin investing in long-term human capacity development. However, without a sustainable peace deal with India that includes an amicable resolution of the Kashmir dispute, this is unlikely to happen. There is a growing realization in India that a failed Pakistan is not in its best interest. Peace in South Asia is attainable if Pakistan, its neighbors, and international stakeholders focus on the following measures:

- Pakistan must set a goal of increasing annual direct bilateral trade with India to more than $5 billion by 2020, as increased economic interactions will expand the space for peace constituencies in both states. As a first step, India should unilaterally lower nontariff barriers to trade with Pakistan. In turn, Pakistan can accord India most-favored-nation trade status.

- Reforming the visa issuance process will help support and strengthen people-to-people contact from both countries, as will further encouraging contacts between civil society groups and student exchange programs in both countries.

- Enhancing energy cooperation between India and Pakistan is a potential avenue of dialogue between the two countries. Cooperative energy projects, such as joint natural gas pipelines, joint electricity-generation projects, and the development of a common grid system, will go a long way toward demonstrating that the people of both countries can benefit from improved relations.

- The governments of Pakistan and India should place a moratorium on the expansion of their nuclear weapons programs. Pakistan's military leaders must realize that more nuclear weapons will neither improve the country's nuclear deterrence capabilities nor help in its fight against terrorism. Furthermore, Pakistan must ensure the safety and security of its nuclear materials.

- By reposturing militarily and becoming less Pakistan focused, India can help ease Pakistan's insecurity. War doctrines such as "Cold Start" should be reviewed and Pakistan's apprehensions about Indian interference in Baluchistan need to be addressed. At the same time, Pakistan must dismantle all armed groups focused on Kashmir.

- Pakistan, India, Afghanistan, and other external powers must recognize that terrorism is by no means a state-specific problem; the entire region will have to confront it together. Cooperation between civilian law enforcement agencies in South Asia should be institutionalized.

- The United States cannot promote an amicable resolution of the differences and disputes between India and Pakistan by supporting one side or the other; it must remain objective. In the case of Afghanistan, a more proactive role for the United States must include bringing all the regional stakeholders to the table, ideally under a United Nations umbrella and with the aim of ending the India–Pakistan rivalry and proxy war in Afghanistan.

Pakistan faces enormous challenges in the years ahead. But the people of Pakistan have shown a remarkable resilience in addressing some of these challenges, and there is a high potential for reform and development in the country. Progressive and constructive policy shifts, as suggested here, are what truly matter in the long term. Moreover, internal and regional factors will define and drive Pakistan's path toward reform, and the international community, especially important allies such as the United States, must play a supportive role.

Critical Thinking

1. Can Pakistan be stabilized? Explain.

2. What do you anticipate Pakistani politics and security to be like in 2020? Explain.

3. Do you believe that Pakistan will be the central foreign policy challenge during the last few years of the Obama administration? Explain.

4. Will the global war against terrorism within the Pakistan-Afghanistan region, as its epicenter, be a continuing tragedy? Explain.

Create Central

www.mhhe.com/createcentral

Internet References

Stabilizing Pakistan through Police Reform — Asia Society
asiasociety.org/files/pdf/as_pakistan_police_exec_sum.pdf

Logic is Variable
http://logicisvariable.blogspot.com/2013/02/pakistan-2020-vision-for-building.html

Pakistan 2020 — Asia Society
http://asiasociety.org/files/pdf/as_pakistan%202020_study_group_rpt.pdf

Voice of America
www.voanews.com/content/musharraf-says-pakistan-can-play-critical-role-in-stabilizing-afghanistan/1593660.html

The Frontier Post
www.thefrontierpost.com/article/26471/

HASSAN ABBAS (Project Director), is Bernard Schwartz Fellow, Asia Society; Quaid-i-Azam Professor, Columbia University's South Asia Institute.

Unit 6

UNIT

Prepared by: Caroline Shaffer Westerhof,
California National University for Advanced Studies

Unelected Government Office: Judiciary, Military, and Bureaucracy in Everyday Politics

We describe the workings of the unelected branches of the government—the judiciary, military, and bureaucracies—to show their impact on policymaking. There is a clear ambivalence regarding these branches of government. In particular, as unelected officers, these officials are able to exert considerable influence as administrators and interpret if and how laws are carried out. Consequently, they have significant influence on the institutional effects over politics and society.

Such analysis reveals that where the executive or judiciary may be dragging its heels on policymaking—on issues ranging from counterterrorism to environmental protection—the judiciaries across a range of countries have executed clearer and more consistent policies in these areas. A look at these judicial decisions reveal that the claim that unelected officers are displacing elected ones is untenable: The judiciaries are ruling in areas where the executives and legislatures have failed to pursue clear policy options. The reality, then, is that the judiciary is expanding "policy space" to facilitate decision making rather than angling for a part as a policymaker. In doing so, the judiciary is engaging the other branches of government—the executive and the legislature—by applying the interpretation of foreign and international laws to cases, or stepping in to give voice to those unrepresented or poorly represented, such as following the Civil War in the United States and during the rise of fascism in Europe.

Such has been recently noted by Alan Dershowitz, one of the United States' most well-known constitutional scholars, who stated on CNBC that "there is no right to an abortion in the (U.S.) constitution. "I can't find anything in the constitution that says you prefer the life of the mother, or the convenience of the mother if it's an abortion by choice, over the potential life of the fetus...." He was referring to the U.S. Supreme Court Case of *Roe v. Wade*, decided in 1973. Thus, this is the type of policymaking framed by the decisions of the United State Supreme Court, whose justices are nominated by the president and confirmed by the vote of the U.S. Senate. We note that the judiciary tends to "make policy" by its decisions, whether in a democratic or authoritarian society.

In the intelligence community in the United States, in the political role of the military in democratic countries, in authoritarian nations, and in the political transition in Egypt, we note that unelected officials are not accountable; they may also behave in ways that destabilize the country. This is the case for transitioning countries such as Egypt, that is, where the military was and is considered an important ally and essential for political stability. The political transition in Egypt took place in part due to the military's withdrawal of support from the previous authoritarian regime; however, since the transition, the military has also established a firm role in politics. This role of the military in Egyptian politics was reduced in August 2012 through changes introduced by Egyptian President Mohammed Morsi; the changes included reversing constitutional decrees issued by the Supreme Council of the Armed Forces (SCAF) that reduced the powers of the presidency in Egypt. In reversing the SCAF's decrees, President Morsi appeared to have restored some oversight of the military and reestablished "civilian control over politics." The military continues to pose a destabilizing threat to civilian power that is likely to be asserted if civilian authorities fail to make the political, social, and economic performance necessary for popular support.

Nor is unaccountability limited to the unelected military and bearer of arms. If the global economic crisis provides any insights, those who wield the pen pose problems as well. Thus, on one side of the Atlantic in the United States, conservatives and liberals alike—although for different reasons—fault the Federal Reserve bureaucracy and the government for the crisis. On the other side, the European Central Bank (ECB) has provided a total of 1.7 trillion euros to ailing banks in the European continent and, consequently, undergirded the European Union. Whether such bureaucratic authority is good or otherwise depends on one's perspectives. Thus, from Germany's perspective, the ECB's policy is tantamount to easy money that delays real solutions such as public administration and wasteful spending; from the perspective of other European leaders, such as in Spain or Italy, the policy helps them compete against economic powerhouses such as Germany.

Can some positions be constitutionally changed and become elected positions? Are there clear advantages for continuing the practice of keeping branches of government unelected? In reviewing unelected officials, it is worthwhile to pay heed to the following argument on accountability:

"Horizontal accountability" (a concept developed by scholars such as Guillermo O'Donnell and Richard Sklar) refers to the capacity of governmental institutions—including such "agencies of restraint" as courts, independent electoral-tribunals, anticorruption bodies, central banks, auditing agencies, and ombudsmen—to check abuses by other public agencies and branches of government. (It is distinguished from, and complements, "vertical accountability," through which public officials are held accountable by free elections, a free press, and an active civil society.)[1]

Clearly, democratic progress in any country must build on both vertical and horizontal accountability. Like all other branches of government, these agencies or branches should not displace policymaking. Instead, an essential may be oversight or checks, so that the influence of these unelected officials do not exceed elected ones. When these unelected officials are countenanced with constraints, they stand as additional venues for citizen access. Then, they are not generally "runaway" policycymakers; instead, they potentially fill in for government failures or oversights. At that level, perhaps the question is not whether they should have influence but, rather, why not.

Senegal has been a bastion of stability and democracy on a continent where such is a regional exception. Here we see that the president and its cohorts offer stability and economic growth. Such can only happen because the president recognizes that the bureaucracy is a vital part of a stable political system. Yet Tunisia and Egypt are linked together because of similarities. Massive demonstrations, as in Egypt and in Tunisia, are polarizing these countries, as we well know. Who forces the issues of quelling these demonstrations? It is the military—the unelected forces of power—that use weapons that kill when the demonstrators do not turn back.

The bureaucracy, also known as agencies within public administration, play a pivotal role in government policymaking. In the United States, many congressional legislators look to the agencies within the administration to write the bills that are sent to the president, after both houses have passed such. It is important to recognize that members of the bureaucracy have lengthy years of service, probably tenure, and therefore know the history and background of issues that warrant the potential of new legislation. Thus the bureaucrats are silently in the forefront of helping elected legislators to write the bills.

The military and the intelligence communities have played a pivotal role, both in stable and unstable political regimes, as unelected power and political actors. "The black bag job" is a "silent part of the Central Intelligence Agency, in the United States; it is the clandestine operations of surveillance of various actions. In war games designed by the military, the question is still asked, " . . . what forces are adequate to the problem of loose nukes?" Then the questions are raised that " . . . will Central Command decline?" How can they when another foreign policy expert writes, "Don't be too sure there won't be another U.S. war in the Middle East?"

Note

1. Harald Waldrauch of the Institute for Advanced Studies (Vienna), and the editors of the International Forum for Democratic Studies Report on the Third Vienna Dialogue on Democracy on "Institutionalizing Horizontal Accountability: How Democracies Can Fight Corruption and the Abuse of Power," 6-29 June 1997, co-sponsored by the Austrian Institute for Advanced Studies (Vienna) and the National Endowment for Democracy's International Forum for Democratic Studies (Washington, D.C.). Available at www.ned.org/forum/reports/accountability/report.html

Article

Prepared by: Caroline Shaffer Westerhof,
California National University for Advanced Studies

The CIA's New Black Bag is Digital

When the NSA can't break into your computer, these guys break into your house.

MATTHEW M. AID

Learning Outcomes

After reading this article, you will be able to:

- Explain the CIA concept of the "black bag job."

- Explain the CIA's Technical Operation Collection and how it carries out assignments.

- Explain the rivalry and present relationship between the CIA and NSA.

During a coffee break at an intelligence conference held in The Netherlands a few years back, a senior Scandinavian counterterrorism official regaled me with a story. One of his service's surveillance teams was conducting routine monitoring of a senior militant leader when they suddenly noticed through their high-powered surveillance cameras two men breaking into the militant's apartment. The target was at Friday evening prayers at the local mosque. But rather than ransack the apartment and steal the computer equipment and other valuables while he was away—as any right-minded burglar would normally have done—one of the men pulled out a disk and loaded some programs onto the resident's laptop computer while the other man kept watch at the window. The whole operation took less than two minutes, then the two trespassers fled the way they came, leaving no trace that they had ever been there.

It did not take long for the official to determine that the two men were, in fact, Central Intelligence Agency (CIA) operatives conducting what is known in the U.S. intelligence community as either a "black bag job" or a "surreptitious entry" operation. Back in the Cold War, such a mission might have involved cracking safes, stealing code books, or photographing the settings on cipher machines. Today, this kind of break-in is known inside the CIA and National Security Agency as an "off-net operation," a clandestine human intelligence mission whose specific purpose is to surreptitiously gain access to the computer systems and email accounts of targets of high interest to America's spies. As we've learned in recent weeks, the National Security Agency's ability to electronically eavesdrop

from afar is massive. But it is not infinite. There are times when the agency cannot gain access to the computers or gadgets they'd like to listen in on. And so they call in the CIA's black bag crew for help.

The CIA's clandestine service is now conducting these sorts of black bag operations on behalf of the NSA, but at a tempo not seen since the height of the Cold War. Moreover, these missions, as well as a series of parallel signals intelligence (SIGINT) collection operations conducted by the CIA's Office of Technical Collection, have proven to be instrumental in facilitating and improving the NSA's SIGINT collection efforts in the years since the 9/11 terrorist attacks.

Over the past decade specially-trained CIA clandestine operators have mounted over one hundred extremely sensitive black bag jobs designed to penetrate foreign government and military communications and computer systems, as well as the computer systems of some of the world's largest foreign multinational corporations. Spyware software has been secretly planted in computer servers; secure telephone lines have been bugged; fiber optic cables, data switching centers and telephone exchanges have been tapped; and computer backup tapes and disks have been stolen or surreptitiously copied in these operations.

In other words, the CIA has become instrumental in setting up the shadowy surveillance dragnet that has now been thrown into public view. Sources within the U.S. intelligence community confirm that since 9/11, CIA clandestine operations have given the NSA access to a number of new and critically important targets around the world, especially in China and elsewhere in East Asia, as well as the Middle East, the Near East, and South Asia. (I'm not aware of any such operations here on U.S. soil.) In one particularly significant operation conducted a few years back in a strife-ridden South Asian nation, a team of CIA technical operations officers installed a sophisticated tap on a switching center servicing several fiber-optic cable trunk lines, which has allowed NSA to intercept in real time some of the most sensitive internal communications traffic by that country's general staff and top military commanders for the past several years. In another more recent case, CIA case officers broke into a home in Western Europe and surreptitiously loaded Agency-developed spyware into the personal computer of a man suspected of being a major recruiter for individuals wishing to fight with the militant group al-Nusra Front in Syria, allowing CIA operatives to read all of his email traffic and monitor his Skype calls on his computer.

The fact that the NSA and CIA now work so closely together is fascinating on a number of levels. But it's particularly remarkable accomplishment, given the fact that the two agencies until fairly recently hated each others' guts.

Critical Thinking

1. How did the CIA and NSA, once fierce rivals, develop a reciprocal relationship at the present time?

2. How does "spy software" operate within "black bag jobs"?

3. Why do some women feel they have a "special genius" for spying?

Create Central

www.mhhe.com/createcentral

Internet References

The Verge
www.theverge.com/2013/7/17/4532788/cia-black-bag-squads-get-data-the-old-fashioned-way

CIA Conducts over 100 Black Bag Jobs in Past Decade: *US Magazine*
http://english.cntv.cn/program/newsupdate/20130724/104107.shtml

With Bags of Cash, C.I.A. Seeks Influence in Afghanistan
www.nytimes.com/2013/04/29/world/asia/cia-delivers-cash-to-afghan-leaders-office.html?_r=0

MATTHEW M. AID is an amateur researcher and historian who figured out that for at least six years, the CIA and the Air Force had been withdrawing thousands of records from the public shelves—and that Archives officials had helped cover up their efforts. Mr. Aid's profession is as a corporate investigator.

Article   Prepared by: Caroline Shaffer Westerhof,
California National University for Advanced Studies

A Cautious Win in Egypt's Power Struggle

Bob Bowker from the Australian National University offers his insight into the unfolding power struggle between the Egyptian military and the Muslim Brotherhood.

BOB BOWKER

Learning Outcomes

After reading this article, you will be able to:

- Examine the role of the military within the political order of Egypt.

- Examine the role and the future of the Muslim Brotherhood within the political order of Egypt.

- Explain the military and the Muslim backlash within Egypt today, which Dr. Bowker did not project in 2112.

The power struggle between the Egyptian military and the Muslim Brotherhood saw a shift in favour of the latter on August 12.

That's when the recently elected president, Mohammed Morsy, sacked the commander in chief of the Egyptian Armed Forces, Field Marshall Tantawi; his chief of staff, General Anan; and the chiefs of the navy, air and air defence forces.

Morsy also reversed a constitutional decree issued by the Supreme Council of the Armed Forces (SCAF) on June 18, shortly before his victory in the presidential election run-off, which significantly reduced the power of the presidency in regard to defence matters and formally placed SCAF in a dominant legislative position. He appointed a judge believed to be sympathetic to the Brotherhood as his vice-president.

Since the lower house of the elected parliament was dissolved by SCAF after the Supreme Constitutional Court ruled the parliamentary election law unconstitutional, Morsy now holds all executive and legislative powers of state.

Morsy could recall the Brotherhood-dominated People's Assembly, but he does not need to do so ahead of the elections, which will follow the emergence of a new constitution and its passage in a referendum. Those processes are expected to be completed before the end of this year, but if the Constituent Assembly tasked with drafting the constitution is dissolved by the Administrative Judiciary Court, it will be Morsy who appoints a replacement, not SCAF.

Unless his moves are successfully challenged by the judicial system, Morsy has therefore taken a significant step towards asserting civilian control over the Egyptian military. He has set the framework for Egyptian politics in ways which the military will find difficult to change.

In making these moves, Morsy played his cards carefully. He appears to have seized an unexpected political opportunity which was created by popular frustration with the military leadership (and according to some reports, among the lower ranks of the officer corps) following an attack on an Egyptian post in the Sinai which saw the deaths of 16 policemen.

Shortly beforehand, he had replaced the editors of major state-owned newspapers with people viewed as compliant or sympathetic to the Muslim Brotherhood. A crackdown on other critical newspapers and broadcasters had also begun.

For its part, the ageing and incompetent Marshall Tantawi was hardly likely to be a rallying point for the military, and General Anan was disadvantaged by being seen as close to the United States. Morsy, however, did not challenge the very considerable depth of residual power enjoyed by the military beyond the political arena. Indeed, he appointed the removed service chiefs to civilian positions consistent with their seniority and experience—including as head of the Suez Canal Authority, as minister of state for military production, and as head of the Arab Organization for Industrialisation, the latter two of which are major revenue sources for the military.

Nor did Morsy give the military cause for concern about its immediate interests: Tantawi's departure was accorded a degree of formal dignity, and his replacement as defence minister, General Abdel-Fattah El-Sissy, had staunchly defended the abysmal human rights record of the military (including its 'virginity testing' of protesters) following the overthrow of the Mubarak regime. Anan's replacement as chief of staff, General Al-Assar, was a high-profile member of SCAF.

While it is clear that neither Morsy nor the military wanted to engage in a confrontation over the system in making or responding to these moves, the effect of the dismissals and appointments lies in its signalling to the military that civilian control over politics has begun. Morsy has initiated a process which will make those occupying senior military positions beholden to him, and those wishing to secure their careers will take note accordingly.

Whether Morsy will move to address corruption and other possible charges against the military for human rights abuses during the Mubarak era and in the revolutionary period remains to be seen. The whole issue of transitional justice and reconciliation has yet to be seriously addressed. At a minimum, however, he has now acquired a formidable bargaining card in that respect. It is also very unlikely that any future civilian government, Islamist or secular, would be willing to cede political power to the military, or to relinquish the power of a civilian president to determine senior military appointments.

While the political battlefield has been tilted in favour of the civilians as a result of the Brotherhood's moves, it is by no means certain that the Brotherhood has secured its long-term political dominance over the political scene as a whole.

The Brotherhood's performance in parliament was disappointing to many. Morsy won only narrowly against his secular opponent in the presidential election, largely because of divisions and abstentions among the voting public.

Popular frustration with the symptoms of a stagnant economy and failing electricity and other infrastructure will cost the Brotherhood at the polls. The bureaucracy remains resistant to reform, but seeking to address its failings and the influence of the military over the economy, business and regional government arrangements would be as challenging for an Islamist government as any other.

While the Brotherhood has presented itself as intent on achieving its social justice agenda through promoting business, and an immediate financial crisis appears to have been averted by receipt of substantial assistance from Qatar, its capacity to manage an economy beset by multiple structural problems remains open to question.

There are also serious doubts about the Brotherhood's capacity to attract and retain talent and experience in key areas such as the banking sector. The financial stringencies that any credible reform program will require will not sit easily with the Brotherhood's own rank and file, let alone with the Egyptian middle class and the wider public.

Egyptian political forces opposed to the Brotherhood face an unenviable choice between working with it in coalition, and reinforcing the Brotherhood's electoral prospects by helping it to achieve a measure of economic success, or seeking to regroup and contesting the forthcoming elections more successfully by attacking the government's record.

So far, the Brotherhood has not been able to draw in much talent from among Egypt's secular and liberal-minded political and intellectual elements: 18 of the 35 members of the newly appointed cabinet, and the prime minister himself, have connections to the disbanded National Democratic Party of the former regime.

The Brotherhood enjoys little popular trust. Some fear it will exploit its present political advantages to cement its grip on power through the constituent assembly and, if necessary, through repopulating the judiciary with judges of its choice. Its moves to limit press freedom are of obvious concern in that regard.

However, such an interpretation of the overall picture is unduly alarmist. The latest developments are part of an inevitable and necessary rebalancing of the relationship between the military and civil authorities, in which the Muslim Brotherhood has played its cards better than its opponent, but where the military is far from being a spent force.

Both sides still see more to be gained at this stage by avoiding a direct and open confrontation. Whether the Muslim Brotherhood emerges as the main beneficiary of that situation in the long-term, whether the checks and balances of a constitutional system will be allowed to function effectively in the medium term, and whether the calculations underlying the positions taken by the contending parties will remain unchanged in the short-term are all far from certain.

Critical Thinking

1. Can there be stabilization within the political order of Egypt?

2. How can democracy ever return to the political order within Egypt?

3. Why is the United States in a quandary with regard to its actions and relationship to Egypt?

Create Central

www.mhhe.com/createcentral

Internet References

Faculty of Arts Asia Institute—University of Melbourne
asiainstitute.unimelb.edu.au/

Mursi Ouster Rooted in Failure to Sprout Egypt Recovery—Bloomberg
www.bloomberg.com/news/2013-07-03/mursi-ouster-has-roots-in-unemployment.html

Egypt: An Islamist Insurrection?—*The Interpreter*
www.lowyinterpreter.org/post/2013/07/10/Egypt-An-Islamist-insurrection.aspx

A Cautious Win in Egypt's Power Struggle—*The Drum*
www.abc.net.au/unleashed/4200892.html

Bishop Suriel's Blog
bishopsuriel.blogspot.com

DR. BOB BOWKER was the Australian Ambassador to Egypt 2005–2008. He is presently a professor at the Australian National University.

Article

Prepared by: Caroline Shaffer Westerhof,
California National University for Advanced Studies

U.S. Army Learns Lessons in N. Korea-like War Game

PAUL MCLEARY

Learning Outcomes

After reading this article, you will be able to:

- Explain the concept and theory behind "war games."

- Explain the types of deployment models that can make war games a success.

- Explain why war games are a benefit to the Army's Training and Doctrine Command.

Washington—It took 56 days for the U.S. to flow two divisions' worth of soldiers into the failed nuclear-armed state of "North Brownland" and as many as 90,000 troops to deal with the country's nuclear stockpiles, a major U.S. Army war game concluded this winter.

The Unified Quest war game conducted this year by Army planners posited the collapse of a nuclear-armed, xenophobic, criminal family regime that had lorded over a closed society and inconveniently lost control over its nukes as it fell. Army leaders stayed mum about the model for the game, but all indications—and maps seen during the game at the Army War College—point to North Korea.

While American forces who staged in a neighboring friendly country to the south eventually made it over the border into North Brownland, they encountered several problems for which they struggled to find solutions. One of the first was that a large number of nuclear sites were in populated areas, so they had to try to perform humanitarian assistance operations while conducting combined arms maneuver and operations.

One way of doing this was to "use humanitarian assistance as a form of maneuver," Maj. Gen. Bill Hix, director of the Army's Concept Development and Learning Directorate, told reporters. The Army dropped humanitarian supplies a short distance from populated areas, drawing the population away from the objective sites, he explained.

Many of the problems encountered were hashed out with Army leaders at a Senior Leader Seminar on March 19 at Fort McNair in Washington. The event—which included the Army chief of staff, Gen. Ray Odierno, and the vice chief, Gen. John Campbell, along with a collection of three- and four-star generals—was off the record, but under terms of the agreement that allowed a handful of reporters to cover the event, unattributed quotes can be reported.

One of the major complications was that "technical ISR was not capable of closing the gap" caused by not having human intelligence assets in the country for years before the fight, one participant said. Also, "our ability to get north was hindered by our operational inflexibility," particularly when it comes to dropping troops into austere, contested areas.

To move soldiers quickly, Marine Corps V-22 Ospreys quickly inserted Army units deep behind enemy lines, but leaders found that inserting troops far in front of the main force so quickly often caused them to be surrounded, after which they had to be withdrawn.

Overall, the friendly force ultimately "failed to achieve the operational agility" it needed to succeed, another participant complained, "largely due to the rigidity" of current deployment models. What's more, the joint force was "able to get the force there quickly, but it was the technical force" that proved more difficult to deploy.

Another participant agreed, adding "the key challenge was timely access to joint enablers" such as ISR and counter-weapons of mass destruction units, which were desperately needed by the general-purpose ground units.

While not all lessons learned from the exercise were fully hashed out in this unclassified setting, some officers involved expressed their views of how the past decade of war has influenced how the Army prepares to fight.

"We've had the luxury in the last several wars of a place called Kuwait" from which to launch troops and stage equipment, one officer said. "I think our skills have atrophied in the call you get in the middle of the night," and in forcible-entry operations from the air and sea. Skills haven't been kept fresh in doing things such as loading trains full of equipment, and in setting up new command posts, he said.

Another leader agreed. "We have been spoiled by a command-and-control network that has been established for a decade" in Afghanistan and Iraq, he said, adding that the Army has to get back to training to operate in an austere environment.

One lesson from Iraq and Afghanistan, reinforced by the Unified Quest game, was that "we're not going to fight a pure military war again," one four-star general opined. Instead, being successful in conflict will require a variety of solutions requiring cultural knowledge, political acumen and other intelligence activities. The problem is, according to another officer, that the service needs to better understand the cultures in which it will fight, since "we tend to focus on the clash, when we need to focus on the will" of the local population.

Gen. Robert Cone, director of the Army's Training and Doctrine Command, said the difficulties the Army faces in moving troops and materiel around the battlefield again reinforced that "we have significant inter-service dependencies on our ability to move" and that any future fight will be a joint fight.

When asked about the potential for conflict in North Korea specifically, Cone said that while he thinks the forces the U.S. has today in South Korea "are adequate . . . the question is what forces are adequate for the problem of loose nukes?"

Critical Thinking

1. What kind of war games, if any, could model "loose nukes"?

2. What are the benefits of conducting the Unified Quest War Games?

3. What are lessons learned in the development of current deployment models?

Create Central

www.mhhe.com/createcentral

Internet References

North Korea Puts Troops on War Footing and Warns of "Horrible Disaster"—*TIME World*

    http://world.time.com/2013/10/08/north-korea-puts-troops-on-war-footing-and-warns-of-horrible-disaster/

USA Thinks North Korea Will Collapse And Lose Control of Its Nukes—*Oceans Vibe News*

    www.2oceansvibe.com/2013/03/27/usa-thinks-north-korea-will-collapse-and-lose-control-of-its-nukes/

Decision Point: Understanding the US's Dilemma over North Korea—*New York Times*

    http://learning.blogs.nytimes.com/2013/03/19/decision-point-understanding-u-s-s-dilemma-over-north-korea/

War Game Exposes Gaps for U.S. Army—*Defense News*

    www.defensenews.com/article/20130331/DEFREG02/303310003/

US Army Learns Lessons in N. Korea-like War Game—*Defense News*

    www.defensenews.com/article/20130326/DEFREG02/303260020/

PAUL MCLEARY is Land Warfare reporter for *Defense News*.

Prepared by: Caroline Shaffer Westerhof,
California National University for Advanced Studies

Article

What Caused the Economic Crisis?

The 15 best explanations for the Great Recession.

JACOB WEISBERG

Learning Outcomes

After reading this article, you will be able to:

- Understand the balance between free market capitalism and social protection.

- Understand why regulatory failures exist.

- Understand the bureaucracy of globalization and monetary policy in the face of economic crises.

As the financial crisis of 2008–09 draws to a close, narratives of the meltdown are flooding bookstores, think tanks are cranking out white papers, and four different congressional committees, along with the official Financial Crisis Inquiry Commission, are investigating what went wrong. Well they might, as the most basic question about the meltdown remains unsettled: Why did it happen?

The only near consensus is on the question of what triggered the not-quite-a-depression. In 2007, the housing bubble burst, leading to a high rate of defaults on subprime mortgages. Exposure to bad mortgages doomed Bear Stearns in March 2008, then led to a banking crisis that fall. A global recession became inevitable once the government decided not to rescue Lehman Bros. from default in September 2008. Lehman's was the biggest bankruptcy in history, and it led promptly to a powerful economic contraction. Somewhere around here, agreement ends.

There are no strong candidates for what logicians call a sufficient condition—a single factor that would have caused the crisis in the absence of any others. There are, however, a number of plausible necessary conditions—factors without which the crisis would not have occurred. Most analysts find former Fed Chairman Alan Greenspan at fault, though for a variety of reasons. Conservative economists—ever worried about inflation—tend to fault Greenspan for keeping interest rates too low between 2003 and 2005 as the real estate and credit bubbles inflated. This is the view, for instance, of Stanford economist and former Reagan adviser John Taylor, who argues that the Fed's easy money policies spurred a frenzy of irresponsible borrowing on the part of banks and consumers alike.

Liberal analysts, by contrast, are more likely to focus on the way Greenspan's aversion to regulation transformed pell-mell innovation in financial products and excessive bank leverage into lethal phenomena. The pithiest explanation I've seen comes from New York Times columnist and Nobel Laureate Paul Krugman, who noted in one interview: "Regulation didn't keep up with the system." In this view, the emergence of an unsupervised market in more and more exotic derivatives—credit-default swaps (CDSs), collateralized debt obligations (CDOs), CDSs on CDOs (the esoteric instruments that wrecked AIG)—allowed heedless financial institutions to put the whole financial system at risk. "Financial innovation + inadequate regulation = recipe for disaster" is also the favored explanation of Greenspan's successor, Ben Bernanke, who downplays low interest rates as a cause (perhaps because he supported them at the time) and attributes the crisis to regulatory failure.

A bit farther down on the list are various contributing factors, which didn't fundamentally cause the crisis but either enabled it or made it worse than it otherwise might have been. These include: global savings imbalances, which put upward pressure on U.S. asset prices and downward pressure on interest rates during the bubble years; conflicts of interest and massive misjudgments on the part of credit rating agencies Moody's and Standard and Poor's about the risks of mortgage-backed securities; the lack of transparency about the risks borne by banks, which used off-balance-sheet entities known as SIVs to hide what they were doing; excessive reliance on mathematical models like the VAR and the dread Gaussian copula function, which led to the underpricing of unpredictable forms of risk; a flawed model of executive compensation and implicit too-big-to-fail guarantees that encouraged traders and executives at financial firms to take on excessive risk; and the non-confidence-inspiring quality of former Treasury Secretary Hank Paulson's initial responses to the crisis.

Other analysts look to the underlying mindset that supported the meltdown. People like to say that the crisis was caused by shortsightedness, stupidity, and greed. But those are weak explanations, unless you think human nature somehow changed in the final decades of the 20th century to make people greedier or more foolish than they were previously. This isn't impossible, but it's hard to support. A subtler psychological argument is that the economy fell prey to recurring delusions about risk and bubbles, which economists Carmen Reinhart and Kenneth Rogoff describe in their book *This Time Is Different*. In another new book, *How Markets Fail*, New Yorker writer John Cassidy focuses on the fallacies of free-market fundamentalists (Greenspan again). Still other writers, like Nobel Prize winner Joseph Stiglitz in his new book, *Freefall*, point to the way globalization spread the toxicity from one country's mortgage market to the rest of the world. Not all such explanations fall according to ideological expectations. The polymathic conservative jurist Richard Posner, argues in his book *A Failure of Capitalism* that the free market itself is to blame for the recent troubles. What these "root causes" explanations have in common is that they don't lend themselves to practical solutions.

This survey leaves out various ideological and esoteric ideas about the cause of the crisis. Their reasons have shifted, but most libertarians and Wall Street Journal editorial page contributors continue to insist that government caused the whole ordeal. In *I.O.U.*, the only truly entertaining book of the many I've now read or browsed on the subject, British writer John Lanchester tosses out the theory that after the West won the Cold War, capitalism could go naked, because governments no longer had to worry about winning converts away from Communism. This is a fascinating idea about the crisis with no evidence whatsoever to support it.

Historians are still debating what caused the Great Depression, so it's not likely this argument will be settled anytime soon. But if we haven't at least learned that our financial markets need stronger regulatory supervision and better controls to prevent bad bets by big firms from going viral, we'll be back in the same place before you can say 30 times leverage.

Critical Thinking

1. What causes regulatory failure?

2. Is regulatory failure due to ineptitude in the bureaucracy, misunderstandings of people, or other circumstances?

3. How does the author expect that the individual "bureaucratic infrastructure across countries in the European Union. . . ." can "adopt labor market reforms . . ." to save the euro?

Create Central

www.mhhe.com/createcentral

Internet References

What Caused the Economic Crisis?—*Slate*
www.slate.com/articles/news_and_politics/the_big_idea/2010/01/what_caused_the_economic_crisis.html

Not Enough House Votes to Pass a Clean CR?—MSNBC
http://video.msnbc.msn.com/now/53209279#53209279

Blaming Rubin—*Reuters*
blogs.reuters.com/felix-salmon/2010/05/01/

What Caused the Financial Crisis?—Marginal Revolution
http://marginalrevolution.com/marginalrevolution/2008/10/what-caused-the.html

JACOB WEISBERG is chairman and editor-in-chief of The Slate Group.

Prepared by: Caroline Shaffer Westerhof,
California National University for Advanced Studies

Article

Rumors of Central Command's Decline are Wishful Thinking

RICHARD L. RUSSELL

Learning Outcomes

After reading this article, you will be able to:

- Examine the actions and issues of sequestration regarding the Central Command's "rumored" decline.

- Examine the role and actions of Central Command in the wake of the September 11, 2001, attacks on the World Trade Center and the Pentagon.

- Understand the lack of security intelligence in Central Command trying to put into place a secure environment conducive to the nurturing of a democratic government in Kabul.

Disclaimer: The views expressed are those of the author alone and do not reflect the policy or position of the U.S. government, the Department of Defense, the National Defense University, or Central Command.

Central Command's Marine four-star combatant commander James Mattis passed the command flag to Army four-star General Lloyd Austin in Tampa, Florida on 22 March. Mattis was widely known for his battlefield tenacity in the 2003 Iraq invasion and Austin is known for ably ending in 2011 American combat operations in Iraq leaving some wondering if Central Command's time in the American national security limelight after the drawdown in Afghanistan in 2014 will be at its end. And the hearing of sharpening of sequester budgetary knives up in Washington on Capitol Hill, in the White House, and across the Potomac River in the Pentagon aren't calming any rumors of Central Command's decline.

The sharpening is reminiscent of that heard in the early 1990s during the Clinton administration. International relations optimists wanted to reap huge "peace dividends" by slashing the defense budget because a "democratic peace" was going to characterize the post-Cold War world. The subsequent decades of international conflict should have sobered the democratic peace enthusiasts, but they are at it again. Today, they are arguing that the drawdowns of American forces in Iraq and soon in Afghanistan are now offering a window of opportunity to reap significant defense budget savings by slashing the armed forces and the U.S. Central Command in charge of military operations in the Middle East and South Asia. These policymakers and lawmakers ought to think again to avoid being "penny wise and pound foolish."

A bit of military history is in order for a wiser perspective on current and future defense strategy challenges. Central Command has come a long way since its humble beginnings and has had to mount a wide range of military interventions in the Middle East and South Asia over the last three decades. It grew from a rapid reaction force into a command during the Cold War to deter the Soviet Union from a feared military drive through Iran to the warm water ports of the Arabian Gulf for the projection of Soviet naval power. As the Cold War wound down, it shifted attention from keeping the Soviets out of the Gulf to balancing the Arab Gulf states against Iran, which threatened off and on to defeat Iraq during the Iran-Iraq war from 1980–1988. The simmering naval war with Iranian forces in the Gulf had not halted for two years before Central Command had to take the lead for a military campaign to liberate Kuwait from Iraqi forces. Central Command had to again jump from the pan into the fire after the tragic 11 September 2001 attacks which necessitated waging war against the Taliban and al Qaeda in Afghanistan and, by subsequent turn of events, marching on to Baghdad. Subsequently the command worked to provide stable security environments in both Afghanistan and Iraq for transitions to polities that looked more like democracy.

American policy makers, military men and women, and the American public writ large have been exhausted by the last decade of war in Central Command's area-of-responsibility. Many commentators clamor for the complete withdraw of American troops from Afghanistan after 2014 much like has been done in Iraq in 2011. President Obama himself appears ready to "wash his hands" of the region and his administration has been making great noises about shifting or pivoting America's strategic attention to Asia. If the Middle East and South Asia in Central Command's purview is seen by many as the lands of death, destruction, and misery, the lands of Asia under Pacific Command's watch, in the minds of many, are the lands of plenty, opportunity, and optimism.

But the reports of Central Command's decline and demise are grossly exaggerated. No matter how much Americans would like to turn our backs on problems and conflicts of the Middle East and South Asia, the more we do the more will we be stabbed in our backs. The grim reality is that Middle East and South Asia will a the cross roads of many of the world's ills at odds with American strategic interests to regrettably give Central Command more than its fair share of security burdens year—and even decades—after our 2014 drawdown in Afghanistan.

The Command's Pick-Up Warfare Game Past

Most people have long since forgotten, but the rationale for an American military command for the Middle East and South Asia stemmed from the Cold War rivalry with the Soviet Union. The Carter administration was especially alarmed by the 1979 Soviet invasion of Afghanistan. It worried that the Soviets, if left undeterred, could take a similar gamble and invade Iran to gain access for the Soviet Navy to the warm water ports of the Arabian Gulf. The Carter administration also was gravely concerned that the Iranian revolution had deprived American security policy of one of its great nation-state regional security pillars, making the Gulf all the more vulnerable to Soviet aggression.

The Carter administration undertook two important steps to deter the Soviets from Iran and the Gulf. It announced what came to be known as the Carter Doctrine, stating that, "An attempt by any outside force to gain control of the Persian Gulf region will be regarded as an assault on the vital interests of the United States of America, and such an assault will be repelled by any means necessary, including military force." The doctrine mentioned by all means necessary, which seemed to include the threat of American nuclear weapons. The Carter administration complemented the nuclear threat with conventional force projection capabilities with the establishment in 1980 of the Rapid Deployment Joint Task Force.[1] After the hostage rescue debacle in Iran, the United States turned in earnest to bolster both special operations and traditional military and force projection capabilities into the Middle East and Southwest Asia with the creation of the Central Command.[2]

The American military's sluggish bureaucratic inertia kept Central Command as "an odd man out" even though the command was waging low intensity conflict throughout the 1980s. All the honor, prestige, and promotions seemed to go to American general and flag officers assigned to European Command and NATO, even though a cold peace prevailed in Europe while their peers were in command of shooting conflicts with Iranian forces in the Middle East. Iran was aiding and abetting Hezbollah surrogate bombings and hostage taking of Americans in Lebanon with impunity while mounting naval guerrilla warfare against oil tankers in the Arabian Gulf being escorted by American and allied ships during the Iran-Iraq war. The Iranians harassed international oil shipping and American and coalition forces by laying mine fields and mounting hit-and-run attacks with Revolutionary Guard naval forces.

The American military built and deployed in the European theater to deter and fight the Soviet and Warsaw Pact militaries came in handy for Central Command in 1990 when Saddam Hussein ordered Iraq military forces to invade Kuwait. The forces and doctrine developed for waging war in temperate European theater proved applicable for fighting in the deserts in and around Kuwait. The Americans surged more than 500,000 troops to Saudi Arabia as the jumping off point for liberating Kuwait. The qualitatively better-trained and equipped American military outclassed the numerically superior and largely Soviet-supplied Iraqi military.

The American-led coalition's decisive battlefield besting of the Iraqi military gave birth to heralds of a "revolution in military affairs." They praised battlefield performances dominated by air power and informed by computers, communications, and intelligence. That enthusiasm dwindled in the years after the war after the awakening of ethnic conflict in the Balkans in the 1990s. Many downgraded expectations for battlefield technology and spoke of the "evolution in military affairs." Central Command spent the 1990s broadening and deepening its military support nodes in the Gulf beyond Saudi Arabia and Bahrain as it policed Saddam's Iraq and its largely non-compliance with the terms of the 1991 ceasefire and through Saddam's ejection of United Nations weapons inspectors from his country in 1998.

From Simmering to Hot Wars

Central Command was back front and center in American defense policy strategy in the wake of the 11 September 2001 al Qaeda attacks on the U.S. homeland that killed more than 3,000 people. If anyone had predicted anytime before that fateful year that the United States would one day dispatch up to 160,000 troops to Afghanistan, they would have been declared insane. But that is where American soldiers found themselves overthrowing the Taliban regime, destroying al Qaeda's leadership and infrastructure, and struggling to put into place a security environment conducive to the nurturing of a democratic government in Kabul.

The American military struggled for years, grappling with Afghanistan's security landscape. The military has imprudently turned-over the generals leading the war effort too rapidly, averaging about one per year. Commanding generals barely had enough time to get their bearings before they were dispatched to their next assignment. The American war effort in Afghanistan too was a struggle within the army between the "big army" advocates who focused on using "kinetics" to kill enemies and the "small army" adherents struggling to nudge an institution indoctrinated for fighting similarly organized and equipped militaries to mount a counter-insurgency campaign. The latter focused less on kinetics and more on providing security for the Afghan civilian population.

The struggle for the "hearts and minds" of the Afghan people—as well as for the American army's leadership—played out too in the parallel war in Iraq launched in 2003. President George W. Bush harnessed the political capital he gained in a politically unified United States in the ruins of the 9/11 attacks to order Central Command to oust Saddam Hussein's regime in Baghdad. Bush was shocked, as was the American public, that despite the pre-war American intelligence warnings about Iraq's reconstitution of its biological, chemical, and nuclear weapons programs, all of them were subsequently discovered to have remained in a shambles since the 1991 war. If the United States had launched the war guided by abysmal intelligence, at least the United States and the United Kingdom which bore the brunt of ground combat had given the Iraqi people a window of opportunity to seek a better future for themselves than they had under Saddam's heinous reign.

Talk of the Command's Future Decline Grossly Exaggerated

More than a decade of war in Central Command's strategic neighborhood has taken its toll on the United States. The wars in Afghanistan and Iraq have lasted longer than the American involvement in the World Wars, Korea, or Vietnam. We tragically have lost more than six thousand men and women in uniform, and thousands have been wounded. The men and women remaining in service are suffering as evident by broken military families burdened by seemingly endless combat tours and alarming suicide rates. We have spent hundreds of billions of dollars on the wars and have worn out our military hardware, to include tanks, infantry fighting vehicles, trucks, fixed-wing aircraft, helicopters, ships, and the like. The United States, its leadership and people, are looking to Central Command's area-of-responsibility and are collectively sighing: "Enough."

President Obama does not say it in public, but one certainly could read it "between the lines" when his administration announces its determination to strategically pivot to Asia. The United States is weary from the chronic problems and pessimism of the Middle East and South Asia and wants to geographically turn around to face and embrace the seemingly endless economic opportunities and optimism offered by the "Asian Tigers" and rising China. This worldview focus on Asia will come into sharper focus as the United States in years ahead starts making some dramatic and drastic strategic and military tradeoffs in order to make budgetary ends and means match in the Pentagon.

Nevertheless, the idea that the United States could simply walk away from the Middle East and South Asia for the sake of interests in Asia is simply an illusion. The United States is going to have to be prepared to wage the full spectrum of war in Central Command's area-of-responsibility whether it likes it or not. Central Command has had to militarily intervene in the Middle East and South Asia over the course of decades with direct action special operations, counter-terrorist operations, naval escort and mine clearing, surface-to-surface naval combat, air reconnaissance and policing no-fly zones, retaliatory and punitive aircraft and cruise missile strikes, hostage rescue missions, establishing sanctuary and safe haven for humanitarian assistance delivery, and for waging high intensity state-to-state warfare.

Central Command has performed these broad ranging and diversified types of operations in the past and undoubtedly, and regrettably, will have to dip into the full spectrum of warfare toolkit in the future. It cannot be stressed enough, however, that a consistent trend has emerged throughout our three decades of conflict in the Middle East and South Asia. We have never have been able to predict what kind of fight the next one will be. Consequently, Central Command will have to plan and prepare contingency plans for the full spectrum of military intervention and war.

Far too much of the world's energy wealth—and power derived from it—are married to the most acute security problems on the globe in Central Command's region. These threats stem from Islamic militancy exercised by terrorist and insurgent groups the likes of al Qaeda and the Taliban, as well as by the leaderships emerging in the post-Arab spring regimes—influenced or controlled by Salafists, Hamas, Hezbollah, or the Muslim Brotherhood. Other threats will stem from ethnic and religious conflict, and the proliferation of chemical, biological, and nuclear weapons. If the United States and its Central Command will continue to be embattled by these threats, Israel increasingly will find itself under outright siege. All of these problems, moreover, are growing in scope and magnitude at a time when the world is seemingly getting smaller with globalization and the revolutions in global travel, computers, and communications. To put it bluntly, what happens in Vegas may stay in Vegas. But what happens in the Middle East and South Asia spreads to the world.

Notes

1. Lawrence Freedman, *A Choice of Enemies: America Confronts the Middle East* (New York: PublicAffairs, 2008), 103–104.

2. For an excellent scholar-practitioner's account of the creation of Central Command, see William E. Odom, "The Cold War Origins of the U.S. Central Command," *Journal of Cold War Studies*, Vol. 8, No. 2 (Spring 2006).

Critical Thinking

1. Challenge the concept that current and future defense interventions are winding down.
2. What was the basis for the Carter doctrine?
3. How do the military and the administration look upon the importance of Central Command when we live today in a world that is "seemingly getting smaller with globalization, global travel, revolutions in computer technology and communications"?

Create Central

www.mhhe.com/createcentral

Internet References

U.S. Central Command
http://centcom.ahp.us.army.mil/en/about-centcom/posture-statement

Rumors of Central Command's Decline are Wishful Thinking—Small Wars Journal

http://smallwarsjournal.com/jrnl/art/rumors-of-central-command%E2%80%99s-decline-are-wishful-thinking

Former Commander of U.S. Central Command Cautions against U.S. Military Involvement in Syria without an Endgame—CNN

http://security.blogs.cnn.com/2013/07/21/former-commander-of-us-central-command-cautions-against-u-s-military-involvement-in-syria-without-an-endgame/

U.S. Military Assistance for Africa: A Better Solution—The Heritage Foundation

www.heritage.org/research/reports/2003/10/us-military-assistance-for-africa-a-better-solution

U.S. Military Bases: a Global Footprint—Geopolitical Monitor

www.geopoliticalmonitor.com/us-military-bases-a-global-footprint-3138/liked/

Dr. Richard L. Russell is Professor of National Security Affairs at the Near East and South Asia Center for Strategic Studies.

Article

Prepared by: Caroline Shaffer Westerhof,
California National University for Advanced Studies

The Revenge of Force Planning

MACKUBIN THOMAS OWENS

Learning Outcomes

After reading this article, you will be able to:

- Understand the future of force planning.

- Understand the strategy of the force planner.

A decade of war has obscured the importance of "force planning," a complex, interactive, inter-temporal art intended to ensure that today's operational and strategic demands are being met while preparing for a future that may resemble the present or differ from it in unexpected ways. The objective of *force planning* is to create a *future force structure* of the *right size* and the *right composition* (force mix) to achieve the nation's *security goals,* in light of the *security environment* and *resource constraints.* In essence, the force planner must answer two questions. First, what *capabilities* do we need to fulfill the requirements of our strategy, in light of the security environment? Second, what is the appropriate size of the force—in other words, *how much is enough?*

Although former Secretary of Defense Donald Rumsfeld's Pentagon attempted to both fight today's wars and "transform" the force at the same time, the emphasis unsurprisingly shifted over time to the latter. Today's force is not only worn out but also perhaps mismatched to an emerging security environment. Thus, as the wars of the last decade wind down, it is time to return force planning to its central place in overall defense planning.

In theory, force planning is a very logical process that flows from the choice of a *strategy.* To implement the chosen strategy, the force planner identifies the *strategic requirements—the military tasks required by the strategy*—that must be fulfilled to implement the strategy and the *operational challenges*—the obstacles—that must be overcome. To overcome these operational challenges and fulfill the strategy-driven requirements, military planners develop *operational concepts* and identify the necessary *military capabilities.* These operational concepts

and required military capabilities help the planner identify the characteristics of the force and drive the acquisition of forces and equipment. Throughout the process, the planner must constantly evaluate any risk that may be created by a potential ends-means mismatch.

Today, U.S. force planning is complicated by several factors: uncertainty about the future security environment; the lack of any real strategic guidance on the part of the Obama Administration to address this uncertainty, and the precipitous decline in U.S. defense spending. To paraphrase the Cheshire cat's comment to Alice, if you don't know where you're going, any road will get you there. A clear conception of strategic ends and the challenges thrown up by the security environment is necessary to minimize the adverse impact of declining resources for defense.

The uncertain security environment requires that the United States be prepared to confront a wide range of adversaries across the spectrum of conflict. At one end of the spectrum is the potential threat to U.S. security by the rise of China. Indeed, the similarities between the cases of Wilhelmine Germany and Great Britain at the turn of the twentieth century, and China and the United States today are compelling. At the other end of the spectrum lies what we confronted in Iraq and Afghanistan, an environment in which our opponents rely on asymmetric, low-tech tactics and networks of people rather than networks of state-of-the-art weapon systems.

Notwithstanding the failure of the Obama Administration to provide strategic guidance, it is possible for planners to infer what must be done by turning to strategy in general as a guide to force planning. Strategy is designed to secure national interests and to attain the objectives of national policy by the application of force or threat of force. Strategy is dynamic, changing as the factors that influence it change. Potential mismatches between ends and means create risks. If the risks resulting from an ends-means mismatch cannot be managed, ends must be reevaluated and scaled back, means must be increased, or strategy must be adjusted. Until the advent of the Obama administration, U.S. presidents took it for granted that the goal of American strategy was to underwrite a liberal world order (free trade, freedom of navigation, liberal governance) by providing the "public good" of global security, while preventing the emergence of a rival seeking to undermine such a liberal world order.

At a minimum, the United States must maintain a force capable of accomplishing certain military tasks: to *defend the territory of the United States* and its strategic approaches against attack, seizure, or interdiction by protecting against a *terrorist attack or missile strike* against U.S. territory, and to *threaten the sanctuaries of would be attackers,* whether state or non-state actors.

Thus, U.S. forces are required to *project and sustain power at great distances* from the continental United States, *shape the security environment* by means of forward presence, reassuring friends and allies and deterring adversaries, and in the event that deterrence fails, *defeat an adversary* in one or more theaters. The major problem U.S. planners face today is that the proliferation of militarily useful technology means that the operational environment will be far less permissive than it has been in the past.

Operational challenges that U.S. force are likely to face in the future include: confronting a wide range of adversaries in a complex battle-space; the absence of access to forward bases and the resulting "tyranny of distance" that U.S. force must overcome to project power; the likely adoption of asymmetrical anti-access strategies (area denial/ anti-access, or AD/A2) by potential adversaries resulting from the proliferation of militarily useful technology; maintaining our own information security while degrading that of an adversary; dealing with the effects of weapons of mass destruction/effects and the necessity of contending with mass population problems such as operations in urban terrain, refugees, and epidemics.

To overcome these operational challenges, U.S. planners need to develop operational concepts and military capabilities that will permit the United States to achieve its goals. For

instance, to overcome the tyranny of distance and project power against an adversary's sanctuary in the face of AD/A2 threats, the United States must be able to dominate the world's commons, especially sea, space, and cyberspace and prevail in the world's contested littorals. The U.S. military must be able to execute operations at intercontinental distances, conduct long-range precision strikes while protecting its forces against ballistic and cruise missile attack; continue to exploit stealth technology in order to perform operations based on stealthy, extended-range, unmanned system-dominated air warfare; and carry out distributed, deep-strike, non-linear ground operations, as well as submersible, distributed, sea-based power projection—both strike and amphibious. But flexibility is critical. As the American experience in Iraq and Afghanistan illustrated, the United States does not always get to choose the area of military competition.

Critical Thinking

1. To what degree does force planning flow from the choice of a strategy?
2. Discuss the quandary affecting the uncertain security environment that requires that the United States to be prepared to confront a global range of adversaries.
3. Understand the inherent difficulties of military opponents that do not rely on networks of state-of-the-art weapon systems.

Internet References

Air Power, National Military Strategy and Policy
www.ausairpower.net/strategy.html

Army's 2014 modernization plan prioritizes Soldiers in fight
www.army.mil/article/104115/

2014 Budget Looks to Balance Ends, Ways, Means, Hagel Says
www.defense.gov/news/newsarticle.aspx?id=119787

MACKUBIN "MAC" OWENS is editor of *Orbis,* FPRI's quarterly journal of international affairs, and Senior Fellow at its Program on National Security. He is also Professor of National Security Affairs at the Naval War College in Newport, Rhode Island.

Prepared by: Caroline Shaffer Westerhof,
California National University for Advanced Studies

Article

We Shall Return

Don't be too sure there won't be another U.S. war in the Middle East.

RICHARD L. RUSSELL

Learning Outcomes

After reading this article, you will be able to:

- Explain the future of conflict and the implications for the Army.
- Explain Secretary of Defense Robert Gates' term, "next-war-it is."
- Explain how the Army can, and whether it will, adapt its practices and culture to 21st century strategic realities.

Shortly before he left office in February 2011, Defense Secretary Robert Gates told West Point cadets that "in my opinion, any future defense secretary who advised the president to again send a big American land army into Asia or into the Middle East or Africa should 'have his head examined,' as General MacArthur so delicately put it." The remark no doubt reflected Secretary Gates's fatigue and frustration from the enormous intellectual and emotional burdens associated with overseeing the wars in Iraq and Afghanistan.

One suspects, however, that in a more reflective moment, Gates would have acknowledged that "never say never" is a wise rule of thumb in planning for military contingencies, especially in the region that makes up Central Command's area of responsibility. Few, for example, predicted the 1979 Soviet invasion of Afghanistan. Gates himself—who was a senior CIA official during the covert war supporting the Afghan resistance—surely did not anticipate then that the United States would have to return to Afghanistan two decades later to oust a Taliban regime that was harboring terrorists. Before 1990, moreover, no one predicted that Iraq, having just ended a bitter eight-year war with Iran, would swing its battered forces south to invade Kuwait.

So if it's conventional wisdom that the United States will not, or should not, intervene militarily in the Middle East or South Asia after it draws down forces in Iraq and Afghanistan, it's also likely dead wrong. What is true, however, is that political and military trajectories in the Middle East and South Asia are likely to increasingly challenge U.S. contingency access in the coming decade. The ability for the United States to surge large-scale forces into the region, as it did in the 1990 and 2003 wars against Iraq, will grow increasingly circumscribed. The United States will have to adapt to this new strategic landscape by developing more nimble, highly-mobile, stealthy, and networked forces, and by abandoning the traditional practice of slowly and steadily building up conventional forces at regional logistic hubs prior to launching war.

Perhaps the most significant factor that portends against further intervention in the Middle East and South Asia is increased political resistance—and outright opposition—from the countries in the region. That resistance is likely to come from the new regimes emerging from the Arab uprisings, as well as a number of Gulf monarchies.

Indeed, the political trends in the region are unlikely to conform to the rosy predictions of democratic peace theorists, whose musings have implicitly informed the security policies of both Republican and Democratic administrations for decades. Old authoritarian regimes seem to be passing the way of the dodo bird, but the new regimes taking shape are heavily influenced by militant Islamic ideology that will make them less likely to engage in security or military cooperation with the United States.

Democracy optimists argue that these ideological regimes, once entrenched in power, will have to moderate their zeal in order to govern. Pragmatism will ultimately trump ideology. That line of reasoning, however, is based on the assumption that the policy decisions of such regimes can be explained by rational choice economic theory. In other words, if they want to attract international capital and participate in the world economy, they are going to have to break with their ideological affinities. But that reasoning ignores a hard fact of international politics: that time and again, political and ideological prerogatives trump economic rationality. It made little economic sense, for example, for Pakistan to pursue a nuclear weapons program in the 1970s, just as it makes little economic sense for Iran to do so today. Clearly, both Pakistan and Iran made major policy decisions based on political-military priorities rather than economic calculations.

As for the surviving monarchies in the Middle East, they too will likely be less accommodating to American military forces than they have been in the past. To be sure, much of the Arab support for past American military operations—like both Iraq wars—was hidden from the public eye. Arab states often loudly and publicly denounced "unilateral American" military action in the region at the same time as they supported it in backroom dealings, quietly authorizing facilities support and air, land, and sea access.

But if Arab Gulf states were quietly supportive in the past, their opposition to American military force is likely to grow in the future. They read the aftermath of the Arab uprisings much differently than did American and European policymakers. The Gulf monarchies were shocked that the United States "abandoned" Egyptian President Hosni Mubarak in his time of need in early 2011. Their leaders expected the United States to push for Mubarak and the Egyptian military to crack down on public protests in Cairo. After all, American policymakers during the Carter administration had at least given this policy option consideration during the Iranian revolution in 1979.

Already, several Gulf states have begun to translate their displeasure into policy independence from Washington. In 2011, for example, a coalition of Gulf states led by Saudi Arabia intervened in Bahrain to quell domestic unrest in the island country. They did so under the banner of the Gulf Cooperation Council (GCC), which for years had been a feckless military force. Largely unnoticed in Western commentary was that the GCC, for the first time in its history, mounted a relatively effective military intervention.

Bahrain today is for all intents and purposes a province of Saudi Arabia, even if it is not polite to say so in diplomatic circles. Since the Iranian revolution, Bahrain—like the United Arab Emirates, Kuwait, Oman, and Qatar—has pursued close ties with the United States, in significant measure to counterbalance Iran and Saudi Arabia. With Washington at their back, they were able to stake out security policies that were at least nominally independent from Saudi Arabia. When Saudi Arabia wanted American forces removed from the kingdom, for example, Qatar was eager to compensate by hosting a more robust American command presence in the region.

The Arab uprisings and subsequent GCC intervention in Bahrain have turned the tables, making Saudi security backing a necessity for the smaller Gulf monarchies. From their perspective, American forces are clearly more capable than Saudi forces, but given the alignment of their interests, Riyadh is a more reliable security partner. Gulf leaders and military commanders in the coming decade will be focused on how to avoid following in Mubarak's footsteps. Part of minimizing that risk will involve decreasing security dependency on the United States. Gulf leaders have to worry that if push comes to shove, the Americans will throw them under a bus just like they did to Mubarak.

★ ★ ★

If the political dynamics in the Middle East and South Asia do not favor further American military intervention in the future, neither do the emerging military trends. The proliferation of supersonic cruise missiles and mines in the region will make for nasty forced entries into narrow maritime confines like the Suez Canal, the Red Sea, and the Persian Gulf.

But the likely proliferation of nuclear weapons—and ballistic missile delivery systems—will pose even more formidable challenges to conventional military surges in the region. In the future, the United States will not be able to take for granted unchallenged surges of naval, air, and ground forces into regional theaters via logistics hubs. These hubs—like the American naval presence in Bahrain—are large, readily identifiable, and will be increasingly vulnerable to future targeting by nuclear weaponry.

Iran's nuclear weapons, assuming it gets them, will pose a direct threat to American military surge capabilities. Although American policymakers and military commanders might feel confident that they could surge forces into the Gulf despite Iranian nuclear threats because of the American nuclear deterrent, Gulf security partners might be more nervous and less willing to cooperate. As a result, they might not grant access to U.S. air, naval, and ground forces out of fear of angering Iran.

American observers who doubt that Gulf states would make such calculations should recall how Kuwait responded in the lead-up to Iraq's invasion in 1990. When faced with a build-up of Iraqi forces along its border, Kuwait decided not to mobilize its military out of fear that the move would provoke Saddam Hussein. The incentives for Gulf states to make similar strategic calculations in the future will be greater when Iran has an inventory of nuclear weapons to match its growing ballistic missile capabilities.

The Gulf states, moreover, will likely reason that the U.S. capability to threaten or use force against a nuclear Iran will be significantly diminished. Even without nuclear weapons, Gulf states have seen, in their view, a long history of American reluctance to threaten or use force against Iran. For example, the United States took no direct military action against Iran after it aided and abetted Hezbollah bombings against Americans in Lebanon in the 1980s, after Iran supported the bombing of Khobar Towers in Saudi Arabia in 1996, or even after Iran supported the deadly campaign of improvised explosive devices (IEDs) against U.S. troops in Iraq. Gulf states will no doubt judge that if the United States was unable and unwilling to attack Tehran under these circumstances, then it is certainly not going to attack Iran in the future, when it will be able to retaliate with nuclear weapons.

American policymakers may counter that Iran would never be foolish enough to threaten or use nuclear weapons against the United States, given its robust nuclear deterrence posture. But the threat or use of nuclear weapons might not look so foolish from Iran's perspective. One of the great strategic lessons drawn from the long history of conflict in the Middle East is this: Do not go to war without nuclear weapons, as Saddam Hussein did when he invaded Kuwait. The corollary is: Do not allow the United States to methodically build up forces in the Gulf prior to invading, as Saddam did both in the run-up to the 1991 re-conquest of Kuwait and in 2003, before the drive to topple the regime in Baghdad.

Drawing upon these lessons, Iran will likely do everything in its power to deny the United States the ability to surge conventional forces into the region—and that might include threatening to target U.S. forces with nuclear weapons. Iran might accept the risk that preemptive use of nuclear weapons could bring on American nuclear retaliation, because failure to do so would mean certain destruction for the regime. The United States would be able to build up conventional forces in the region and oust Iran's leaders just as it did in Baghdad.

This line of strategic reasoning runs counter to conventional wisdom in the West, but we actually know little or nothing about what Iranian decision-makers think about nuclear weapons or deterrence theory. Since the Iranian revolution in 1979, opportunities for the exchange of professional views between Western and Iranian scholars, policymakers, and military leaders on these critically important issues have been extremely limited. Therefore, it's not unreasonable to assume that the Iranians, like American policymakers in the early stages of developing their nuclear triad doctrine, will think of nuclear weapons as merely "big artillery." Unfortunately, the United States and its security partners lack formal and informal exchanges with the Iranians akin to the Cold War discussions and arms control negotiations between the Americans and Soviets, which allowed both parties to develop mutual understandings of the other's perception of nuclear weapons. These understandings were essential for crisis management in the Cold War strategic relationship after the Cuban missile crisis.

Meanwhile, the Gulf states, led by Saudi Arabia, are likely to look for their own nuclear deterrents. Much like France wanted its own nuclear *force de frappe* during the Cold War, the Gulf states will want their own nuclear weapons to deter Iran. Saudi Arabia and the smaller Gulf states will worry that the United States would be deterred from coming to their defense in future regional crises by Iran's nuclear weapons.

Saudi Arabia and other Arab states are likely to see nuclear weapons as a quick fix for all of their security woes. Although they have been on a shopping spree in the past decade, buying expensive and sophisticated Western military technology, they have had a tough time absorbing the new technology and fully utilizing and integrating weapons systems. To be sure, in a rough net assessment, Saudi Arabia and its allies in the Gulf have significantly greater conventional capabilities than Iran. But if Iran goes nuclear, they will want to follow suit.

★ ★ ★

Americans may be weary of conflict in the Middle East and South Asia, but strategic prudence demands that we contemplate future military interventions in the Central Command theater. A scan of the horizon reveals that both political and military trends in the region pose formidable obstacles to conventional force surges into the region.

But there is another wrinkle in this story that U.S. policymakers must contend with as they plan for the future. As Gulf monarchies seek to reduce their dependence on American military power, they will increasingly look to China for security assurances. China does not have a political agenda devoted to promoting democratization, and it maintains political and diplomatic ties with both Arab states and Iran. China's military activity in the region is modest but increasing, as evidenced by its recent peacekeeping dispatches to the region and naval port visits in the Gulf. Beijing is likely to send more naval forces to the Gulf to increase its presence there and enhance its ability to protect the sea lanes which bring oil to China's thirsty

economy. China is keenly aware that the United States has naval supremacy in the Gulf, but will be working to erode that strategic edge in the future.

Faced with these realities, there is a need for new thinking and innovative conceptualizations of surges into Centcom's area of responsibility. Theater campaign planners will have to think about contingencies in which the United States cannot slowly and methodically build up forces in the region and then kick off campaigns after most troops, arms, and equipment are in place. Future U.S. force build-ups in the region will be far too vulnerable to preemptive nuclear strikes. As a result, planners will have to devise campaign plans in which the insertion of U.S. military forces begins with an immediate rolling and flowing start. The United States will have to work from smaller troop footprints and be prepared to start fighting even as follow-on forces are on the way. Ideally, these forces would flow from multiple staging positions to reduce vulnerability to nuclear attack. The politics of the region, however, will work against securing a multitude of staging areas from which to deploy.

The region under the purview of Centcom has always been riddled with political violence that has posed formidable challenges to military operations. But in plotting a course over the horizon, the political and military obstacles for American military surges into the region are poised to grow even larger. As a result, theater contingency planners will have fewer good options for projecting American military power into the region—and they'll have to do more with the bad and the ugly.

Critical Thinking

1. How must the military service change to empower its leaders in the 21st century?

2. How has the Army, as an institution, been transformed by war?

3. Critique the meaning of the quote from the Revolutionary War that Secretary of Defense Gates often refers to: In a letter Abigail Adams wrote to her son, John Quincy Adams, "these are times in which a genius would wish to live. It is not in the still calm of life or in the repose of a pacific station that great characters are formed . . . great necessities call out great virtues."

Create Central

www.mhhe.com/createcentral

Internet References

U.S. Department of Defense—Speech
www.defense.gov/speeches/speech.aspx?speechid51539
Interview with Former Defense Secretary Robert Gates—CNN
transcripts.cnn.com/TRANSCRIPTS/1306/26/ampr.01.html
Robert M. Gates—*New York Times*
http://topics.nytimes.com/top/reference/timestopics/people/g/robert_m_gates/

Richard L. Russell, Ph.D., is Professor of National Security Affairs at Near East and South Asia Center for Strategic Studies, National Defense University, and Political, Military Analyst, Central Intelligence Agency.

Russell, Richard L. Reprinted in entirety by McGraw-Hill with permission from *Foreign Policy*, February 5, 2013. www.foreignpolicy.com. © 2013 Washingtonpost.Newsweek Interactive, LLC.

Article

Prepared by: Caroline Shaffer Westerhof,
California National University for Advanced Studies

Economy Slows "Due to Rebalancing"

Chen Jia, He Wei, and He Yini

Learning Outcomes

After reading this article, you will be able to:

- Understand the slower economic growth in China and economic restructuring.

- Understand measures that will react to liquidity outflows.

- Understand the reality of GDP growth rates in China and why the country coud be increasingly vulnerable to a chaotic adjustment.

China's economy grew by 7.6 percent year-on-year in the first half, a marked slowdown in comparison with near double-digit growth recorded just two years ago.

A government spokesman said that reducing the growth rate is necessary for rebalancing the economy. The nation is capable of keeping growth momentum steady for the rest of the year, even though the economic environment is expected to remain grim and complicated, he added.

The government's yearly GDP growth target for 2013, set earlier this year, is 7.5 percent.

Sheng Laiyun, spokesman for the National Bureau of Statistics, said that despite the slowdown, China's growth is still higher than that in other major economies.

The nation saw economic growth fall to 7.5 percent in the second quarter, from 7.7 percent in the first and 7.9 percent in the fourth quarter of 2012.

Investment was the biggest growth driver in the first half of the year, contributing 4.1 percentage points to the 7.6 percent rate, while consumption contributed 3.4 percentage points and net exports 0.1 percentage point, the bureau said.

Industrial output in the first six months grew by 9.3 percent from a year earlier, compared with a 10.5 percent increase in the first half of 2012.

Annual growth of fixed-asset investments in the first half lost some steam, rising 20.1 percent year-on-year, down from 20.9 percent.

Meanwhile, consumer goods retail sales rose by 12.7 percent, 1.7 percentage points lower than in the first two quarters of 2012.

The slowdown was caused by the weak global economic recovery and measures taken by the new leadership, Sheng said.

Jonathan Holslag, a research fellow at the Brussels Institute of Contemporary China Studies, said the figures send a very strong signal that the central government is trying to rebalance the economy.

"The growth rate is still optimistic considering the scale of China's economy and is still contributing a lot to the global economy," Holslag said.

But he said this year will be very challenging as the country restructures the economy against a backdrop of global hardship. Holslag stressed that the risks the government faces come from the banking sector and the stock market.

Slowdown to Continue

Wang Jun, a senior economist at the China Center for International Economic Exchanges, a government think tank in Beijing, said China still faces pressure from downside risks in the second half.

"It may push the government to take measures ... to further expand domestic demand. Otherwise, difficulties may arise from tight local government financing and increasing unemployment," Wang said.

He denied that a large stimulus package will be needed, as the new leadership might tolerate a growth rate of no less than 7 percent.

After the statistics bureau released the first-half growth figures, JPMorgan Chase downgraded its forecast for the year's growth to 7.4 percent from 7.6 percent, saying manufacturing investment and overseas demand remain weak.

"A slowdown of GDP growth to 7.5 percent will not trigger a change in policy," said Zhu Haibin, chief economist in China with the US bank.

"The new government made it clear that it is willing to tolerate slower growth for better quality of growth. Economic restructuring is the priority task going ahead."

On July 15, Nomura Securities said it will keep its GDP growth forecast for this year at 7.5 percent, but lower it to 6.9 percent for 2014.

"We expect growth to bottom in the second quarter of 2014 at 6.5 percent," said Zhang Zhiwei, the company's chief economist in China.

An adjusted growth target of 7 percent may emerge in 2014, setting the country on a temporary but turbulent journey toward a more balanced economy, according to Michael McDonough, senior economist at Bloomberg LP.

But for the next six months, the government may still accelerate investment projects and cut interest rates, among other efforts to defend a 7.5 percent GDP growth target, he noted.

This year, China's macroeconomic data have consistently come in below analysts' forecasts, leading to a series of growth downgrades, he said. For instance, the government's 2013 GDP goal is 7.5 percent, well below January's consensus forecast of 8.1 percent.

It is interesting to note that historically the government's target has acted more as a floor than a legitimate estimate. But this year that is very likely to change, McDonough said.

"They won't set next year's target below 7 percent, but I do think a general trend is going to be a continued slowdown. Slower growth will be a good thing, though it will inevitably cause some short-term pain. But in order to rebalance, you need to lessen the reliance on investment," he said.

The 4 trillion yuan ($651 billion) stimulus package enacted following the 2008 financial crisis boosted growth, but essentially led to a surge in credit expansion and generated extensive industrial overcapacity, which McDonough said was responsible for much of the current slowdown.

The overcapacity was especially obvious in the manufacturing sector, where the Producer Price Index, a main gauge of inflation at the wholesale level, has dropped for 16 consecutive months, indicating tepid domestic demand.

Another case in point was the surging amount of social financing after the 2008 input. An increasing portion of these loans, which targeted lower-valued projects, may struggle to stay afloat in an environment of slowing growth.

Annual new yuan loan-issuance between 2008 and 2012 was on average more than 140 percent above the 2007 level.

Private Sector Encouraged

McDonough noticed a change in the response to the slowdown compared with five years ago.

"While the government still has room to increase investment in certain infrastructure projects that may boost urbanization, a goal the new leadership has highly valued, officials are showing a restrained response and instead are attempting to encourage more private-sector involvement," he noted.

He said urbanization-driven infrastructure investment is going to be a value-added, smart use of money to bring people to cities and would produce a decent return in the long run, whereas the stimulus program only resulted in industry bubbles.

While these types of investment may accelerate in the second half of the year, the aim will probably be to achieve the government's official target, rather than what investors might perceive as market-friendly 8 percent growth, McDonough added.

While officials have publicly recognized that China's economy needs to lessen its dependence on investment, there has yet to be tangible change on that front.

Investment's share of GDP rocketed to 48.3 percent in 2011, while household consumption shrank to just 35.4 percent, compared with 50 percent in 1989.

McDonough said that the rising contribution of investment has meant that slower growth is almost a "necessity" if China is to shift toward consumption and the private sector as a major growth engine.

"An economic slowdown is like a forest fire (that gets rid of the underbrush) in a forest. It's terrible at first, but then it cleans out the excesses of the current system, and everyone will be better off when the economy starts over from a sound base," Jim Rogers, an international investment guru, said in an exclusive interview with *China Daily*.

"It's happening in China at the moment as the government stays tight to cool things down. But I think it's a good thing."

The government said in a guideline issued on July 5 that it would continue belt-tightening and scale back the supply of funds in the market to a reasonable level to contain a debt-fueled economic boom.

The guideline came after a liquidity crunch, which triggered a dive in the stock market and pushed interbank rates to record highs, had eased. But economic concerns linger.

"The Chinese government does have a plan to stay tight to calm things down. Some people are going to suffer, and that's what's happening. But that will be good for China in the end," Rogers said.

"Even if some sectors of the Chinese economy have a hard landing and some people go bankrupt, people (doing business) in other sectors, such as agriculture, culture, pollution control, etc, will not be affected at all, because these fields will enjoy great prosperity in the years to come."

These fields, Rogers said, will be new sweet spots for investment in China.

He said all countries that rise have periodic setbacks along the way.

Critical Thinking

1. Why is the growth rate that really matters considered to be the average household income?

2. Why are ordinary Chinese most concerned about real disposable income, rather than per capita share of country's GDP?

3. What would affect the risk of a credit crisis in China?

Create Central

www.mhhe.com/createcentral

Internet References

National Forex
http://nationalforex.com/2013/07/15/

Chinese Economic Slowdown and Its Implications—The Frontier Post
www.thefrontierpost.com/article/41247

China's Economic Growth and Rebalancing—European Central Bank
www.ecb.europa.eu/pub/pdf/scpops/ecbocp142.pdf

China's Economic Rebalancing and the Impact on the Australian Economy—The Daily Reckoning
www.dailyreckoning.com.au/chinas-economic-rebalancing-and-the-impact-on-the-australian-economy/2013/07/04/

CHEN JIA is chief correspondent of *China Daily USA* in San Francisco and covers topics including business, technology, politics, and education.

Article   Prepared by: Caroline Shaffer Westerhof,
                                    California National University for Advanced Studies

Democracy in Cyberspace: What Information Technology Can and Cannot Do

IAN BREMMER

Learning Outcomes

After reading this article, you will be able to:

- Examine the reality of how information technology has demolished time and distance.

- Identify the spread and the concept of the "freedom virus."

- Examine how the Internet is promoting pluralism and human rights around the world.

"Information technology has demolished time and distance," Walter Wriston, the former ceo of what is now Citigroup wrote in 1997. "Instead of validating Orwell's vision of Big Brother watching the citizen, [it] enables the citizen to watch Big Brother. And so the virus of freedom, for which there is no antidote, is spread by electronic networks to the four corners of the earth." Former Presidents Ronald Reagan, Bill Clinton, and George W. Bush have articulated a similar vision, and with similarly grandiose rhetoric. All have argued that the long-term survival of authoritarian states depends on their ability to control the flow of ideas and information within and across their borders. As advances in communications technology—cellular telephones, text messaging, the Internet, social networking—allow an ever-widening circle of people to easily and inexpensively share ideas and aspirations, technology will break down barriers between peoples and nations. In this view, the spread of the "freedom virus" makes it harder and costlier for autocrats to isolate their people from the rest of the world and gives ordinary citizens tools to build alternative sources of power. The democratization of communications, the theory goes, will bring about the democratization of the world.

There seems to be plenty of evidence to support these ideas. In the Philippines in 2001, protesters sent text messages to organize the demonstrations that forced President Joseph Estrada from office. In the lead-up to the 2004 presidential election in Ukraine, supporters of Viktor Yushchenko, then the leader of the opposition, used text messaging to organize the massive protests that became the Orange Revolution. In Lebanon in 2005, activists coordinated via e-mail and text messaging to bring one million demonstrators into the streets to demand that the Syrian government end nearly three decades of military presence in Lebanon by withdrawing its 14,000 troops. (Syria complied a month later, under considerable international pressure.) Over the past few years, in Colombia, Myanmar (also known as Burma), and Zimbabwe, demonstrators have used cell phones and Facebook to coordinate protests and transmit photographs and videos of government crackdowns. The flood of words and images circulated by protesters following Iran's bitterly disputed 2009 presidential election—quickly dubbed the "Twitter revolution"—seemed to reinforce the view that Tehran has more to fear from "citizen media" than from the U.S. ships patrolling the Persian Gulf.

But a closer look at these examples suggests a more complicated reality. Only in democracies—the Philippines, Ukraine, Lebanon, and Colombia—did these communications weapons accomplish an immediate objective. In Myanmar, Zimbabwe, and Iran, they managed to embarrass the government but not to remove it from power. As Wriston acknowledged, the information revolution is a long-term process, cyberspace is a complex place, and technological advances are no substitute for human wisdom. Innovations in modern communications may help erode authoritarian power over time. But for the moment, their impact on international politics is not so easy to predict.

There are many reasons why the optimistic view of the relationship among communications, information, and democracy has taken root in the United States. First, these communications tools embody twenty-first-century innovation, and Americans have long believed in the power of invention to promote peace and create prosperity. And with good reason. Admirers of Reagan argue that the United States' ability to invest in strategic missile defense sent the Soviet leadership into a crisis confidence from which it never recovered. The light bulb, the automobile, and airplane have changed the world, greater personal autonomy to many Americans. Similarly, Americans believe that the millions of people around the world who use the Internet, an American invention, will eventually adopt American political beliefs, much like many of those who wear American jeans, watch American movies, and dance to American music have. Champions of the Internet's power to promote pluralism and human rights point to bloggers in China, Russia, and the Arab world who are calling for democracy and the rule of law for their countries, sometimes in English.

But of the hundreds of millions who blog in their own languages—there are more than 75 million in China alone—the vast majority have other priorities. Many more of them focus on pop culture rather than on political philosophy, on pocketbook issues rather than political power, and on national pride rather than cosmopolitan pretensions. In other words, the tools of modern communications satisfy as wide a range of ambitions and appetites as their twentieth-century ancestors did, and many of these ambitions and appetites do not have anything to do with democracy.

Net Neutrality

A careful look at the current impact of modern communications on the political development of authoritarian states should give pause to those who hail these technologies as instruments of democratization. Techno-optimists appear to ignore the fact that these tools are value neutral; there is nothing inherently pro-democratic about them. To use them is to exercise a form of freedom, but it is not necessarily a freedom that promotes the freedom of others.

In enabling choice, the introduction of the Internet into an authoritarian country shares something fundamental with the advent of elections. Some have argued that promoting elections in one country in the Middle East will generate demand for elections elsewhere. A free Iraq is going to help inspire others to demand what I believe is a universal right of men and women," Bush said in July 2006; elections in Iraq would prompt the citizens of Iraq's neighbors to ask why Iraqis were now free to choose their leaders whereas they were not. Similarly, some have argued that the freedom that comes with the Internet will inevitably democratize China. Once Chinese people read about the freedoms of others, the thinking goes, they will want the same for themselves. The tools of modern communications will reveal to Chinese citizens the political freedoms they do not yet have and provide the means to demand them.

But the limited history of elections in the Middle East shows that people do not always vote for pluralism. Sometimes, they vote for security or absolutism, sometimes to express outrage or defend local interests. The same pattern holds true for the Internet and other forms of modern communications. These technologies provide access to information of all kinds, information that entertains the full range of human appetites—from titillation to rationalization, from hope to anger. They provide the user with an audience but do not determine what he will say. They are a megaphone, and have a multiplier effect, but they serve both those who want to speed up the crossborder flow of information and those who want to divert or manipulate it.

Cyberspace can be a very dark place. In *You Are Not a Gadget*, Jaron Lanier argues that the anonymity provided by the Internet can promote a "culture of sadism," feeding an appetite for drive-by attacks and mob justice. In China, the Internet has given voice to wounded national pride, anti-Western and anti-Japanese resentment over injuries both real and imagined, and hostility toward Tibetans, Muslim Uighurs, and other minority groups. It has also become a kind of public square for improvised violence. In an article for *The New York Times Magazine* earlier this year, Tom Downey described the "human-flesh search" phenomenon in China, "a form of online vigilante justice in which Internet users hunt down and punish people who have attracted their wrath." The targets of these searches, a kind of "crowdsourced detective work," as Downey put it, can be corrupt officials or enemies of the state, or simply people who have made other people angry.

These problems are hardly unique to China. In Russia, skinheads have filmed murderous attacks on dark-skinned immigrants from the Caucasus and Central Asia and posted the footage online. Also in Russia—and in the United States and Europe—hate groups and militants of various kinds use the Internet to recruit new members and disseminate propaganda. Of course, beyond all this fear and loathing, many more people around the world use the Internet as a global shopping mall and a source of entertainment. The Internet makes it easier for users with political interests to find and engage with others who believe what they believe, but there is little reliable evidence that it also opens their minds to ideas and information that challenge their worldviews. The medium fuels many passions—consumerism and conspiracy theories, resentment and fanaticism—but it promotes calls for democracy only where there is already a demand for democracy. If technology has helped citizens pressure authoritarian governments in several countries, it is not because the technology created a demand for change. That demand must come from public anger at authoritarianism itself.

Stateside

Citizens are not the only ones active in cyberspace. The state is online, too, promoting its own ideas and limiting what an average user can see and do. Innovations in communications technology provide people with new sources of information and new opportunities to share ideas, but they also empower governments to manipulate the conversation and to monitor what people are saying.

The collapse of Soviet communism a generation ago taught authoritarian leaders around the world that they could not simply mandate lasting economic growth and that they would have to embrace capitalism if they hoped to create the jobs and the higher standards of living that would ensure their long-term political survival. But to embrace capitalism is to allow for dangerous new freedoms. And so in order to generate strong growth while maintaining political control, some autocrats have turned to state capitalism, a system that helps them dominate market activity through the use of national oil companies, other state-owned enterprises, privately owned but politically loyal national champions, state-run banks, and sovereign wealth funds.

Following precisely the same logic, authoritarian governments are now trying to ensure that the increasingly free flow of ideas and information through cyberspace fuels their economies without threatening their political power. In June, the Chinese government released its first formal statement on the rights and responsibilities of Internet users. The document "guarantee[d] the citizens' freedom of speech on the Internet as well as the public's right to know, to participate, to be heard, and to oversee [the government] in accordance with the law." But it also stipulated that "within Chinese territory, the Internet is under the jurisdiction of Chinese sovereignty." That caveat legitimates China's "great firewall," a system of filters and re-routers, detours and dead ends designed to keep Chinese Internet users on the stateapproved online path.

The Chinese leadership also uses more low-tech means to safeguard its interests online. The average Chinese Web surfer cannot be sure that every idea or opinion he encounters in cyberspace genuinely reflects the views of its author. The government has created the 50 Cent Party, an army of online commentators that it pays for each blog entry or message-board post promoting the Chinese Communist Party's line on sensitive subjects. This is a simple, inexpensive way for governments to disseminate and disguise official views. Authoritarian states do not use technology simply to block the free flow of unwelcome ideas. They also use it to promote ideas of their own.

Nonaligned Movement

The techno-optimists who hope that modern communications tools will democratize authoritarian states are also hoping that they will help align the interests of nondemocracies with those of democracies. But the opposite is happening. Efforts by police states to control or co-opt these tools are inevitably creating commercial conflicts that then create political conflicts between governments.

In January, Google publicly complained that private Gmail accounts had been breached in attacks originating in China—attacks that Chinese officials appeared to tolerate or even to have launched themselves. In protest, Google announced that it would no longer censor the results of users' searches in mainland China, which it had reluctantly agreed to do when it entered the Chinese market in 2006. Beijing refused to back down, and Google automatically redirected searches by Chinese users to the uncensored Hong Kong version of the site. But much to the relief of mainland users, mostly students and researchers who prefer Google's capabilities to its main domestic rival, Baidu, Chinese officials eventually announced the renewal of Google's operating license. (It is possible that they backtracked because they believed that they could control Google or use it to monitor the online activities of political dissidents.)

As Chinese technology companies begin to compete on a par with Western ones and the Chinese government uses legal and financial means to more actively promote domestic firms that see censorship as a routine cost of doing business, there will be less demand for Google's products in China. In August 2010, the state-run Xinhua News Agency and China Mobile, the country's largest cell-phone carrier, announced plans to jointly build a state-owned search—engine and media company. In response to these developments, U.S. technology companies

will undoubtedly turn to U.S. lawmakers for help in creating and maintaining a level commercial playing field in China. Far from aligning American and Chinese political values and bringing the citizens of the two countries closer together, conflicts over the flow of information through cyberspace will further complicate the already troubled U.S. Chinese relationship.

Signs of strife are already visible. When Google first went public with its complaints about cyberattacks and censorship, Beijing looked past the company, which it sees as a high-tech arm of the U.S. government, and addressed its response directly to Washington. A Chinese Communist Party tabloid ran an editorial under the headline "The World Does Not Welcome the White House's Google"; it argued, "Whenever the U.S. government demands it, Google can easily become a convenient tool for promoting the U.S. government's political will and values abroad." In response, U.S. Secretary of State Hillary Clinton urged companies such as Google not to cooperate with "politically motivated censorship," further emphasizing the difference, not the convergence, of political values in the United States and China.

Revealing similar fears about the future of its political control, the United Arab Emirates and Saudi Arabia took action earlier this year against Research in Motion (RIM), the Canadian company that makes the BlackBerry, for equipping its devices with encryption technology that authorities cannot decode. Arguing that terrorists and spies could use BlackBerries to communicate within the uae without fear of being detected, Emirati officials announced in August that they would soon suspend BlackBerry service unless RIM provided state officials with some means of monitoring BlackBerry messaging. Within two days, Saudi Arabia announced a similar shutdown, although Riyadh and RIM have since reached a compromise that requires RIM to install a relay server on territory, which allows Saudi officials monitor messages sent from and within country. The UAE will probably also a deal with RIM: there are half a millon BlackBerry users in the UAE (about percent of the population), and the country wants to remain the Arab world's primary commercial and tourist hub. Yet far from promoting Western values in non-Western police states, the BlackBerry has sparked a new round of debate over the willingness of Western technology companies to protect their market shares by making concessions that help authoritarian governments spy on their citizens.

In fairness to these governments, the world's leading democracies are no less concerned about potential terrorist threats posed by unmonitored messaging. The Indian government has also threatened to ban BlackBerries unless RIM gives it access to certain data, and counterterrorism officials in the United States and Europe are considering the option as well. Via efforts to amend the Electronic Communications Privacy Act, the Obama administration has already taken steps to help the FBI gain access to "electronic communication transactional records"—recipients' addresses, logs of users' online activities, browser histories—without a court order if investigators suspect terrorism or espionage. Politicians and technology companies such as Google and RIM will be fighting these battles for years to come.

Of course, authoritarian governments, unlike democracies, also worry that individuals who are neither terrorists nor spies will use new communications tools to challenge their political legitimacy. China, Iran, Myanmar, North Korea, Saudi Arabia, and other authoritarian states cannot halt the proliferation of weapons of modern communications, but they can try to monitor and manipulate them for their own purposes. That struggle will continue as well, limiting the ability of new technologies to empower the political opposition within these countries and creating more conflicts over political values between democratic and authoritarian states.

Feedback Loops

The Internet may have changed the world, but now the world is changing the Internet. For 30 years, new communications technologies have driven globalization, the defining trend of the times. The companies that created these products made longterm plans based on the wants and needs of consumers, not governments. Their profits rose as they connected billions of customers with one another; borders became increasingly less important.

But now, the pace of technological change and the threat of terrorism are forcing policymakers to expand their definitions of national security and to rethink their definitions of "critical infrastructure." As a result, governments are turning to high-tech communications firms to help shore up emerging security vulnerabilities, and high-tech communications firms have begun to think more like defense contractors—companies whose success depends on secrecy, exclusivity, political contacts, and security clearances.

As a result, political borders, which the rise of information technology once seemed set to dissolve, are taking on a new importance: if greater openness creates new opportunities, it also creates new worries. Unable to match U.S. defense spending, China and Russia have become adept at information warfare. The Pentagon reported last August that China continues to develop its ability to steal U.S. military secrets electronically and to deny its adversaries "access to information essential to conduct combat operations." In 2007, a massive cyberattack launched from inside Russia damaged digital infrastructure in neighboring Estonia. The United States' vulnerabilities range from its nuclear power plants and electrical grids to the information systems of government agencies and major U.S. companies. Despite their political and commercial rivalries, the United States, China, Russia, India, and many other states also share a vulnerability to cyberattacks, and they have pledged to work together to build a joint cybersecurity strategy But when it comes to espionage, governments can never fully trust one another. And of course the Obama administration does not want to share technologies that would make it easier for security officials in Beijing or Moscow to track the online activities of political dissidents.

Other problems will exacerbate international tensions. Technology firms in the United States and Europe, mindful of Google's recent troubles in China, will increasingly turn to their governments for help with their own security needs. As cyberthreats become ever more sophisticated, these companies will collaborate more actively with national security agencies on developing new technologies. This will pull more technology companies into the orbit of the military-industrial complex. That, in turn, will make them even more suspect to authoritarian regimes and likelier targets for hackers and spies of all kinds. Borders are about to become much more important.

The result will be a world that has not one Internet but a set of interlinked intranets closely monitored by various governments. The Internet is not about to disappear, but the prediction that a single Internet could accommodate both the West and the evolving demands of authoritarian states was never realistic. American and European users will access the same Internet as before, but the Chinese government has already made clear its intention to declare sovereignty over an Internet of its own. Other authoritarian states have every incentive to follow its lead.

There are far too many variables at work to predict with confidence the full, longterm impact of modern tools of communications on the political development of authoritarian states. But it seems safe to expect that their effects will vary as widely as the motives of the people and the states that use them.

Critical Thinking

1. How has the Internet developed a "multiplier" effect?
2. Can the Internet threaten authoritarian governments with loss of political power?
3. How is the globalization of the world changing the use and misuse of the Internet?

Create Central

www.mhhe.com/createcentral

Internet References

Ian Bremmer
www.ianbremmer.com/book/every-nation-itself-winners-and-losers-g-zero-world

Challenges of Democratization
www.brandonkendhammer.com/democratization_Spring2013/schedule

Who's in Charge of the World? No One—Reuters
blogs.reuters.com/ian-bremmer/2012/04/30

Ian Bremmer—World Policy Institute
www.worldpolicy.org/ian-bremmer

IAN BREMMER is president of the Eurasia Group and is a geopolitical analyst.

From *Foreign Affairs*, vol. 89, issue 6, November/December 2010, pp. 86–94. Copyright © 2010 by Council on Foreign Relations, Inc. Reprinted by permission of Foreign Affairs. www.ForeignAffairs.com

Unit 7

UNIT

Prepared by: Caroline Shaffer Westerhof,
California National University for Advanced Studies

Global Trends: Institutional Change, Progress, and Threat

The systematic treatment of the political behaviors of citizens, interest groups, parties, the executive, legislature, and unelected officers in government, such as the military, lobbyists, and others reflects other dimensions of policy and decision making within regimes. The discussions make clear the relevance of institutions and institution building in providing formal venues to regulate and regularize political behaviors so that they are clear-cut, comprehensible, constant, and, thus, predictable. But, if institutions affect political behaviors, it is also indisputable that political behaviors shape institutions. In this unit, we examine the "what, how, and why" of institutional changes. In the process, we consider the extent to which political behaviors shape institutions in general, and democratization in particular.

What are institutional changes? Institutional changes refer to the creation or alteration of political organizations, conventions, or participation. They include modifications in political or legal processes, bureaucracy and technology, enhanced by all types of electronics, including cyberspace. They may be radical or gradual; they may reflect democratic governments, as well as authoritarian. They may involve the creation of new political organizations, or they may involve the liberalizing trends in some Asian state institutions, and they may seek to project the future. It is more realistic "to project" what may or may not happen than "to predict." The science of projection is easier to develop than the database of predictions.

How do institutional changes occur? Institutional changes are brought on by a combination of the following: domestic demand, such as by citizens, interest groups, and the government; or new pressures from new climate-related disasters and globalization. Institutional changes generated by domestic demand often hinge on changes in values and attitudes, and the state of the economy. Can we project the future when we study climate destruction and an economy based on poverty? Does one destroy the other or can the destruction be corrected?

Can there ever be a definitive discussion of the events in the Middle East? Is it one's perspective versus another's? In surveying political behaviors and institutions across a wide net of countries we realize that this full circle returns to this: Institutional changes occur in response to demands for better or more representative venues within which citizens and government may interact. While onlookers may fault institutions or even countries for failing to be more accountable, representative, or just, it is primarily the demands of domestic constituents—the citizens—that will usher in and support changes. Supporting nation-states and non-supporting play a role in the manipulation of political power in such nation-states as Lebanon, Egypt, and Syria. We have not simultaneously witnessed such Middle East chaos on so many fronts, as in the present.

Representation and accountability are sorely lacking at the present time in many nations within the Middle East. It is not necessarily the spirit that will "move systems." Understanding comparative politics generates a greater awareness of actions leading to changes in organizational structures, or more turbulence, or why the actors are and must change. We are each part of multi-stakeholder behavioral patterns, economic rebalancing, and changes in governmental structures; there is explicit acknowledgment and awareness that the processes toward a global, regional and nation-state solution are far outpaced by the unknown of world problems, present and in the future. As a result, the first step—even if it is an "insufficient" one—is to try to understand what is presently happening and the undercurrents of the present and continuing changing actors. Thus it is crucial that all elements and actors in the institutions, including outlets, academics, military, governmental and nongovernmental organizations, work together to share information.

Any faith that providing more information and disseminating it widely will usher in better or more representative political and social environs by galvanizing the citizens misreads and misunderstands that there is as much information on the Internet that is deliberately planted and monitored. Similarly, if we expect that international or regional agencies are able to step in to provide a hand, and that the descriptions of global political development and actions that span across the boundaries of countries, then we, as responsible global citizens, should be informed about institution building and policy choices through understanding and knowledge. We continue to survey democratic theory and how citizens' behavior and institutional performance relate to democratization, and other political systems, typical and atypical. In doing so, we are better able to outline for the international community what it means to nurture and support citizen demands, without imposing our own preferences and impatience, in the interests of promoting stability and development within countries, intra-nations, and in inter-nation relations.

Article

Prepared by: Caroline Shaffer Westerhof,
California National University for Advanced Studies

The Coming Wave

LARRY DIAMOND

Learning Outcomes

After reading this article, you will be able to:

- Explain why democracies have gained ground in areas of the world except the Middle East.

- Explain the liberalizing trends that Larry Diamond notes in some Asian state institutions, besides Japan and South Korea.

- Explain how the political aftermath of the Arab Spring of 2011 continues to shape world politics.

I f there is going to be a big new lift to global democratic prospects in this decade, the region from which it will emanate is most likely to be East Asia.

With the eruption of mass movements for democratic change throughout the Arab world in 2011, hopeful analysts of global democratic prospects have focused attention on the Middle East. Three Arab autocracies (Tunisia, Egypt, and Libya) have fallen in the past year. At least two more (Yemen and Syria) also seem destined for demise soon, and pressures for real democratic change figure to mount in Morocco, Jordan, the Palestinian Authority, and perhaps Kuwait, and to persist in Bahrain. Yet among these and other countries in the Middle East (including Iraq and Iran), only Tunisia has a good chance of becoming a democracy in the relatively near future. Aspirations for more democratic and accountable government run deep throughout the Middle East, and for years to come the region will be a lively and contested terrain of possibilities for regime evolution. But if a new regional wave of transitions to democracy unfolds in the next five to ten years, it is more likely to come from East Asia—a region that has been strangely neglected in recent thinking about the near-term prospects for expansion of democracy. And East Asia is also better positioned to increase the number of liberal and sustainable democracies.

Unlike the Arab world, East Asia already has a critical mass of democracies. Forty percent of East Asian states (seven of the seventeen) are democracies, a proportion slightly higher than in South Asia or sub-Saharan Africa, though dramatically lower than in Latin America or Central and Eastern Europe, where most states are democracies. As a result of the third wave of global democratization, East Asia has gone from being the

cradle and locus of "developmental authoritarianism," with Japan as its lone democracy—and a longstanding one-party-dominant system at that—to at least a mixed and progressing set of systems. Today, Japan, South Korea, and Taiwan are all consolidated liberal democracies. East Timor, Indonesia, Mongolia, and the Philippines are at least electoral democracies with some resilience.

Moreover, as I will explain, there are now significant prospects for democratic change in a number of the region's remaining authoritarian regimes. Thailand is progressing back toward democracy; Malaysia and Singapore show signs of entering a period of democratic transition; Burma, to the surprise of many, is liberalizing politically for the first time in twenty years; and China faces a looming crisis of authoritarianism that will generate a new opportunity for democratic transition in the next two decades and possibly much sooner. Moreover, all this has been happening during a five-year period when democracy has been in recession globally.

There are three democracies in East Asia today that rank among the stable liberal democracies of the industrialized world: Japan, South Korea, and Taiwan. They are not without stiff economic and political challenges and large numbers of disenchanted citizens who in surveys express only tepid support for democracy. Yet in each of these countries, overwhelming majorities of citizens reject authoritarian regime options while voicing reasonably robust support for broadly liberal values such as the rule of law, freedom of expression, and judicial independence.[1] Comparative data on political rights, civil liberties, and the quality of governance confirm that these are liberal democracies. They could become better, more liberal ones, however, by deepening the rule of law and civil liberties and improving mechanisms of accountability and transparency to control corruption and political favoritism.

East Asia's merely electoral democracies have further to go toward deepening and consolidating democracy, of course. Mongolia scores relatively well in Freedom House ratings of political rights and civil liberties, but in this phenomenally mineral-rich country the judiciary remains underdeveloped, the rule of law is weak, and corruption remains a grave problem widely recognized by the public. Indonesia's democratic performance over the past decade has been much better than what many experts on that country might have expected. The Philippines has returned to democracy with the 2010 election, in which Benigno Aquino III won the presidency. Yet semi-feudal elites retain a strong hold on the politics of many Philippine provinces and constituencies, and their presence in the country's Congress has so far largely blocked basic reform. In the World Bank's annual governance ratings, Indonesia and the Philippines rank in the bottom quartile of all countries in corruption control and not much better (the bottom third) in rule of law. In 2010, among big (mainly G-20) emerging-market democracies such as Argentina, Bangladesh, Brazil, India, Mexico, South Africa, and Turkey, only Bangladesh did worse on these two governance indicators.[2]

In each of these three electoral democracies—Mongolia, Indonesia, and the Philippines—at least three-quarters of citizens agree that "Democracy may have its problems, but it is still the best form of government." In each, likewise, only about half the public is satisfied with the way democracy is working, but majorities believe that democracy remains capable of solving the country's problems. One possible reason for this faith in democracy is suggested by the wide majorities in each country (up to 76 percent in Mongolia and 80 percent in the Philippines) who say that they believe the people retain the power to change the government through elections.[3]

Prospects for Further Democratization

It is by now widely appreciated that Singapore is by any standard a massive anomaly. As we see in the Table (next page), Singapore is far richer today than any major third-wave countries were when they made their transitions to democracy (this includes Spain and Greece, which do not appear in the Table). Singapore is the most economically developed nondemocracy in the history of the world. But Singapore is changing, and this change will probably accelerate when the founding generation of leaders, particularly Lee Kuan Yew (who turned 88 last September), passes from the scene. In the May 2011 parliamentary elections, the ruling People's Action Party (PAP) recorded its weakest electoral performance since independence in 1965, winning "only" 60 percent of the vote. Although the PAP still won (yet again) well over 90 percent of parliamentary seats thanks to a highly rigged electoral system, the opposition Workers' Party broke through for the first time to win a five-seat group constituency, and a total of six seats overall—a record for the Singaporean opposition. While a postelection survey failed to reveal a general increase in support for greater political pluralism since the last elections (in 2006), the expressed preference for a more competitive political system did increase dramatically in the youngest age cohort (those from 21 to 29), shooting up from 30 to 44 percent.[4] If Singapore remains in the grip of a half-century-long single-party hegemony, that hegemony now seems to be entering a more vulnerable phase, as opposition parties find new energy and backing, as young people flock to social media to express themselves more openly, as independent media crop up online to provide a fuller range of news and opinions, and as the ruling party feels compelled to ease censorship and other controls. Singapore, in other words, has already joined the ranks of the world's "competitive authoritarian" regimes—the

class of autocracies among which democratic transitions are most likely to happen.[5]

Singapore's exceptionalism is widely known. Less well known is that Malaysia now also has a higher per capita income than most third-wave countries did when they made their transitions to democracy. In fact, among the prominent cases in the Table, only Taiwan had a higher per capita income than Malaysia when it completed its democratic transition. Moreover, Malaysia's score on the UNDP's Human Development Index—which, in measuring not only per capita income but also levels of health and education, is arguably a truer measure of development—is now significantly higher than the levels in Brazil, Chile, Mexico, and even Hungary, Poland, and Ukraine when they made their respective transitions to democracy. From the standpoint of modernization theory, then, Malaysia is also ripe for a democratic transition.

For more than a decade, Malaysia's competitive authoritarian regime has faced a much more serious challenge than anything Singapore has so far seen. As the opposition has gained in unity, credibility, and mobilizing power, the long-ruling United Malays National Organization (UMNO) feels under increasing threat. Much of what is driving change in Malaysia is not only exhaustion with half a century of rule by one party (formally through a ruling coalition), but also a much better educated and more pluralistic society, with the attendant growth in independent organizations and the intense and innovative use of social media (including one of the most influential online newspapers in the world, *Malaysiakini*).

Alarmed by the upheavals that began sweeping the Arab world at the end of 2010, Malaysia's Prime Minister Najib Razak pledged to appoint a broad committee to review the country's electoral system and recommend reforms, and then vowed to repeal the draconian Internal Security Act. Many opposition and civil society leaders, however, saw these promises as empty, citing Razak's push to enact stiff new security laws in place of the old ones. After winning control of five of the thirteen states in 2008, opposition forces are poised to do better in the next elections, which could come in 2012. The new opposition alliance, Pakatan Rakyat, is gaining momentum, and the regime's renewed effort to destroy former deputy prime minister Anwar Ibrahim with trumped-up charges of homosexual misconduct seems even less credible than when the ploy was first tried some years ago. To be sure, Malaysia's authoritarian establishment still has a lot of resources, but Razak's proposed reforms now seem "too little too late," as "cynicism still pervades the country."[6] A transition to democracy could happen any time in the coming years, through the familiar instrument that has brought it about in other competitive authoritarian regimes: the electoral process.

Thailand is less developed than Malaysia, but also has far more democratic experience and now, once again, more freedom and pluralism. Although Thais remain deeply polarized between a camp that backs ousted premier Thaksin Shinawatra and one that clusters around the institution of the monarchy, national elections are highly competitive and seem to meet the "free and fair" standard of electoral democracy. With the decisive opposition victory of the new Pheu Thai Party (led by

Thaksin's sister Yingluck Shinawatra) in the May 2011 parliamentary elections, the political force that the military deposed in the 2006 coup has returned, and Thailand has apparently become once again an electoral democracy. Yet it faces a rocky road ahead, as the stabilizing presence of long-reigning King Bhumibol (b. 1927) draws toward a close. If the end result is a weaker monarchy (and military), this might ultimately help to ease the country's intense polarization and create a more mature and securely institutionalized politics. At least the military seems to have learned from the political turbulence and polarization of the last decade that its own direct intervention will not solve the country's political problems. Though it clearly preferred the incumbent Democrat Party, the military made a point of declaring its neutrality in the recent election. If the 2006 military coup does prove to be the last in Thailand's history, democracy will put down firmer roots over the coming decade as modernization further raises incomes and education. Already, Thailand has a per capita income and human-development score roughly equivalent to those of Poland when it made its transition to democracy around 1990 (see Table).

It is not only Southeast Asia's wealthier countries that are experiencing the winds of democratic change. As Burma's iconic democratic leader Aung San Suu Kyi has recently acknowledged, that country's political opening, launched in 2008 amid widespread skepticism with many voters abstaining from a constitutional referendum, suddenly seems quite serious. Labor unions have been legalized, Internet censorship has been eased, and a number of political prisoners have been freed. Now, Suu Kyi's National League for Democracy (which won the aborted 1990 elections) is preparing to register for and run in parliamentary by-elections to be held probably later in 2012. As has happened with other authoritarian regimes that opted to liberalize politically, Burma's authoritarian rulers seem to have been influenced by democratic developments elsewhere in the world, as well as by the prospective economic benefits—chiefly flowing from closer integration with the global economy—that political liberalization might bring. As an advisor to Burma's President Thein Sein noted in December 2011, "The president was convinced about the global situation; he saw where the global stream was heading."[7]

The Coming Change in China

Annual per capita income in China is still little more than half what it is in Malaysia, but it has been rising rapidly and now approaches the level that South Korea could boast at the time of

Table—Development Levels and Democratic Transitions

Country	Year of Transition	GDP per Capita, PPP$ (2009 international dollars)	HDI Score (year of transition)
Turkey	1984	6,316	—
Brazil	1985	7,596	0.687
Philippines	1986	2,250	—
South Korea	1988	9,086	—
Pakistan	1988	1,722	—
Hungary	1990	12,979	0.692
Poland	1990	8,376	0.683
Chile	1990	6,896	0.675
Bangladesh	1991	748	0.186
Thailand	1992	4,732	0.685
South Africa	1994	7,235	0.716
Taiwan	1996	19,938	—
Indonesia	1999	2,666	0.681
Mexico	2000	12,662	0.698
Ghana	2000	1,653	0.431
Ukraine	2005	6,037	0.696
Asia (Current)			
Singapore	—	56,522	0.866
Malaysia	—	14,670	0.761
Thailand	—	8,505	0.682
China	—	7,519	0.687
Vietnam	—	3,134	0.593
Laos	—	2,436	0.524
Burma	—	1,256	0.483

Source: for HDI: http://hdr.undp.org/en/data/trends; for GDP per capita: www.imf.org/external/pubs.
Note: GDP per capita and HDI (Human Development Index) scores in the bottom index are for the years 2010 and 2011, respectively. All GDP per capita figures have been transformed into the value of constant 2009 dollars using the GDP deflator.

its democratic transition in 1987–88. In fact, by IMF projections, China could surpass that level (about US$9,000 in 2009 Purchasing Power Parity [PPP] dollars) by next year. In 1996, Henry Rowen predicted on the basis of data and projections regarding economic development that China would become what Freedom House would call a Partly Free country by 2015, and a Free one (with political-rights and civil-liberties scores as good as those of India or Indonesia today) by 2025.[8] More recently, Rowen affirmed that analysis, estimating that even if China's growth in GDP per capita slowed to 5 percent annually starting in 2015, it would have by 2025 a per capita income roughly equivalent to that of Argentina's in 2007 (about $15,000 in current PPP dollars—which is roughly where Malaysia is today).[9] And if China's growth in per capita income were to slow immediately to 6 percent annually, it would still reach $13,000 in current PPP dollars before 2020—the level of Hungary in 1990 and Mexico in 2000 when they transitioned to democracy.

It is not only modernization—the spread of democratic values and capacities in tandem with rising incomes and information—that is feeding the escalating pressure for democratic change in China. As Yun-han Chu notes in his contribution to this set of essays, the growing density of ties between mainland China and Taiwan—including direct access (through travel and satellite television) to political news from the highly competitive and even raucous democracy that is Taiwan—is serving as an additional stimulant to the growth of democratic norms and aspirations in China. The irony of Communist China's relentless push for closer integration with Taiwan is that it may well begin to generate political convergence—but not in the way that the Communist leaders imagined.

Rowen's projections were a bit mechanical in assuming that economic growth would necessarily drive *gradual* political change toward democracy in China. Instead, it seems increasingly likely that political change in China will be sudden and disruptive. The Communist Party leadership still shows no sign of embarking on a path of serious political liberalization that might gradually lead to electoral democracy, as their counterparts in Taiwan's then-dominant Nationalist Party did several decades ago. Instead, the rulers in Beijing are gripped by a fear of ending up like the USSR's Mikhail Gorbachev, who launched a process of political opening in hopes of improving and refurbishing Soviet Communist rule only to see it crumble and the Soviet Union itself fall onto the ash heap of history. Torn by intense divisions within their own ranks and weakened by the draining away of power and energy from the center to the provinces and a congeries of increasingly divergent lower-level authorities, China's political leaders seem as frozen and feckless on the grand question of long-term political reform as they are brisk and decisive in making daily decisions on spending and investments.

As Francis Fukuyama notes in the essay that follows, the one flaw in the otherwise impressive institutionalization of Chinese Communist rule is its lack of adaptability. For a regime whose specialty is producing rapid economic change, such rigidity is a potentially fatal defect. With every month or year that ticks by while corruption, routine abuses of power, and stifling constraints on expression go unchecked, citizens' frustration mounts. Already, protests erupt with ominous frequency across tens of thousands of Chinese localities every year, while subversive and democratic ideas, images, and allusions proliferate online, despite the best efforts of fifty-thousand Internet police to keep Chinese cyberspace free of "harmful content." As Minxin Pei has been arguing for some time and as he asserts again in his essay here, the strength of the authoritarian regime in China is increasingly an illusion, and its resilience may not last much longer. As frustration with corruption, collusion, criminality, and constraints on free expression rise, so do the possibilities for a sudden crisis to turn into a political catastrophe for the Chinese Communist Party (CCP).

Beyond the ongoing frustrations with censorship, insider dealing, abuse of power, environmental degradation, and other outrages that can only be protested by antisystem activity of one sort or another, there are, as Fukuyama notes, the big looming social and economic challenges that China faces as the consequences of its one-child policy make themselves felt in a rapidly aging (and disproportionately male) population. Jack Goldstone reports that China's labor force stopped growing in 2010 and has begun shrinking half a percent a year, which "will, by itself, knock 2.2 percentage points off China's annual economic growth potential." Urbanization, a key driver of productivity increases, is also slowing dramatically, and the growth of education "has clearly reached a limit," as the number of college graduates has expanded faster than the ability of the economy—even as it faces labor shortages in blue-collar industries—to generate good white-collar jobs.[10]

The Chinese economy will have to pay for rapidly rising wages and cope with industrial labor shortages even as it comes under pressure to finance pension, welfare, and healthcare benefits for the massive slice of the populace that is now moving toward retirement. Moreover, as it manages all this, China will need to address growing frustration among college graduates who cannot find jobs to match their expectations. If the suspected bubbles in the real-estate and financial markets burst as these twin generational challenges are gathering force, political stability in the world's most populous country may well become no more than a memory.

Increasingly, the CCP faces the classic contradiction that troubles all modernizing authoritarian regimes. The Party cannot rule without continuing to deliver rapid economic development and rising living standards—to fail at this would invite not gradual loss of power but a sudden and probably lethal crisis. To the extent that the CCP succeeds, however, it generates the very forces—an educated, demanding middle class and a stubbornly independent civil society—that will one day decisively mobilize to raise up a democracy and end CCP rule for good. The CCP, in other words, is damned if it does not, and damned if it does. The only basis for its political legitimacy and popular acceptance is its ability to generate steadily improving standards of living, but these will be its undoing.

For some time, I suspected that Henry Rowen's projections were a bit optimistic and that China's democratic moment, while foreseeable, was still 25 to 30 years away. Now, as the need for a more open, accountable, and law-based regime becomes as obvious as the current leaders' inability to bring one about, I suspect that the end of CCP rule will come much sooner, quite possibly within the next ten years. Unfortunately, a sudden collapse of the communist system could give rise, at least for a while, to a much more dangerous form of authoritarian rule, perhaps led by a nationalistic military looking for trouble abroad in order to unify the nation at home. But this would likely represent only a temporary solution, for the military is incapable of governing a rapidly modernizing, deeply networked, middle-class country facing complex economic and social challenges.

Whatever the specific scenario of change, this much is clear: China cannot keep moving forward to the per capita income, educational, and informational levels of a middle-income country without experiencing the pressures for democratic change that Korea and Taiwan did more than two decades ago. Those pressures are rising palpably now in Singapore and Malaysia. They will gather momentum in Vietnam as it follows in China's path of transformational (even if not quite as rapid) economic development. In Thailand, continuing modernization over the next decade will change society in ways that will make democracy easier to sustain. In short, within a generation or so, I think it is reasonable to expect that most of East Asia will be democratic. And no regional transformation will have more profound consequences for democratic prospects globally.

Notes

1. See, for example, Yun-han Chu et al., *How East Asians View Democracy* (New York: Columbia University Press, 2008), and various reports of the Asian Barometer, *www.asianbarometer.org*.

2. World Bank Group, Worldwide Governance Indicators, 2011, *http://info.world-bank.org/governance/wgi/index.asp.* Indonesia and the Philippines were rated in the 27th and 22nd percentiles, respectively, on control of corruption and the 31st and 24th percentiles, respectively, on rule of law. South Korea, by contrast, was in the 69th and 81st percentiles on these two measures.

3. Data is from Round III of the Asian Barometer.

4. Institute for Policy Studies (Singapore), "IPS Post-Election Survey 2011." My thanks to Tan Ern Ser for sharing a copy of the summary findings.

5. Stephan Ortmann, "Singapore: Authoritarian but Newly Competitive," *Journal of Democracy* 22 (October 2011): 153–64.

6. Ooi Kee Beng, "In Malaysia, Reforms Take a Staggered Path," *TodayOnline*, 3 December 2011, available at *www.todayonline.com/Commentary/EDC111203-0000021/In-Malaysia-reforms-take-a-staggered-path.*

7. "In Myanmar, Government Reforms Win Over Some Skeptics," *New York Times*, 30 November 2011.

8. Henry S. Rowen, "The Short March: China's Road to Democracy," *National Interest* 45 (Fall 1996): 61–70.

9. Henry S. Rowen, "When Will the Chinese People Be Free?" *Journal of Democracy* 18 (July 2007): 38–52.

10. Jack A. Goldstone, "Rise of the TIMBIs," *Foreign Policy*, 2 December 2011, available at *www.foreignpolicy.com/articles/2011/12/02/rise_of_the_timbis?page=0,1.*

Critical Thinking

1. Why are there no Arab democracies in the Middle East?

2. Could you compare the Arab Spring of 2011 to the tearing down of the Berlin Wall? Why or why not?

3. Has Thomas Jefferson's prophecy any reality with regard to the Arab Spring "I hope our wisdom will grow with our power, and teach us, that the less we use our power, the greater it will be"?

Create Central

www.mhhe.com/createcentral

Internet References

Stanford
http://fukuyama.stanford.edu/files/Patterns%20of%20History.pdf

Thinking about Hybrid Regimes—Project Muse
http://muse.jhu.edu/login?auth=0&type=summary&url=/journals/journal_of_democracy/v013/13.2diamond.html

Harvard
www.hks.harvard.edu/fs/pnorris/DPI403%20Fall09/DPI403_Powerpoint_Slides_Fall2010/3%20DPI403%20Applying%20the%20analytical%20framework.pdf

Larry Diamond Speaks on Governance and Democracy in Africa—United States Africa Command
www.africom.mil/Newsroom/Article/7522/larry-diamond-speaks-on-governance-and-democracy-i

Democracy's Third Wave
www.rickweil.com/s4421/Readings/Huntington.pdf

Larry Diamond—Stanford Center on Democracy, Development, and the Rule of Law
http://cddrl.stanford.edu/people/larry_diamond

LARRY DIAMOND is senior fellow at the Hoover Institution and the Freeman Spogli Institute for International Studies at Stanford University, director of Stanford's Center on Democracy, Development, and the Rule of Law, and coeditor of the *Journal of Democracy*. His forthcoming book, In *Search of Democracy*, will be published by Routledge later this year.

Article   Prepared by: Caroline Shaffer Westerhof, *California National University for Advanced Studies*

Iran Press Report: Reactions to Developments in Lebanon, Egypt, and Syria

MEHRUN ETEBARI

Learning Outcomes

After reading this article, you will be able to:

- Explain why some Middle East leaders felt that Morsi's fall from power became a losing strategy when he put trust in the Americans.

- Understand why Iran is compared to North Korea.

- Understand the fears of Prime Minister Netanyahu of Israel when he says if Iran were to reverse course and push for a nuclear bomb, Israel would have to retaliate.

In reaction to the week's bad news for Iran's close ally in Lebanon, there was all-around condemnation in the Iranian press this week for the European Union's decision to add Hezbollah's military wing to its list of terrorist groups. Mohammad Safari in the conservative *Siasat-e Rooz* argued that the move was likely to poison the atmosphere for future negotiations between Iran and the P5+1 over the nuclear program. He added that it was yet another example of the Western service of the Zionists: "The occupying regime [Israel] . . . has stood to this day only thanks to the West and the European nations, and if, one day, the West stops its support for the Zionists, that day will be the day of the definitive fall of the regime." Hossein Sheikholeslam in the reformist *Etemaad* agreed that the move was dishonorable, suggesting that much as European nations resisted against Nazi occupation in World War II, they are going against their historical principles in calling a group which is fighting Israel for its "occupation of Lebanon and Syria" terrorists.

The situation in Egypt has continued to draw reflection from Iranian commentators, many of whom focused their attention on where they thought deposed president Mohammad Morsi had gone wrong. Yadollah Javani in the hardline *Javan* said that Morsi's mistake had been trying to secure the Muslim Brotherhood's grip on power by reaching out to the United States,

Israel, and their allies, who could not be trusted. "After his victory, Morsi's first foreign trip was to Saudi Arabia . . . but after his fall from power, the Saudi king was the first person to congratulate the interim president who replaced Morsi," he wrote, adding that the coup had vindicated the anti-American nature of Iran's Islamic Revolution. He posed the rhetorical question, "If the American Embassy [in Tehran] had not been captured, would the Islamic Revolution still be around in its fourth decade?" In *Qods,* Mohammad-Mehdi Shirmohammadi agreed that Morsi had put his faith in the wrong partners, saying, "Instead of relying on the Egyptian nation he relied on the reactionary regimes and America," and argued that Turkish Prime Minister Recep Tayyip Erdogan should view Morsi's downfall as a cautionary tale and change his behavior. Meanwhile, Amir Mousavi added in a *Hamshahri* interview that the Muslim Brotherhood's rejection of cooperation with other parties and the retreat of Qatar from active support played roles in Morsi's fall.

Not all articles put the primary blame on Morsi and the Brotherhood. Despite Iranian problems with the Brotherhood, however, and despite the mistakes that Morsi made in government, Mohammad-Mehdi Mazaheri argued in *Hamshahri* that the Muslim Brotherhood being allowed an active role in politics is the only way Egypt can reclaim its democracy. In a more convoluted analysis, Hassan Hanizadeh claimed in Tehran-e Emrooz that instability in Egypt has been deliberately stoked by Washington as part of a conspiracy to create chaos that will prompt the partitioning of the nation between Christian and Muslim regions, with the Christian region used by America to provide greater security to Israel.

Commentators also discussed what they saw as weakness of countries that had been acting against the interests of Iran and the "resistance axis." In his interview, Amir Mousavi added that Turkish distraction with domestic protests, Qatar's retreat from the stage during the transfer of power to the new Emir, Sheikh Tamim bin Hamad, and the downfall of Morsi's presidency meant most of the regional actors who had been supporting the Syrian opposition were increasingly absent from the scene, leaving Saudi Arabia on its own there with little chance for success. This dynamic, wrote Seyyed Emad Hosseini in the reformist daily *Etemaad,* left one-time staunch Iranian ally Hamas, and its political leader Khaled Meshaal, in a tough situation. Citing the retreat of Hamas's new anti-Iranian supporters, he wrote that Meshaal has made a "180-degree turn" and is asking for Iranian support, and questions whether the resistance axis should welcome Hamas back. He suggests that Meshaal might be too ungracious to deserve it: "[Meshaal], meanwhile, has not explained why, in spite of the widespread support that the government of Bashar Assad had given his movement, he sharply criticized the Damascus government."

Critical Thinking

1. How has the condemnation of the European Union's decision to add Hezbollah's military wing to its list of terrorist groups affected Iran, Lebanon, and its neighbors?

2. What do commentators allege when they say, "Tehran is not Pyongyang"?

3. Why do commentators feel that it is a weakness of countries that had been acting against the interests of Iran and the "resistance axis"?

Create Central

www.mhhe.com/createcentral

Internet References

Iran—Press TV
www.presstv.ir

Iran Focus News and Analysis
www.iranfocus.com

Opinion Polls | The Arab American Institute
www.aaiusa.org/pages/opinion-polls

Prepare for the Worst—Brookings
www.brookings.edu/research/opinions/2013/07/25-middle-east-peace-talks-fall-apart-sachs

What to Read on Iran This Week: Looking Ahead to the Rouhani Presidency—Brookings
www.brookings.edu/blogs/iran-at-saban/posts/2013/08/02-what-to-read-on-iran-this-week

---

MEHRUN ETEBARI is an Iran analyst in Washington, D.C., and Senior Research Assistant, Saban Center for Middle East Policy.

Article

Prepared by: Caroline Shaffer Westerhof,
California National University for Advanced Studies

A New Growth Paradigm

VINOD THOMAS

Learning Outcomes

After reading this article, you will be able to:

- Understand how the Philippines' vulnerability to floods and storms is sapping the commitment of the government.

- Explain how the present weather disasters have hindered growth in the economy of the Philippines.

- Explain the microfinance programs in the Philippines.

The economy of the Philippines stands out for its relatively robust 6.6-percent growth in 2012 amid lackluster economic growth in most places around the world. The crucial question, however, is how the country can sustain this performance to generate far more jobs and reverse the rise in poverty seen in the past decade.

Domestic reforms are paramount to the Philippines' growth prospects, but cross-border factors matter, too, in our highly globalized world economy. Perhaps surprisingly for some, the danger of climate change arguably presents a greater threat than the current global economic malaise. If sustained growth is to take place, this challenge must be met. Specifically, we need to strengthen disaster resilience, care more for the urban environment, and confront climate change as part of the growth paradigm.

Climate-related disasters have crowded the headlines worldwide in recent years. East and Southeast Asia top the list of the regions affected. Floods and storms have cut significantly into annual growth rates in Australia, China, Indonesia, Korea, Thailand and Vietnam—a trend that is set to worsen. The Philippines, often the first major landfall for typhoons arising in the western Pacific, is among the most vulnerable.

Multiple factors, of course, explain these mounting disasters. First, many more people now live in harm's way, particularly in low-lying megacities like Manila. Second, soil erosion, deforestation, and just plain overcrowding leave people more vulnerable to natural hazards. And third, the hazards are growing more menacing.

Scientists are nevertheless cautious in linking any particular disaster to climate change, whether it is Typhoon "Pablo" in Mindanao or Hurricane "Sandy" on the US East Coast. In the same way, economists are reluctant to pin higher inflation in any given month on rising money supply. But, as with inflation, the broader associations are unmistakable.

For some, the front-and-center needs of the Filipino poor will apparently heighten a dilemma balanced on growth versus the environment. But the dilemma presents a false choice. Relying on a longstanding growth pattern that fuels economic momentum with environmental destruction will only aggravate climate change. And it is the poor who stand to lose most from the ravages of global warming.

So, as Einstein is said to have observed, we can't do the same things over and over again and expect different results. We must grow fast, but we also need to grow differently.

In essence, we need a new strategy that values all three forms of capital—physical, human and natural. Sound growth policies have long been understood as those that expand investments in physical and human capital. But unless we also invest in natural capital, all bets are off.

First, we should build disaster resilience into national growth strategies. Japan invests some 5 percent of GDP in this area: While paying a heavy price, it has avoided much worse economic damage and deaths from disaster because of this investment.

And high returns on such investment are evident even where the total spending is far less. In the Philippines, the effects of flooding in Manila after heavy monsoon rains in August 2012 contrasted strongly with the devastation in the city from Tropical Storm "Ondoy" in 2009.

The response to the most recent storm demonstrated the vast payoff from measures such as social media alerts, better relief operations, and early warning systems. It also highlighted the benefits of the hazard maps and upgraded rain and water-level monitoring systems promoted by Project NOAH (the Nationwide Operational Assessment of Hazards).

Second, planners need to raise the priority of urban management as a strategic thrust. The five cities considered most vulnerable to natural hazards are all in Asia: Dhaka, Manila, Bangkok, Yangon, and Jakarta. These urban centers are overcrowded and situated in ecologically fragile settings. The massive agglomeration notwithstanding, fewer than 50 percent of Asians live in cities, compared to 80 percent in Latin America. Further urbanization would seem inevitable. It is hard to overstate the high priority for careful physical planning, environmental care and judicious urban management.

Third, climate action needs to be part of the national plan. Economic growth will not be automatic if climate change is not dealt with. Adapting to the changing climate through better management of location decisions of people and businesses and protecting the natural environment assume urgency. But realistically, adaptation measures will not come nearly soon enough, so it is essential to mitigate climate change as well. No single country can make a difference in this respect. However, Asia, which is the most at risk, must be a powerful voice by switching to a low-carbon path and calling on others to do the same.

At the end of the day, we need to change our mindset on how growth is generated. Old-style growth at the expense of the environment will be self-defeating—a realization driven home by the stark reality of climate change.

Critical Thinking

1. Is the Philippines ever going to raise itself from poverty? Explain.

2. Can Vinod Thomas, the author, as a member of the Asian Development Bank, be instrumental in improving the economic growth in the Philippines? Explain.

3. What are the results, to-date, and what has been accomplished implementing the microfinance programs?

Create Central

www.mhhe.com/createcentral

Internet References

Vinod Thomas—Inquirer Opinion
http://opinion.inquirer.net/byline/vinod-thomas

Preparing Better for More Frequent Natural Disasters—Inquirer Opinion
http://opinion.inquirer.net/56761/preparing-better-for-more-frequent-natural-disasters

'More Funds Should Go to Disaster Preparedness'—ABS CBN News
www.abs-cbnnews.com/business/08/21/13/more-funds-should-go-disaster-preparedness

Bank Warns That Asian Growth Could Collapse—UCA News
www.ucanews.com/news/bank-warns-that-asian-growth-could-collapse/68640

VINOD THOMAS is the director general of independent evaluation at the Asian Development Bank and is responsible for the assessment of its many projects and programs in Asia and the Pacific.

Article

Prepared by: Caroline Shaffer Westerhof,
California National University for Advanced Studies

Towards a Renewed Global Partnership for Development

The global partnership for development that underpins the Millennium Development Goals (MDGs) was captured as a standalone goal (MDG8) in 2000. It has played a crucial role in the achievement of the MDGs by facilitating resources and an overall environment conducive to development. A report assessing MDG8 will be released in March and later followed by a chat on Facebook.

DEPARTMENT OF ECONOMIC AND SOCIAL AFFAIRS

Learning Outcomes

After reading this article, you will be able to:

- Understand the shared framework for the global development agenda, action, and cooperation as the world approaches 2015.

- Understand the work of the United Nations System Task Team.

- Identify the Global Partnership Thematic Think Pieces.

As the conversation gears towards the 2015 development agenda, there is great interest to learn from the experience of implementation of MDG8 and ways to strengthen the global partnership for development in the post-2015 era. In this sense, the Secretary-General's High-level Panel of Eminent Persons will place this important issue at the centre of its upcoming meeting in Indonesia at the end of March.

The UN System Task Team (UNTT) on the Post-2015 UN Development Agenda has prepared a report on global partnership which will be published in early March on the UNTT website. Titled 'Towards a renewed global partnership for development' the report presents an assessment of MDG8 and it reviews new challenges for the global economy as well as new trends in development cooperation. The report proposes possible contours, alternative formats and a robust accountability mechanism for a renewed global partnership for the post-2015 era.

Recognizing New Challenges

MDG8 served as an important advocacy tool to stress the important role of the international community in achieving the globally agreed development goals outlined in the MDG framework. Based in the context of 2000, when the MDGs were conceived, the focus of MDG8 is primarily in the areas of Official Development Assistance (ODA), debt relief, trade, technology and access to essential medicines. It also gave special attention to the needs of the least developed and most vulnerable countries.

Going forward, a renewed global partnership for development needs to recognize the challenges of the world we live in today and formulate adequate global efforts that corresponds with global challenges in the areas of climate change, rising inequalities, changing population dynamics, and remaining governance and human rights deficits. Fragile countries have seen the least progress in terms of MDG achievement and thus any attention to most vulnerable countries needs to include fragile states.

Sustainability at the Core

In the discussion about the characteristics of the post-2015 development agenda, there is broad consensus among all stakeholders that sustainability must be at the core of the new agenda. Larger financing needs can be anticipated which cannot be met by ODA alone. While ODA commitments will continue playing a key role supporting the development efforts of the poorest countries, the recent years have seen the rise of a more multipolar economy leading to a significant shift in global economic balance. Given the rise of middle-income countries, the face of poverty has changed significantly.

Today, 75 per cent of the poor live in middle-income countries and further progress to eradicate poverty will require greater policy coherence at global and national levels. Based on the emergence of new economic powers, South-South cooperation has increased and a large array of non-governmental actors (including the private sectors, philanthropy and civil society organizations) have engaged in various forms of global partnerships, often focusing on specific sectors, mainly in the areas of health, education and food security.

Reshaping Donor-Recipient Relationships

A renewed global partnership will need to move away from the traditional donor-recipient relationship that characterized MDG8 and consider a wider range of actors and mechanisms to make the most effective contribution to global development. Unlike MDG8, the new agenda should also build a robust accountability mechanism to address, on a continuous basis, possible shortcomings from commitments made as part of a renewed global partnership for development.

When speaking at an event recently, Secretary-General Ban Ki-moon also described the need for renewed global partnership. "The current global partnership for development needs to be rebalanced and redefined—taking into account emerging economies, South-South partnership, private sector engagement and innovative financing," he said.

Looking at the various challenges at hand and the need for consistent global responses with participation from multiple actors, the discussion about the characteristics of a renewed global partnership for development in the post-2015 era is rather complex. The report of the UN System Task Team provides an overview of the key challenges involved and makes recommendations on ways to address some of these questions with clear suggestions about the format and the contours of a renewed global partnership.

Critical Thinking

1. How has DESA achieved solutions in addressing the world's more pressing concerns?

2. Is DESA NEWS beneficial in understanding the United Nations' actions in the areas of economic and social development policy?

3. What have the Millennium Development Goals achieved to date moving toward the goal date of 2015?

Create Central

www.mhhe.com/createcentral

Internet References

DESA News Announces Release of Second UNTT Report—International Institute for Sustainable Development
http://post2015.iisd.org/news/desa-news-announces-release-of-second-untt-report

United Nations
www.un.org

IOM position on the Post-2015 United Nations Development agenda
www.iom.int/files/live/sites/iom/files/What-We-Do/docs/IOM-Position-Paper-on-Post-2015.pdf

United National Department of Economic and Social Affairs
www.un.org/en/development/desa/newsletter/desanews/2013/03.html

The United Nations Department of Economic and Social Affairs (DESA) works closely with governments and stakeholders to help countries around the world meet their economic, social and environmental goals. DESA News is an insider's look at the United Nations in the area of economic and social development policy.

Article

Prepared by: Caroline Shaffer Westerhof
California National University for Advanced Studies

Climate Change Is a Challenge for Sustainable Development

RACHEL KYTE

Learning Outcomes

After reading this article, you will be able to:

- Understand how sustainable development, in its various aspects, affects global poverty and creates uncertainties for policymakers around the world.
- Understand the global concept of "robust" decisions when implemented in the field of sustainable development.

Climate change is the most significant challenge to achieving sustainable development, and it threatens to drag millions of people into grinding poverty.

At the same time, we have never had better know-how and solutions available to avert the crisis and create opportunities for a better life for people all over the world.

Climate change is not just a long-term issue. It is happening today, and it entails uncertainties for policy makers trying to shape the future.

Effects on Russia

In 2008, the Russian National Hydrometeorological Service (Roshydromet) found that winter temperatures had increased by 2–3 degrees Celsius in Siberia over the previous 120–150 years, while average global temperature rose about 0.7 degrees during the same period.

Russia is projected to cross the 2°C threshold earlier than the world on average if significant and effective mitigation is not forthcoming. By 2100, the northern half of Asia, including Russia, is likely to experience a temperature increase of 6–16°C, compared to approximately 4°C global mean temperature increase.

While warming might have some potential gains for Russ the adverse effects include more floods, windstorms, he waves, forest fires, and the melting of permafrost.

Globally, permafrost is thought to hold about 1,700 gig tons of carbon—and near-shore seabeds in the Eastern Sib rian Sea hold a similar amount in methane hydrates that cou potentially be destabilized in a warmer world, as well. This compared to 850 gigatons of carbon currently in the Earth atmosphere. Of this, 190 gigatons are stored just in the upp 30 cm of permafrost, the layers that area most vulnerable melting and the irreversible release of methane. The release even a small portion into the atmosphere could dramatica compound the challenge already presented from anthropoger sources, potentially wiping out any hard-won mitigation gair

Russia hosts perhaps 70 percent of methane in circumpo permafrost, as well as the methane hydrates in the East Siberi Sea. Permafrost warming of up to 2°C in parts of the Europe Russia has already been observed.

Russia will be front and center for any efforts to deal w thawing permafrost and Russian leadership is much need to better understand its effects for the global climate as w as finding solutions for effective adaptation. There is no ti to lose.

In Yakutsk, collapsing ground caused by melting permafre has damaged buildings, airport runways, and other infrastru ture. In 2010, the Ministry of Emergency Situations estimat that a quarter of the housing stock in Russia's Far North wou be destroyed by 2030.

Analyses indicate that about 60 percent of infrastructure the Usa Basin in Northeast European Russia is located in "high risk" permafrost area, which is projected to thaw in future. This region is an area of high industrial and urban dev opment, like coal mines, hydrocarbon extraction sites, railwa nd pipelines. Yet the timing of this thaw remains uncertain—otentially a few decades or as long off as a century away.

Decision Making Under Uncertainty

olicy makers all over the world are facing similar challenges. While we certainly know that the climate will change, there is reat uncertainty as to what the local or regional impacts will e and what will be the impacts on societies and economies. oupled with this is often great disagreement among policy makers about underlying assumptions and priorities for action.

Many decisions to be made today have long-term consequences and are sensitive to climate conditions—water, energy, griculture, fisheries and forests, and disasters risk management. We simply can't afford to get it wrong.

However, sound decision making is possible if we use a different approach. Rather than making decisions that are optimized to a prediction of the future, decision makers should seek identify decisions that are sound no matter what the future rings. Such decisions are called "robust."

For example, Metropolitan Lima already has major water hallenges: shortages and a rapidly growing population with million underserved urban poor. Climate models suggest at precipitation could decrease by as much as 15 percent, or crease by as much as 23 percent. The World Bank is partnerg with Lima to apply tested, state-of-the-art methodologies ke Robust Decision Making to help Lima identify no-regret, bust investments. These include, for example, multi-year ater storage systems to manage droughts and better management of demand for water. This can help increase Lima's longrm water security, despite an increasingly unpredictable future.

Working Where It Matters Most

ach country will need to find its own ways to deal with uncerinties and find its best options for low-carbon growth and missions reduction. While they vary, every country has them.

One example: Russia has made remarkable progress since 005 in reducing the flaring of gas from oil production, but it is ill the world's largest gas flarer. And it is situated in a region om where black carbon from the flares reaches the Arctic ow and ice cap, which diminishes the cap's reflective power lbedo). The World Bank Group is appreciative of the success-l cooperation with Russia's Khanty-Mansiysk region in the lobal Gas Flaring Reduction partnership (GGFR). With more ussian partners, in particular from Russian state oil compaes, the impact could be even greater.

Russia's forests provide the largest land-based carbon store in the world. Better forest management and improving

forest fire response—a long-standing field of cooperation between Russia and the World Bank Group—are another example to reconcile growth and emissions reductions.

Options for countries all over the world include a mix of technology development that lowers air pollution; increasing investment in renewable energy and energy efficiency, expanding urban public transport; improving waste and water management; and better planning for when disasters strike.

Each of these climate actions can be designed to bring short-term benefits and lower current and future emissions.

To move forward on the global level at the required scale, we must drive mitigation action in top-emitting countries, get prices and incentives right, get finance flowing toward low-carbon green growth, and work where it matters most.

Prices: Putting a price on carbon and removing harmful fossil fuel subsidies are necessary steps toward directing investment to low-carbon growth and avoiding a 4°C warmer world. We are working with others to help lay the groundwork for a robust price on carbon and supporting the removal of harmful fossil fuel subsidies. An ambitious global agreement could help establish stronger carbon prices and should include commitments to accelerate fossil fuel subsidy reform and other fiscal or tax policy measures in support of low carbon and climate resilient development.

Finance flowing: Progress on the provision of climate finance is critical. Governments must deliver a clear strategy for mobilizing the promised $100 billion in climate finance. This $100 billion is doubly important in that it must be used to mobilize effectively private investment and other finance.

Climate change increases the costs of development in the poorest countries by between 25 and 30 percent. For developing countries, the annual cost of infrastructure that is resilient to climate change is around $1.2 trillion to $1.5 trillion, resulting in a yearly $700 billion gap in financing. It will take combining efforts of development banks, financial institutions, export credit agencies, institutional investors, and public budgets to meet the climate and development challenge.

All public finance should be used to leverage private capital and fill gaps in the market where private finance is not flowing. Also, it must be deployed in a way that the least amount leverages the maximum amount from public and/or private sources. We are not dealing with how to jump start something in which the private sector is not interested, but how we create the framework within which the now small but significant momentum is captured, disseminated, and accelerated and the speed-bumps are removed and setbacks avoided.

At the World Bank Group we are committed to working where it matters most:

By 2050 two-thirds of the world's population will be living in cities. Helping developing country cities access private financing and achieve low-carbon, climate-resilient growth and avoid locking in carbon intensive infrastructure is one of the smartest investments we can make. Every dollar invested in building creditworthiness of a developing country city will mobilize $100 dollars in private financing for low-carbon and climate-resilient infrastructure.

To feed 9 billion people nutritiously by 2050 we need to make agriculture resilient, more productive in changing landscapes, and aggressively reduce food waste. Making agriculture work for the people and the environment is one of the most pressing tasks at hand. We need climate-smart agriculture that increases yields and incomes, builds resilience, and reduces emissions while potentially capturing carbon.

The World Bank Group supports the Sustainable Energy for All goals of doubling both the rate of improvement of energy efficiency and the share of renewable energy in the global energy mix from 18 percent to 36 percent by 2030. Reaching these goals is key to low-carbon growth.

Critical Thinking

1. Define the global challenging tasks affecting sustainable development.

2. Why is climate change considered the most significant challenge in achieving sustainable development?
3. Can long-term decision making be successful if there are poli disagreements in determining priorities for action?

Internet References

China's Urbanization Plan—Sustainable Development?
www.thediplomat.com/2014/04/chinas-urbanization-plan-sustainab development

Climate Change Is a Challenge for Sustainable Development
www.worldbank.org/en/news/speech/2014/01/15/climate-change-challenge-for-sustainable-development

Sustainable Development Knowledge Platform
www.sustainabledevelopment.un.org

UNESCO World Conference on Education for Sustainable Dev opment 2014
www.unesco.org/new/en/education/events/calendar-of-events/educati global-conferences

RACHEL KYTE is World Bank Group vice president and special env for climate change. She oversees work on climate change adaptatic mitigation, and climate.

Prepared by: Caroline Shaffer Westerhof,
California National University for Advanced Studies

rticle

2014: A Risky Year in Geopolitics?

The biggest political risks ahead.

N BREMMER

earning Outcomes

ter reading this article, you will be able to:

Discuss the geopolitical risks and concerns within the year 2014.

Discuss why the international community perceives U.S. foreign policy behavior as "unpredictable."

What are the biggest political sks for 2014?

ere are plenty of potential crises to keep us up at night in 14. There are tensions between China and Japan in the East ina Sea and elite-level executions in North Korea. Violence ntinues to worsen in the Middle East with a resurgence of a re localized Al Qaeda, a deteriorating security environment Iraq, and 2014's biggest geopolitical pivot point: the make-break Iran nuclear agreement. If the P5 + 1 and Iran strike a al, it would be a huge boon for the Obama administration, but would leave Iran economically emboldened and looking to ckstop Shia initiatives across the region, putting it even more odds with Saudi Arabia. A deal is, on balance, more likely n not. But if it falls through, it means a spike in oil prices, addition to the likelihood that Israel strikes Iran before it can int to nuclear-breakout capacity. All of these geopolitical ncerns are front and center for the coming year.

But above all, two essential questions best categorize the jor political risks of 2014. For many of the world's predomi-t emerging markets, it's an internally focused question: w will key developing countries adapt to upcoming elections implement ambitious agendas—and what does it mean for ir behavior beyond their borders? For the United States, the estion is externally focused. The international community

perceives America's foreign-policy behavior as increasingly unpredictable. Is the United States disengaging internationally? How will policymakers define the role that the US should play in the world? Much depends on these concerns, as America's relationships with its allies become increasingly fraught.

When you add these two questions to the more conventional geopolitical security uncertainties, there is one clear answer: the erosion of global leadership and coordination will become more apparent and pronounced in 2014.

How will emerging markets respond to internal challenges?

This year, we will see domestic distractions in emerging markets, from election cycles to unprecedented reform agendas; do not expect them to play a significant role internationally that does not cohere with their more pressing priorities at home. We are in the midst of a new era of political challenges for emerging markets, as slowing growth, sputtering economic models, and rising demands from newly enfranchised middle classes create heightened uncertainty. As recent protests in Brazil, Turkey, Thailand, Colombia, Ukraine, and Russia have shown, new middle classes have new demands—and are willing to take to the streets if they go unmet.

It is in this context that six of the world's largest emerging markets—Brazil, Colombia, India, Indonesia, South Africa, and Turkey—will hold national elections in 2014. In all six countries, the incumbent party will have ruled for a decade or more, but since coming to power, few of them will have faced an electoral cycle quite like this. Political, social, and economic dynamics in each of these countries vary immensely, but elections raise the risk of prevote populist policymaking in all of them. As emerging-market growth wanes, many of these countries need to implement economic reforms in order to enhance productivity and continue enriching their citizens. But as elections loom, the fears of politicians grow, and substantive reform of pensions, privatization, labor markets, and taxation will stall. Nor will the outlook improve substantially post-elections. We are likely to see second mandates of weaker leaderships—a political environment that is by no means ideal for big-bang reforms.

While these six emerging markets are the most important players for the global economic community, the emerging market elections story extends much further. A total of 44 democratic emerging-market countries accounting for 36 percent of the world's population will hold national elections this year. Growing middle classes across the emerging market space are expecting more and better services precisely as governments' capacity to deliver (economically and politically) is diminishing. That leaves emerging market governments with their hands full at home.

Among emerging markets, Turkey is especially vulnerable in 2014. The country faces spillover effects from the civil war in Syria and a re-emergence of the Kurdish insurgency. More worryingly, Prime Minister Erdogan's increasingly aggressive behavior is a huge variable at a time when he is likely to become president. Expect uncertainty and conflict over the division of powers between him and the prime minister.

Critical Thinking

1. Why could there be a spike in oil prices?
2. Can emerging markets respond to internal challenges?
3. Can you explain the potential erosion of global leadership in 2014?
4. Can you analyze who will be the leader among emerging markets in 2014?
5. Can you analyze which nation-state will be the leader among emerging markets in 2014?

Internet References

Global Geopolitics & Political Economy
    www.globalgeopolitics.net/wordpress/2014/04
The Geopolitics of the Eurasian Economic Union
    www.counterpunch.org/2014/06/03/the-geopolitics-of-the-eurasia economic-union
The Vineyard of the Saker
    www.vineyardsaker.blogspot.in/2014/02/the-geopolitics-of-ukraini conflict.html

---

IAN BREMMER is president of the Eurasia Group.